RESTORATION DRAMATISTS

RESTORATION DRAMATISTS

A COLLECTION OF CRITICAL ESSAYS

Edited by
Earl Miner

Prentice-Hall, Inc. 

Englewood Cliffs, N. J.

 Library of Congress Catalog Card Number 66-28108. Printed in the United States of America—C. P77490, C77491

Current printing (last number):
10 9 8 7 6 5 4 3 2 1

Contents

Introduction, *by Earl Miner* 1

The Significance of Dryden's Heroic Plays,
by D. W. Jefferson 19

The Significance of Dryden's *Aureng-Zebe,*
by Arthur C. Kirsch 37

All for Love, by Eugene M. Waith 51

George Etherege and the Form of a Comedy,
by Jocelyn Powell 63

The Comic Language, *by Dale Underwood* 87

William Wycherley, *by Anne Righter* 105

The Satiric Design in *The Plain Dealer,*
by Rose A. Zimbardo 123

Otway Preserved: Theme and Form in *Venice Preserv'd,*
by David R. Hauser 139

Love for Love, by Norman Holland 151

Congreve's Last Play, *by Thomas H. Fujimura* 165

Chronology of Plays 175
Notes on the Editor and Authors 177
Selected Bibliography 179

RESTORATION DRAMATISTS

Introduction

by Earl Miner

The fact that Restoration drama has long been the problem child of English literature has not prevented people from making up their minds about it. The history of its criticism from its own day to ours shows that the effort to evaluate it has raised fundamental questions about the conventions, techniques, range, sociology, and morality of literature. Much of its fascination has indeed been extra-literary, and settled judgments have often been made upon very little literary evidence. If only a lively literary period could arouse such personal responses, only the combination of real literary merit and a relevance to our day can account for the remarkable rise in the quality as well as quantity of criticism of Restoration drama in the past twenty years. The subject has proved to be quite difficult, but numerous writers have combined historical knowledge and critical acumen to advance our understanding. Most of the best work, which is represented in the essays that follow, has earned the right to evaluate by accepting the discipline of historical or critical analysis. Although the reinterpretation is far from complete, the result, to paraphrase Dryden, has been to reveal to us almost a whole new drama. My purpose in this Introduction is the more modest one of description, both of Restoration drama and of fruitful approaches to it.

I

Restoration drama must be described as three groups of works. For most people it is still limited, unfortunately, to Wycherley's *Country Wife,* Etherege's *Man of Mode,* and Congreve's *Way of the World.* A rough division of interpretations and of responses might in fact be made purely upon the basis of preferences among the three, often with an accompanying insouciance for the rest of the achievement of four or five prolific decades of theatre. It must be confessed that many professional students of Restoration drama have not cast their nets much more widely. At least he who addresses himself to the dull task of combing bibliographies will discover that the twentieth century critical view of Restoration drama is confined, with but few exceptions, to Dryden, Wycherley,

Etherege, Congreve, and Otway, a fact that has determined the nature of this collection. There are signs of change, but the common reader may rejoice to concur with the professional critic.

A second description of Restoration drama must, however, take a larger province into view. If we accept the usual dates of inclusion, from about 1660 to about 1700, there are to consider about two hundred dramatists and almost one hundred plays of unknown authorship. The bouncy Shadwell alone wrote twenty, his satiric commentator Dryden nearly thirty. It cannot be said that this vast wood has been wholly uncharted, much less that it is all enchanted forest. But neither can it be measured by the three familiar landmarks. A full description of what Restoration drama means would have to include the sum of the productions appearing, for short runs of three days or so, during those same four decades. That is what Pepys and the other theatregoers saw, applauded, hissed, described in their diaries and letters, or criticized in the coffeehouses. In this larger sense, it includes the dramatists of "the former age"—Shakespeare, Jonson, Beaumont and Fletcher, Webster, and others—whether in pristine form or in adaptation. It includes translations and adaptations of foreign plays, the beginnings of English opera, puppet shows, variety theatre, pageants, masques, and cantatas, in addition to the staples of comedy, tragedy, and heroic play in their numerous mutations and combinations.

From time to time the general public has had the opportunity of seeing revivals. The early and basically mindless play by Newcastle and Dryden, *Sir Martin Mar-all,* keeps an audience in constant laughter. A late play like Farquhar's *Recruiting-Officer* moves by the naturalness of its language and feeling. The Tate-Purcell *Dido and Aeneas* and the cantatas based upon Dryden's St. Cecilia Day odes evoke admiration whenever they are heard. What we so easily term Restoration drama is extremely varied and very much in need of careful discriminations. It not only includes many types of theatrical experience but also changes markedly in a normal literary evolution from those first days when the theatres were reopened under Charles II to the time when a softer eighteenth century taste led to a preference for moral tears over the bracing laughter of comedy and to a rejection of tragedy darkened by fate or illicit love and of the high astounding terms of the heroic play. The real problem of Restoration drama is that it is too little known.

There is, however, a more familiar problem, sexual morality. So fascinating has the problem been to the moralists and the prurient that consideration of Restoration comedy, with which the problem has been associated, has directed attention away from the other forms. Although the comedy has attracted consistent moral criticism, the nature of the censure has varied. Restoration criticism charged it with profanity in the strict sense; eighteenth and nineteenth century critics found it guilty of sexual license. Aware that neither of these censures is quite suited to the twentieth century, modern traducers of Restoration comedy have sophisticated the charge into one of sterile preoccupation with sex. Undoubtedly the comedy is openly occupied with sexual behavior. Worse still, to the moralists of all periods, the characters persist in talking about their sexual notions and ideas, in overturning received notions of social behavior. Some people find it annoying to have moral problems constantly discussed, especially in the seemingly topsy-turvy Restoration terms. The adverse critics—including those among our contemporaries—are annoyed by the sexual chatter, and it would be difficult to say whether the ingenuity of some of our defenders of Restoration comedy responds more to the plays or their critics.

So much critical smoke must arise from some degree of literary fire; at least it is generally conceded that in the next century comedy turned moral and dull (not that these qualities were, or are, inseparable). One might wish that the moral problem had been treated by critics in the larger terms of personal exploitation of others or of economic morality, but one must take history as one finds it and say that the critics' discussion in fact revolves about sex, which the dramatists treat by no means uniformly. Wycherley is largely satiric, though possessed of some ambiguity about sexual freedom. Etherege condones license within the limits of a reasoned code. Dryden usually allows his characters to reach for, but not to grasp, forbidden fruits. Congreve likes to place the license in the past and to adapt attitudes found in his predecessors. Other writers bring other variations, but with Farquhar and Vanbrugh sex approaches the melodramatic and so admits a degree of growing hysteria or uncertainty about the subject. It was clearly an age when marriage customs and relations between the sexes occupied men's thoughts and conversation. Conventional notions were often ridiculed as writers groped for more satisfactory norms. Two short, not very attractive stories published together early in the Restoration as *The Ephesian and Cimmerian Matrons* illustrate the complexity of attitude. The first tells how a widow mourns her dead husband only to yield to a passing soldier in a charnel-house atmosphere. The other is even less edifying. Each is, however, interlarded with disquisitions on love—the first in a neo-Epicurean vein justifying the woman and denying the validity of the "Platonicks" of the century, the second (despite its sordid tale) justifying an idealistic code of love. The two plots of these stories and the two attitudes toward them give four versions of love which, along with the numerous contemporary treatises on marriage and polygamy, show that the age was like our own in possessing an irresistible urge to talk about matters that frightened and fascinated it. The persistency of the concern and the seeming cynicism in which it is cast are what continue to upset people.

We may dismiss from consideration the foolish old lechers, the cuckolds, and the willing widows, all of whom are comic types inherited from sources as distant as Chaucer and Elizabethan drama. But we cannot ignore the prudes, the rakish men of sense, or the witty virgin ladies seeking husbands. The prudes and the virgin ladies are foils to the witty rakes, either in revealing that the openness of the men entitles them to sexual freedom or by affirming, in whatever modified fashion, conventional moral standards. The prudes become stock comic types, and their frequent sober equivalents, the seriously virtuous characters, are usually rarefied to the point of becoming symbols. It is the virgin, witty young women who determine the end of the action, namely marriage. The normal movement of English comedy from disorder to order is confirmed by reinstatement of the characters after numerous trials into the most basic social unit, the family, and is strengthened by persuasive economic settlements. The threats to such movement come not so much from outside pressures as from rebellious impulses within, giving characters a more complex motivation than in earlier comic drama. The movement of a Restoration comedy is, therefore, perversely like that of romantic drama. Only the virgin woman is permitted her choice of husband; and the man's code, though freer, is nonetheless a code.[1] How strong the final reconciliation is can be judged by the ritual dance that concludes so many of the comedies.

In other words, the Restoration discovered in the freedom of action of the young men and the freedom of speech of the young women a way of testing and even mocking the social values centering on marriage. Youth challenged the forms and conventions inherited from age, wittily mocking those elders who like Congreve's Lady Wishfort sought youth's freedom, or heartlessly dismissing the women who did not wait till marriage. Yet male Youth had to yield finally and become Age. The fact that marriage was the basis of the society economically as well as personally and that it repeatedly involves estates, lawyers, priests, and parents suggests the extent to which sex is commonly a shorthand for social freedom and convention throughout a wide range of subjects. The realism of detail and the witty questioning of social standards should not blind us to the romantic and socially affirmative conclusions. Plays as far separated in time and nature as Dryden's *Marriage a-la-mode* (1672) and Farquhar's *Beaux' Stratagem* (1707) concern the nature of marriage and finally support either normal Restoration or very modern views of it. Ultimately, the strongest adverse criticism that can be made of Res-

[1] See John Harrington Smith, *The Gay Couple in Restoration Comedy* (Cambridge, Mass., 1948), pp. 75-78; and Jean Gagen, "Congreve's Mirabell and the Ideal of a Gentleman," *Publications of the Modern Language Association of America,* LXXIX (1964), 422-27. Smith's book is indispensable to study of Restoration drama, but as with some other admirable studies, the length of its chapters precludes inclusion here.

toration comedy is that both its questioning and affirmation are too often conventional and mechanical. The many plays, however, that make these elements fresh yet again, or which are as profoundly ironic as *The Country Wife,* show that the concern with sex was a powerful, positive motive force. When that force diminished, when youthful disorder disappeared, comedy became sentiment, and morality became dull.

II

What is of greater significance than the use of sexual subjects is the playwrights' attitudes toward them. Our proper literary and sociological concern is with the way the plays mirror or distort the social reality on the one hand and the moral ideal on the other. Because the question of the relation between literature and morality is so difficult and because (it must be insisted again) Restoration comedy is so various, no one critical answer holds. The traditional explanations are (1) that the dramatists, themselves depraved, enjoyed picturing immoral actions; (2) that they created a fanciful never-never land which no one should take seriously; and (3) that they were only describing their age.

The first charge originated with the latter-day puritanical attackers of the stage, of whom the liveliest was the Jacobite Anglican cleric, Jeremy Collier.

> To sum up the Evidence. A fine Gentleman is a fine Whoring, Swearing, Smutty, Atheistical Man . . . a Man of Breeding and Figure that burlesques the *Bible,* Swears, and talks Smut to Ladies, speaks ill of his Friend behind his Back, and betraies his Interest: A fine Gentleman . . . Fine only in the Insignificancy of Life, the Abuse of Religion, and the Scandals of Conversation. These worshipful Things are the *Poets* Favourites.[2]

Collier notoriously took offense at the comic representation of priests and was, as Dryden observed, obscene where the dramatists were wanton. He is of the kind given to moral outrage at literature in any age. Yet there is a germ of truth in what he says. To some extent the dramatists did delight in depicting behavior immoral or profane by the standards of the day. The lives of Etherege, Sedley, Buckingham, and Rochester are notorious, in Dryden's words on Buckingham in *Absolom and Achitophel,* "all for Women, Painting, Rhiming, Drinking;/Besides ten thousand freaks that dy'd in thinking." But the fact is that the plays use their sexual concerns to raise other serious matters and that their bawdry is at least of an open, healthy kind.

[2] *A Short View of the Immorality and Profaneness of the English Stage,* Ch. 4, *Critical Essays of the Seventeenth Century,* ed. J. E. Spingarn (3 vols.; Bloomington, Ind., 1957), III, 255-56.

The second view, propounded by Charles Lamb,[3] sees in Restoration comedy a pleasant fantasy, a cloud-cuckoo land in which nothing is meant seriously and nothing therefore should give offense. It is difficult to believe that he had read the plays seriously or that, if he had, he was not ironically glossing them over with a fanciful pre-Victorian prudery. Yet his view, too, has a certain validity if taken rightly. To some extent Restoration comedy does enact a fairy tale in which the improvident, brilliant young rascal of essentially sound principles ultimately gets wife and fortune and settles down. Regarded in these terms Restoration comedy has a plot movement like the novels of Jane Austen or, even more, like Fanny Burney's *Evelina,* with the romantic roles of men and women reversed. In a strange way there is something of romance and fairy tale in this drama. Although no one nowadays would be likely to consider it dominant, the romantic element is significant, as the combination of comic with heroic strains in many plays shows.

The third view, that Restoration comedy merely holds up a mirror to society, has been most cogently expressed by H. F. B. Brett-Smith: we "must adopt the point of view of the age, and not blame the author for picturing what he saw." [4] The trouble with this view is both literary and sociological. It fails to account for most of what is in the plays and is refuted by the lives of the dramatists' contemporaries, great and small, which differed morally very little from our own. Yet this view, too, is a useful reminder of the accuracy of the dramatists in picturing London with the Mulberry Garden, the Mall, the New Exchange, or Locket's, with the dress and occupations of the time, and with the felt sense of life in the national metropolis. Such fidelity to actual life counters the wish-fulfilment in the movement of the plot and gives Restoration comedy a firm basis in social realities.

None of the interpretations just described has wide currency today, although touches of them will be found implicitly or explicitly in the essays collected here. The two prevailing views treat Restoration comedy either as expressive of a coherent philosophy shared by the heroes and dramatists or as fundamentally satiric in a criticism of social institutions and individual behavior.

The philosophy attributed to the dramatists is variously characterized as naturalism, libertinism, or neo-Epicureanism. Drawing, it is said, upon classical naturalism, Renaissance scepticism, and French libertinism, the

[3] "On the Artificial Comedy of the Last Century," in *Works in Prose and Verse,* ed. Thomas Hutchinson (2 vols.; Oxford, 1908), I, 648-65. Lamb remarks of Congreve's plays that "they are a world of themselves, almost as much as fairy-land . . . It is altogether a speculative scheme of things, which has no reference to the world that is"—and much else in a similar vein.

[4] *The Dramatic Works of Sir George Etherege* (2 vols.; Oxford, 1927), Percy Reprints No. 6, I, lxxxii.

dramatists exhibit "the naturalistic, skeptical, and libertine temper of the times." [5] It is said that the dramatists who hold such views express them in the ambiguously good and bad versions of reality and appearance, art and nature[6] which will be discussed subsequently. The philosophy offered a dignified, although almost despairing, comic vision into the nature of human experience and was a late humanist offshoot at once inimical to rational humanism and yet part of it. The contention that this philosophy is at work is most persuasive with respect to Etherege. For other writers it is not so much wrong as partial. For Dryden, it is almost wholly inadequate, for Congreve somewhat more relevant. It suits what is often called "the comedy of manners" far better than "the comedy of humours" practiced by Shadwell and others. But without question it has materially advanced our understanding of Restoration comedy, and I have accordingly reprinted here essays by two of its strongest proponents.

At first sight the belief that Restoration comedy is satiric seems merely to confirm the obvious. Everyone knows that in it the wits dismiss fools, fops, cuckolds, bumpkins, prudes, and other enemies of good sense. But not all critics have agreed that satire is the decisive element, that the truewits are themselves judged and found wanting. The view that the comedy is often dark because it shows the triumph of experience over hope has not been widely held. Yet it is the repeated tribute to Wycherley by writers as diverse as Dryden, Lansdowne, and Farquhar that the direction of his genius was satiric. Moreover when Dryden, in one of his many such passages, wrote of "The satire, wit, and strength of manly Wycherley" in his poem to Congreve, he explicitly claimed the same for Congreve. He might have done the same for himself, for Etherege (although *The Man of Mode* is somewhat ambiguous), and for others. The most explicit evidence that Restoration comedy is to be understood satirically, or at least ironically, is found in the banter of the prologues and epilogues, of which Dryden and Sir Car Scroop are masters, and in the Latin tags and the prefaces attached to the plays. The sociological evidence is yet more formidable. Restoration audiences often protested what they thought had gone too far (Congreve's characterization of Maskwell and Lady Touchwood in *The Old Bachelor,* for example), and it is impossible to believe that the "Cits" and other sober persons who heard themselves attacked would have continued to attend if they did not believe that the fine wits and ladies also smarted under the lash. The most elementary fact to be understood about Restoration comedy is one which the critics have had most difficulty in setting forth: that to it we must bring normal human assumptions to be shared with the

[5] Thomas H. Fujimura, *The Restoration Comedy of Wit* (Princeton, 1952), p. 197.

[6] See Dale Underwood, *Etherege and the Seventeenth-Century Comedy of Manners* (New Haven, 1957), Yale Studies in English No. 135, pp. 3-40.

dramatists and, at a distance of three centuries, with the original audiences; and that the judgment shared is based upon ethical and even social norms common to us and the Restoration. Once we understand this, we are in the theatre again as it has been known in every period and place where it has thrived. Living theatre, and pre-eminently comedy, is impossible without the assumption that we are seeing a play, a representation of reality to be judged by the shared experiences of normal human beings.

III

All of these interpretations of Restoration comedy are partial and, in varying degrees, conflicting. The conflict is no cause for surprise, for the comedy is not a simple or single thing; it is complex in every major instance and various in its decades of development. To understand that diversity and complexity it shares with other major periods of stage comedy, it is necessary to introduce further considerations. We may begin with the simple fact that the audience was by no means exclusively the court audience it is often claimed to be. The highly romantic assumptions about its differences from Shakespeare's are not verified by evidence. Like the Elizabethan, the Restoration theatre brought in many kinds of people. Pepys is respectable to those who know him well. Evelyn is respectable even to those who do not. More significantly, the Dorset Garden theatre of the Duke's Company had the reputation of drawing a bourgeois city audience, yet the plays performed there differ not at all from those performed by the other company.[7] Throughout the Restoration, Tory plays were hooted at by Whig claques, whose vitality came from people antagonistic to the court. The audience included the mercantile "Cits," members of the country gentry on annual visits to London, lawyers and doctors, fine ladies and prostitutes, booby lords and wits. It is true that city and country found themselves laughed at in the plays, but the satiric compass of the plays included the wits and ladies as well, and the audience judged what were after all comedies and not documentaries by normal human standards. The mixed character of the audience is particularly involved in the resolution of the plays. The courtly wits certainly get their virgin brides and fortunes, but they get them by marrying into country or city families. The broad-based audience had the repeated satisfaction of seeing the young wits yield to the

[7] The coincidence of the tastes and attitudes of the bourgeoisie with those attributed to the Court is shown in such a work as the anonymous, ironic *Ten Pleasures of Marriage* (1682), which attacks marriage lustily and slily in a wholly bourgeois situation. It is significant that modern historians of the Restoration have found great difficulty in distinguishing between Court, City, and Country as three separate parties in the Restoration, and certainly the difficulty in distinguishing their culture became greater as the Restoration wore on.

society they had spent so much of the play in rejecting and bow before forces from which they had claimed to be farthest removed. The profitable marriages they managed brought them under the control of, indeed reconciled them to, the familiar bonds of marriage and family, so uniting them with the normal human concerns of the diverse audience and affirming the vitality of the nation it represented. The cynics might yield with witty protest, but they yielded. No matter how witty and bold, the Harriets and Millamants retained their virginity, and their final triumph affirmed not only the wishes of the audience but also the realities and hopes of human life.

So regarded, Restoration comedy can be understood to resemble the comedy of other periods and languages, and this is probably the point most in need of understanding. Once that is accepted, we are entitled to ask how the comedy of these decades may be characterized so as to differentiate it from other English comedy. The most common term for it is of course "comedy of manners," a phrase which, like most other literary characterizations, is useful if not taken too seriously. It has been sharply questioned in recent years, some critics wishing to ban it altogether and others seeking to substitute such alternatives as "comedy of wit." What the objectors have in mind is the function of "wit" in attacking the society of the day. Manners, they argue, are precisely what is under attack, and the comedy deals with far more fundamental individual and social issues than can possibly be implied by that term. Such objections are well founded. Whether through satire, wit, libertinism, or humours, the dramatists are in search of truth, especially that true source of personal happiness and integrity which social forms may obscure or imperil. The proviso scene in *The Way of the World* is but one of many in which this effort is explicitly enacted on the stage. Less explicit enactments mark the plays from Dryden to Vanbrugh. The sense of anger, of danger, of despair, and sometimes almost of terror only half-concealed shows that the best of these plays are far more serious than a phrase like "comedy of manners" can imply.

Yet the idea of manners has some value. The plays *are* concerned with good form, do depict the social life of London, and do seek to formulate a meaningful role for the individual in society. Such concerns are better expressed by Miss Kathleen Lynch's phrase, "the social mode of Restoration comedy," which defines "manners" more meaningfully. It must, after all, be admitted that whatever the essences involved, the surface of Restoration comedy is far more social than any earlier English comedy except Jonson's. If the risk of Elizabethan "romantic comedy" lay in an effort to free human nature from the accidents of time and place that might go too far and take the plays out of touch with reality, the risk of Restoration comedy is that the effort to secure individual integrity and happiness in the face of society has little room for maneuver. Women may still disguise themselves as young men, but fairies with their magic potions, aerial spirits, and enchanters are as dead as Pan. The sea captain who could tell a Viola, "This is Illyria, Lady," is replaced by the servant announcing a guest or taking Lady Wishfort her ratafia. Only by traversing that narrow isthmus between foppery and boorishness and by defining his individuality in social terms could a character qualify for dignity and sympathy. We observe that Wycherley's Manly in *The Plain Dealer* wishes to leave London society for the New World, but also that Aphra Behn's play *The Widow Ranter* shows Virginia to be a social copy of England, and that Thomas Southerne's *Oroonoko* (though a tragedy of a kind) presents a blackamoor hero with manners yet more polished than those of the transplanted English, who themselves behave as if London had been transported with them to Surinam. The fact that Restoration comedy is almost always located in a real historical place, and that place London, and set in a historical time, the present, means that existing society sets the backdrop for the plays. The characters may challenge or alter it, but they cannot evade it. Whether or not their actions can be said to make up a comedy of manners, the arena in which they must act is the public, social one that is known, for all its comic distortions, to be a valid image of London. No one could quarrel with the description of this drama as social comedy.

In these plays the polarity of the individual and society is related to a thematic polarity commonly referred to as art and nature. Both terms are ambiguously positive and negative. Art is positive in suggesting that which human beings can add to life to make it more bearable and attractive; it is a positive symbol of what is good in society and civilization. It is also negative in suggesting the artfulness, artifice, sham, cant, and hypocrisy created by human beings to deceive others and themselves; it is a negative symbol of what is wrong in society and civilization. Nature is positive in suggesting what the individual feels and knows to be true in himself and others; it is a vital, unsullied norm within. But it is also negative in suggesting the selfishness, brutality, and anarchy that Thomas Hobbes saw in "a state of nature"; it represents that which would bring human decencies to ruin. My description is schematic in the interest of brevity. The comedies, which are not schematic, show how thoroughly the values and dangers represented by the terms mingle. Their complex implications are sorted out only with the utmost difficulty, and the characters are driven to adjust their conduct to ambiguous standards. In fact, the plays often suggest that man is caught in the dilemma of his inability to take the positive without the negative, to adjust his own drives to social needs, or the world to himself. If it turns out that marriage is the only solution advanced, that is only partly because marriage is the conventional ending of comedy. More importantly it brings order to individual lives within an orderly society and affords, in its promise of generation, man's deep hopes for a meaningful future.

IV

The dilemma just described appears in different guises in other forms of Restoration drama. If the problem is posed "seriously" rather than "comically," we are in the world of the heroic plays and tragedies. Since these are relatively less known, I shall deal with them more briefly. Heroic plays are an acquired taste. Dryden, the undoubted master of the form, wrote that a heroic play "ought to be an imitation, in little, of an heroic poem [i.e., epic]; and, consequently, that Love and Valour ought to be the subject of it." [8] He went on to justify spectacle and other imaginative effects, saying that they were necessary to convince spectators of the reality represented, and to say that he would refuse to weigh "love and honour . . . by drams and scruples." [9] Yet in his heroic plays "Love and Valour" are usually found defined as "love and honour" and weighed carefully, if not as minutely as in contemporary French drama. Moreover what Dryden speaks of as a single subject ("Love and Valour") is closely related to the "nature" and "art" of the comedies. Instead of treating society in terms of contemporary London, however, the heroic play seeks liberation in another time and place, thereby slackening the hold of contemporary society over individuals, taking man closer to the "state of nature," and allowing for grander conflict between natural individualism and civilized society. Nature and art are, then, magnified in special ways by heroic drama, and it is not surprising that it should be Dryden who introduced into the language (in Part One of *The Conquest of Granada*) the phrase, "the noble savage." His "heroic" rather than sentimental definition of the conflict of individualism with society produced those operatic flights of tough-minded rhodomontade that have been hard for many critics to accept.

The heroic play is related to comedy in another major respect, growing from the rhetorical conception of poetry. Both are distortions in the artist's mirror of the norm of nature, the comic in the lower direction of satire, the heroic in the higher of panegyric and heroic. No doubt the departure seems greater for heroic drama, but it is nonetheless a departure from the same normative standard. Dryden explains the matter well in his "Account" prefixed to *Annus Mirabilis:*

> Such descriptions or images . . . are, as I have said, the adequate delight of heroic poesy; for they beget admiration, which is its proper object; as the

[8] Preface to *The Conquest of Granada,* in *Of Dramatic Poesy and Other Critical Essays,* ed. George Watson (2 vols.; London, 1962), I, 158.

[9] *Ibid.,* I, 161-62, 164-65.

images of the burlesque, which is contrary to this, by the same reason beget laughter: for the one shows nature beautified, as in the picture of a fair woman, which we all admire; the other shows her deformed, as in that of a lazar, or of a fool with distorted face and antic gestures, at which we cannot forbear to laugh, because it is a deviation from nature.[10]

It is not true, therefore, that the heroic plays represent a norm and the comedies divergence from it. There are ideal norms in some of the comedies and real villains in the heroic plays. More than that, the "admiration" or wonder evoked by the heroic plays involves its own distortions; they are closer to the comedies than is usually acknowledged. In *Marriage a-la-mode* or *The Spanish Friar,* comic scenes alternate or are integrated with heroic, and in both Southerne's *Oroonoko* and Aphra Behn's *Widow Ranter,* to name but two of many examples, scenes of comedy sandwich the heroic plot. Both comedy and heroic drama further employ a central love plot complicated by intrigue; heroic argument is the counterpart of comic repartee; and the code of valor is a heroic equivalent of comic canons of sensible behavior. Both forms involve artistic distortions, but what is heightened is recognizable human life.

There is a further respect in which, despite the differences, the heroic play and comedy share common ground. Viewed in seventeenth century terms, their wit and much of their metaphor are not those of imagination (or "fancy"), which discerns resemblances in things unlike, but of reason (or judgment), which discerns the differences between things that seem alike. Whatever the purely imagistic strands of the plays, far-fetched comparisons are repeatedly given to the fops to reveal their false wit. The close discrimination of fops from wits, of permissible self-interest from exploitation, and of art from nature provides a major occupation for the comedy. Similarly, the heroic play discriminates (with more minuteness than Dryden chose to admit) between rival claims of love pressed upon a man or woman, between the cross-purposes of honour, and between the claims of love and honour themselves. At root both forms are arts of discrimination and judgment, although their imaginative configurations, selections of experience, and rhetorical heightenings of course differ.

In the Restoration, the prevailing comic language is prose, the heroic, rhymed verse, and the tragic, rhymed or blank verse. Yet the cadence and tone are again remarkably alike, as in these passages treating the agonies of love.

Why, whither in the devil's name am I a-going now? Hum—let me think—is not this Silvia's house, the cave of that enchantress, and which consequently I ought to shun as I would infection? To enter here, is to put on the envenomed shirt, to run into the embraces of a fever, and in some rav-

[10] *Ibid.,* I, 101.

ing fit be led to plunge myself into that more consuming fire, a woman's arms. Ha! well recollected, I will recover my reason, and begone. (Congreve, *The Old Bachelor,* III, ii).

O heav'ns! is there not punishment enough
In loving well, if you will have't a crime,
But you must add fresh torment daily to't,
And punish us like peevish rivals still,
Because we fain would find a heaven here?
But did there never any love like me,
That, untried tortures, you must find me out?
Others, at worst, you force to kill themselves;
But I must be self-murdress of my love,
Yet will not grant me pow'r to end my life,
My cruel life; for when a lover's hopes
Are dead and gone, life is unmerciful. [. . . *weeps*]

(Wycherley, *The Plain Dealer,* IV, ii)

I'm pleased and pained, since first her eyes I saw,
As I were stung with some tarantula.
Arms, and the dusty field, I less admire,
And soften strangely in some new desire;
Honor burns in me not so fiercely bright,
But pale as fires when mastered by the light . . .
I fear it is the lethargy of love!
'Tis he; I feel him now in every part:
Like a new lord he vaunts about my heart;
Surveys, in state, each corner of my breast,
While poor fierce I, that was, am dispossessed.
I'm bound; but I will rouse my rage again;
And, though no hope of liberty remain,
I'll fright my keeper when I shake my chain.

(Dryden, 1 *The Conquest of Granada,* III, i)

For all their obvious differences, the three passages share a common ethos and similarity in imagery. What is most interesting, however, is the tone. Congreve's Heartwell is foolish but psychologically just. Wycherley's Fidelia (who, disguised as a man, must woo the faithless mistress of the man she loves) is less psychological than sentimental and tragic. Dryden's Almanzor is the best self-analyst of the three. But how does the tone of his speech compare with those of Heartwell and Fidelia? I think that the concluding triplet is crucial. It shows that we are intended to smile—a little. He is no poor dove like Fidelia, and in fact his predicament is very close to Heartwell's. Whether he knows it or not, his speech mingles the admirable with the excessive. Proof that this modern response was shared by Dryden's contemporaries can be found in Colley Cibber's recollections of the faults of the able actor Booth in playing Morat, a Herculean villain in Dryden's heroic play, *Aureng-Zebe*.

> There are in this fierce Character so many Sentiments of avow'd Barbarity, Insolence, and Vain-glory, that they blaze even to a ludicrous Lustre, and doubtless the Poet included those to make his Spectators laugh while they admir'd them; but *Booth* thought it depreciated the Dignity of Tragedy to raise a Smile in any part of it, and therefore cover'd these kind of Sentiments with a scrupulous Coldness and unmov'd Delivery.[11]

The mingling of laughter with admiration in the heroic play, like that of unsullied feminine fidelity with depravity in Wycherley's comedy, shows how much alive contemporary audiences were to shades of tone, and how mature were sensibilities that could accept contradictory emotions in a single experience. The audiences and playwrights had an interest in, and a literary language for, psychological shades of meaning and responses to them. More fundamentally, their rhetorical conceptions of art enabled them to glide easily from the admirable to the ludicrous or to mix them finely, as is shown not only by Dryden's heroic plays but also by much of his nondramatic poetry.

V

I have chosen to speak in the main of elements common to the comedies and the heroic plays, hoping to make intelligible a form of serious drama which is little known and less understood by comparing it with the relatively more familiar comedies. But a few words must be said about their differences, which are those of atmosphere, subject, and theme. The comedies take place in St. James's Park or the Mall, from which the heavens are visible but are seldom looked at. The heroic plays take place in a celestial realm, and their characters are brilliant comets burning fiercely through the sky and not seldom crashing to earth. What they were like on the stage can best be represented by quoting Colley Cibber again, this time on the heroic actor Kynaston.

> He had a piercing Eye, and in Characters of heroick Life a quick imperious Vivacity in his Tone of Voice that painted the Tyrant truly terrible. There were two plays of *Dryden* in which he shone with uncommon Lustre; in *Aurenge-Zebe* he play'd *Morat,* and in *Don Sebastian, Muley Moloch;* in both these Parts he had a fierce, Lion-like Majesty in his Port and Utterance that gave the Spectator a kind of trembling Admiration! [12]

Restoration tragedy is less easily defined, because it varies so much more. The "heroic" variation is best represented by Dryden's *All for*

[11] *An Apology for the Life of Mr. Colley Cibber,* ed. Robert W. Lowe (2 vols.; London, 1889), I, 122. For further evidence, see pp. 124-25.

[12] *Ibid.,* I, 121.

Love, the "fatalistic" variation by his *Don Sebastian,* and the "emotional" variation by Otway's *Venice Preserv'd* and *The Orphan.* In all these, emotion as it is usually understood in tragedy plays a larger role than it does in the heroic play. It is felt more directly, is subjected to less rational analysis. In writing tragedy, the dramatists usually held to the same distance in time and space from the English present that marked heroic tragedy, although the tragic scene showed man in a European or classical state rather than in a state of nature. The tragedies did, however, tend to touch upon the more domestic elements that are closer to comedy. They are chiefly concerned with love, whose domesticity the tragic dramatists seek to transcend by treating it as illicit, exotic, or fated. Apart from Dryden, the public mode of Restoration literature is surprisingly absent from tragedy, and even in his tragedies, the center is most often love or fate, rather than power, justice, or kingship such as are typical of Shakespeare. Whether the proper word for this aspect of the love tragedy is domestic or romantic may be open to question, but the experience is brought closer to the conditions of the audience than it had been in the earlier period. As Rowe said in his Prologue to *The Fair Penitent,* "We ne'er can pity what we ne'er can share." The tragedy of fate in Dryden and Lee's *Oedipus* and in Dryden's later plays raises metaphysical concerns commonly harmonized with love.

If pity and fear are the emotions aroused and purged by classical tragedy, it was pity and admiration which most Restoration tragedy emphasized. Cibber's tribute to Mrs. Barry, though confined to one actress, suggests the character of the tragic as distinguished from the heroic drama.

> Mrs. *Barry,* in Characters of Greatness, had a Presence of elevated Dignity, her Mien and Motion superb and gracefully majestick; her Voice full, clear, and strong, so that no Violence of Passion could be too much for her: And when Distress or Tenderness possess'd her, she subsided into the most affecting Melody and Softness. In the Art of exciting Pity she had a Power beyond all the Actresses I have yet seen, or what your Imagination can conceive. Of the former of these two great Excellencies [i.e., Dignity] she gave the most delightful Proofs in almost all the Heroic Plays of *Dryden* and *Lee;* and of the latter [Pity] in the softer Passions of *Otway's Monimia* and *Belvidera.*[13]

Tragedy maintained the pressure of society upon the individual felt in comedy and heroic plays but dealt with a thwarted passion rather than with reason or volition, evoking pity rather than terror. Although in some respects the least sentimental period in our literature, with Otway and also at times with Lee the age found full scope for tears.

A second important emotion aroused by Restoration tragedy was ad-

[13] *Ibid.,* I, 160.

miration, and it is perhaps this response which most distinguishes the tragic drama of the age from that in other periods. Its introduction as a dramatic ideal came immediately from the epic impulse of the age and through the heroic drama. Its earlier antecedents lie in the addition of *admiratio* to the *dulce et utile* set by Horace as the ends of poetry and in the heroic or "Herculean" drama that had continued since antiquity as an important but rather minor strain. We have already observed how the admirable in the heroic plays admitted the comic, but it also admitted the softer emotion of pity by combining "Love and Valour" into a single dramatic subject. Cibber's comments on Booth, Kynaston, and Mrs. Barry may be recalled. Admiration (with its Restoration sense inclusive of wonder), pity, and laughter are not responses we have lost. But since the Romantics, perhaps since the eighteenth century, we have forgotten how to experience the three together. Dryden is the last to create characters in the tradition of heroic admiration, and *Don Sebastian* is the last of his great plays to show that element in strength. What seems to have happened after him is that a growing tendency of moralism gradually supplanted the heroic with a moral form of the admirable. The tendency is evident in Dryden himself, although never to the point of dominant moral sentiment. For him, the sublimity of the heroic provided that element of exaggerated scope which admitted something of tragic fear, even while absorbing it in admiration. Significantly, the fear lasts longer in his villains than in his tragic heroes, who achieve greater, less comic credibility by the encounters with fate and love.

Instead of fear or admiration, Otway and Lee supplied melodrama, and they had their lesser imitators. The development of this element is often laid to the disturbed personalities of the two men. But in fact, the plays exhibit an element of hysteria related to passion that was found to be highly effective on the stage, even if we may agree that it lacks the dignity of the highest tragedy. There are some signs of comic forms of hysteria in the later Restoration comic writers as well, and in both genres it is due partly to sensationalism and partly to a diminishing of theatrical nerve in the face of the audience's growing appetite for moral and tearful sentiment. No dramatist after Dryden writes convincingly as if fate or its equivalent in metaphysical terms were a reality. Having left behind these larger forces, the other dramatists had to content themselves with conflicts within and between individuals, working them up to pitches of passion that provoked pity. To turn again to faculty psychology, the role of the will is the crucial factor in accounting for changes in the forms of Restoration drama. In the libertine code of the comedies and in the glorious posings of the heroic plays, the will determined the action of the heroes and heroines. They exulted in their freedom—at least till the end, when reason or society or both brought the will under control. Dryden's tragedies show the will in a dilemma, struggling with or against reason or passion, pitted against larger forces such as fate. With Otway the passions rather than the will are the center of things, challenging will and reason alike, as if a suppressed sexuality lay at the root of it all. Theatrically, all forms of Restoration drama are high-pitched, far different from the mood of all passion spent in Milton's *Samson Agonistes,* the greatest closet drama published in the age.

VI

Since this essay is an Introduction, its emphasis has been upon the common elements and resemblances that make a general characterization possible. A proper historical or critical reading of the plays themselves would of course reveal many differences between playwrights, numerous mixed forms, and steady change. Plays like *The Rehearsal* (written by Buckingham and others) do not fit into any of the forms discussed, except possibly as parody. More important, my account has left out the sheer delight the comedies gave their audiences and the moving images of tragic dignity seen on those candlelit stages. In the following century people were not quite sure what to do with Restoration plays, but they went on cutting and applauding them, emerging with the remarkable judgment that Otway was second only to Shakespeare. That judgment, like the loss in popularity of the heroic play, tells us more about the new century than the old. For the Restoration, it is more significant that Dryden should do what no one else has been able to do, seek to draw, as he said, the bow of Ulysses and in *All for Love* attempt to rival Shakespeare on his highest ground. The result was not *Antony and Cleopatra,* but it was a fine play and gave evidence both of the continuity of English drama and of the vitality of the dramatic impulse in the age. It was an age of great theatre, for though the plays ran for short runs, they were acted by some of the greatest players in English theatrical history, and in a physical theatre of very considerable ingenuity and flexibility. The Restoration produced no Shakespeare, and has thereby something in common with all other periods save Shakespeare's own. But it did achieve the second great harvest of English drama and was the last for many generations in which the theatre lived as a creative force.

Editor's Note. The essays appearing here represent the best current criticism of Restoration dramatists, selected with a view to scope, quality, and freshness rather than, necessarily, the editor's agreement. Some essays that might have been included were too long; others have been omitted because their brevity limited their scope. Still others are omitted

because their general nature was not suited to this collection. As readers will discover, a considerable variety of approach and opinion remains.
I wish to acknowledge the kind permission of the authors and their publishers to reprint these essays; and to express my thanks to Miss Jeanette Dearborn for her very generous assistance in the compilation.

The Significance of Dryden's Heroic Plays

by D. W. Jefferson

The rhymed heroic plays are, perhaps, the least understood of all Dryden's works. The general failure to appreciate them is due to the assumption that they are intended, throughout, to be taken seriously—a very natural assumption since Dryden never confessed to any other than a serious and, indeed, orthodox attitude to his subject-matter. In the preface to *The Conquest of Granada,* where he defends his treatment of heroism, he is anxious to show that his work is based on the most respectable ancient and modern precedents. But Dryden could be very disingenuous when it suited his purpose, and this preface, though it probably served as an effective smoke screen against criticism, is by no means a statement of his real views on the subject. The truth is that he had a purpose in these plays which, for want of a better word, may be described as "comic." He chose not to admit it to his public, and his critics ever since have failed to recognize it.

It is instructive to compare Dryden's heroic plays with those of contemporary dramatists; for example, the Earl of Orrery. In Orrery's plays, heroism is always associated with moral idealism. *Mustapha* and *Henry V* are dominated by the theme of self-sacrifice, the triumph of loyalty and friendship over personal desires. There is no violence, no display of heroic force and virtuosity; the action takes place in the moral rather than the physical sphere. This conception of heroism is derived largely from the French romances of Mlle. de Scudéry and others. The atmosphere in Crowne's play, *The History of Charles the Eighth of France,* is somewhat different. Here there is vigorous action, but moral idealism is also present. The victorious hero, realizing the nobility of his vanquished enemy, behaves with great magnanimity towards him, with the result that they lay down their arms and become friends. In Dryden's plays, this moral emphasis is entirely lacking. What attracted him was the "power" element in heroism. His typical hero, Almanzor, is an irresistible conqueror, a creature of immensely dynamic personality who

"The Significance of Dryden's Heroic Plays." From the *Proceedings of the Leeds Philosophical and Literary Society,* V (1940), 125-39. Reprinted by permission of D. W. Jefferson and the Leeds Philosophical and Literary Society.

dominates every situation and reduces his rivals or enemies to pitiful insignificance. The atmosphere is one of violent melodrama.

Why Dryden should have chosen this conception of heroism, is an interesting question, which we must try to answer. We may begin by quoting from the preface to *The Conquest of Granada,* where he tries to justify himself; though, as we have suggested before, his arguments are not to be taken at their face value—

> For, otherwise, what can be more easy for me, than to defend the character of Almanzor, which is one great exception that is made against the play? 'Tis said, that Almanzor is no perfect pattern of Heroick virtue: that he is a contemner of Kings; and that he is made to perform impossibilities.
>
> I must therefore avow, in the first place, from whence I took the Character. The first image I had of him was from the Achilles of Homer; the next from Tasso's Rinaldo (who was a copy of the former), and the third from the Artaban of Monsieur Calprenede: (who has imitated both). The original of these (Achilles) is taken by Homer for his heroe, and is described by him as one, who, in strength and courage surpassed the rest of the Grecian army: but, withall, of so fiery a temper, so impatient of an injury, even from his King and General, that, when his mistress was to be forc'd from him by the command of Agamemnon, he not onely disobey'd it; but returned him an answer full of contumely, and in the most opprobrious terms he could imagine. . . . Tasso's chief Character, Rinaldo, was a man of the same temper: for, when he had slain Gernando in his heat of passion, he not onely refused to be judg'd by Godfrey, his General, but threat'ned that if he came to seize him, he would right himself by arms upon him. . . .
>
> You see how little these great Authors did esteem the point of Honour, so much magnify'd by the French, and so ridiculously ap'd by us. They made their Hero's men of honour; but so, as not to divest them quite of humane passions and frailties. They contented themselves to shew you, what men of great spirits would certainly do, when they were provok'd, not what they were oblig'd to do by the strict rules of moral vertue; for my own part, I declare myself for Homer and Tasso; and am more in love with Achilles and Rinaldo, than with Cyrus and Oroondates. I shall never subject my characters to the French standard; where love and honour are to be weighed by drachms and scruples. . . .

Dryden thus screens his hero from criticism by proving that there is ample precedent for all his excesses. He undoubtedly wanted his readers to believe that Almanzor was intended as another Achilles or another Rinaldo. But no one who has read *The Conquest of Granada* carefully can possibly accept Almanzor in this way, or believe that Dryden really thought of him in this way himself.

The charge brought against Dryden in his own day, and by later critics, is that his treatment of heroism carries extravagance to the point of absurdity. A contemporary critic[1] suggested that "Almanzor is not more

[1] Martin Clifford, whom Dr. Johnson quotes in his life of Dryden.

copied from Achilles than from Ancient Pistol." The following paragraph by George Saintsbury, who wrote as an admirer of Dryden, contains the suggestion that, excellent though the heroic plays are, they are not free from a certain element of unintentional comedy—

> Never, perhaps, was there a better example of what can and what can not be done by consummate craftsmanship in the teeth of artistic error. That Shakespeare could have transformed the heroic play, as he transformed everything he touched, is quite possible. Dryden could not transform it altogether, but he did with it, in the old phrase, "what a man of mould might," and he showed, in the doing, of what a mighty mould he was. With a certain adaptability of temperament, and some little variety of experience in literature, it is easy, even with *The Indian Emperor,* easier with *Tyrannic Love,* and easiest of all with *The Conquest of Granada* to "get the atmosphere," to submit to the conditions, and to drive at full speed with the poet in his distinctly wild but still calculated career. Even when Almeria hectors her suitors, her sister, her rival, her conquerors, and everybody; even when Maximin makes a cushion of his assassin, and stabs it now and then to keep it quiet as he perorates; even when Almanzor makes Drawcansir not so much a caricature as a faded photograph—it is not impossible to gulp the sense of the ludicrous, and pursue the triumph of tempestuous petticoat-worship and roistering declamation. And there are passages where no gulp is necessary. I am not myself fond of the theatre, but I should like to see one of these plays acted. The very boards might dissolve in laughter at the first scene or two; but if this danger could be surmounted, I do not see why Valeria's modern representative—let us hope she might have a tithe of Nelly's well-attested charm—should not speak the famous epilogue (softened, of course) in a tempest and torrent of cheers.[2]

It is this quality of extravagance bordering on absurdity which makes Dryden's heroic plays different from the works which he invokes as his models. Saintsbury assumes that it is an unintentional absurdity, but the contention of the present writer is that the plays can only be understood if we recognize this effect as the result of a conscious artistic purpose. It is, after all, a little unlikely that Dryden, whose sense of the ludicrous was so keen, should have been capable of lapsing into gross absurdity himself without realizing it. He was one of the most deliberate of artists.

Dryden's character presents a strange mixture of positive and negative attitudes to life. This is not in itself remarkable, a certain ambivalency being normal in human nature. What is remarkable is that he could, as it were, exploit this ambivalency in his poetry. He seems to have taken a pleasure in playing off opposing attitudes against each other. When his subject is serious, the positive attitude may prevail, but the negative attitude usually lurks in the background, ready to show itself at any time unexpectedly.

His position in relation to religion affords an example of this habit.

[2] Introduction to selection of Dryden's plays in the Mermaid Series.

Dryden was, as he confessed himself, sceptical by nature; and his scepticism was not confined to matters of doctrine. Throughout his work we continually find passages where the worth-whileness of human existence is called into question, "When I consider life, 'tis all a cheat," is the best known. Resentment against life, flavored by a kind of genial cynicism, is one of the recurring *motifs* in Dryden. It is against this background of scepticism and pessimism that his religious poems become so interesting. The genuine humility, and desire to believe in and live according to the Christian faith, which are expressed there, are all the more moving because his other self is not entirely suppressed. Passages of solemn beauty in *The Hind and the Panther* contrast strangely with touches of wit, where the pagan, earthy side of him comes out. Prior to the period of the religious poems, when religion, we may imagine, had not yet become an urgent personal issue for him, he wrote his dramatic version of Milton's *Paradise Lost*—the opera entitled *The State of Innocence*. Here we have an instance where the intrusion of a negative note into an otherwise respectful presentation of the subject, has the effect of studied incongruity. Adam is visited by Gabriel and Raphael, whose task is to instruct him in the mysteries of the divine purpose. But when the conversation turns on the thorny issue of free-will and divine foreknowledge, it becomes apparent that Adam is capable of holding his own in debate with the angels; and he is not prepared to swallow all that they say. Finally, they are compelled to cut the argument short with a hurried farewell. Adam is left perplexed and not a little resentful—

> Hard state of life! Since Heav'n fore-knows my will,
> Why am I not ty'd up from doing ill?
> Why am I trusted with myself at large,
> When hee's more able to sustain the charge?
> Since Angels fell, whose strength was more than mine,
> 'Twould show more grace my frailty to confine.
> Fore-knowing the success, to leave me free,
> Excuses him, and yet supports not me.[3]

Dryden's treatment of heroism shows a similar mixture of attitudes. He was attracted to this theme because of the ideas of power and grandeur which it suggested. It filled his mind with large conceptions, and gave him unlimited opportunities for exercising his gifts of rhetoric. To this extent, then, he *believed* in heroism. But it also stimulated another side of his nature—his satirical and sceptical spirit, and his sense of the ludicrous. There are a number of passages in the plays where he deliberately introduces sentiments which have the effect of pricking the bubble of heroic idealism. Whether the speech is uttered by a sympathetic

[3] *The State of Innocence,* IV.

character or otherwise does not matter, as it is always quite apparent that it is Dryden himself who is speaking, and that he is doing so for his own pleasure. The following lines on love spoken by Almanzor are a comparatively mild example—

> Love is that madness which all Lovers have;
> But yet 'tis sweet and pleasing so to Rave.
> 'Tis an Enchantment where the reason's bound:
> But Paradice is in th' enchanted ground.
> A Palace void of Envy, Cares and Strife,
> Where gentle hours delude so much of Life.
> To take those Charms away; and set me free
> Is but to send me into misery;
> And Prudence, of whose Cure so much you boast,
> Restores those Pains which that sweet folly lost.[4]

The implication here is that love is very sweet while it lasts, but has no enduring quality. It is an illusion which takes possession of the soul when reason is not in command. The sentiment is not very far removed from that expressed in the speech, "When I consider life 'tis all a cheat" —which Dryden puts into the mouth of his hero, Aureng-Zebe. (The fact that Aureng-Zebe is in adversity at the time gives the speech some degree of dramatic appropriateness, but its tone suggests a settled view of life—the view of life which is, in fact, habitual to Dryden.)

There are other passages where a distrust of the spiritual values proper to the heroic code, and a cynical attitude towards human nature in general, are given more blatant expression. Negative comments on Honour occur frequently—

> The points of Honour Poets may produce;
> Trappings of life, for Ornament, not Use:
> Honour, which onely does the name advance,
> Is the meer raving madness of Romance.[5]
> Honour is but an itch of youthful blood,
> Of doing acts extravagantly good;
> We call that Vertue, which is only heat
> That reigns in Youth, till age findes out the cheat.[6]

These definitions are offered by persons of unheroic disposition. Let us turn to a character who might be expected to speak well of Honour—

> *Cydaria:* What is this Honour which does Love controul
> *Cortez:* A raging Fit of Vertue in the Soul;

[4] *The Conquest of Granada,* Part II, III. iii.
[5] *Aureng-Zebe,* II.
[6] *The Indian Queen,* III.

> A painful burden, which great minds must bear
> Obtain'd with danger, and posses'd with fear—[7]

A much more positive attitude, but even here there is the suggestion that honour may, after all, be only quixotic folly.

General comments on life are very plentiful in the heroic plays. However superficially appropriate to the person speaking and to his or her situation, they usually give the impression of having been put there for non-dramatic reasons. Dryden deliberately uses every occasion that presents itself for saying those things which he enjoys saying, and his comments have added piquancy because they seem all wrong in such a setting.

It is in his characterization that the intrusion of satirical or comic attitudes is most interesting.

The idea of the aggressive, invincible hero appealed to Dryden, but he realized that, with its essential unreality and extravagance, it could easily lead to absurdity. He was not merely aware of these possibilities, but, in the person of Almanzor, he exploited them. This does not mean that he resorted to burlesque. Burlesque merely belittles; its object is entirely negative. Dryden developed both the grandiose and the comic aspects of his theme at the same time, the one being continually modified by the other. His methods are worthy of analysis. They are akin to those with which we are familiar in the later, satirical poetry.

Dryden makes Almanzor an immensely convincing figure. The power and solid weight of his verse suffice to convey an impression of irresistible force of character—

> No man has more contempt than I, of breath;
> But, whence hast thou the right to give me death?
> Obey'd as Soveraign by thy Subjects be;
> But know that I alone am King of me.
> I am as free as Nature first made man,
> 'Ere the base Laws of Servitude began,
> When wild in woods the noble Savage ran.[8]

But there is more here than simple heroic rhetoric. There is statement and argument, and these elements make the effect more complex. Dryden finds in his subject not merely poetical stimulus, but also intellectual amusement. He endows his hero with first-rate powers of debating, with which he makes him expound his own unique nature. It is here that Almanzor becomes "comic." The claims he makes for himself are so monstrous—and yet so convincing, because the whole weight of his overwhelming personality is behind them—that we accept him as a creature

[7] *The Indian Emperor,* II, 2.
[8] *The Conquest of Granada,* Part I, 1.

apart from the human species; a prodigy, at the same time magnificent and grotesque.

Dryden displays great skill in giving a show of plausibility to a completely outrageous argument—

Boabdelin: Since, then, no pow'r above your own you know,
Mankind shou'd use you like a common foe.
You shou'd be hunted like a Beast of Prey;
By your own law, I take your life away.

Almanzor: My laws are made but only for my sake;
No King against himself a Law can make.
If thou pretend'st to be a Prince like me,
Blame not an Act which should thy Pattern be.
I saw th' oppresst, and thought it did belong
To a King's office to redress the wrong:
I brought that Succour, which thou ought'st to bring
And so, in Nature, am thy Subjects' King.[9]

His gift of arguing in verse has always been recognized, but the extent to which he exercised it in the heroic plays has not been sufficiently realized. We shall have occasion to quote several more examples later in this essay.

The imagery of Almanzor's speeches deserves attention. Van Doren, the author of what is perhaps the standard critical estimate of Dryden to-day, remarks that he was somewhat deficient in imagery; but this statement is only true—and then not wholly so—of the satirical and controversial poems, where imagery is not called for to any great extent, and which, moreover, were the product of the poet's later years, when his style, though admirable in its vigor and lucidity, was perhaps less colorful than that of his earlier period. Far from being deficient in imagery, Dryden was very rich in it, and it is of a remarkably original quality. In Almanzor's speeches it is used as a direct instrument in characterization.

The passage quoted below is one which has been referred to by more than one critic as an example of Dryden at his worst. In the opinion of the present writer, this view is the result of the usual failure to understand Dryden's purpose in these plays. The speech occurs in the scene where Almanzor first meets Almahide, and suddenly falls in love with her. His manner of falling in love is entirely in keeping with his tempestuous nature—

I'me pleas'd and pain'd since first her eyes I saw,
As I were stung with some *Tarantula:*
Armes, and the dusty field, I less admire;
And soften strangely in some new desire;

[9] *Ibid.*

Honour burns in me, not so fiercely bright,
But pale as fires when master'd by the light.
Ev'n while I speak and look, I change yet more;
And now am nothing that I was before.
I'm numm'd, and fix'd, and scarce my eye-balls move;
I fear it is the Lethargy of Love!
'Tis he; I feel him now in every part:
Like a new Lord, he vaunts about my Heart,
Surveys in state each corner of my Brest,
While poor fierce I, that was, am dispossesst.
I'm bound; but I will rowze my rage again:
And though no hope of Liberty remaine,
I'll fright my Keeper when I shake my chaine.[10]

Dryden parodies and exaggerates the conventional psychology of love, the imagery being deliberately made crude to suggest an emotional upheaval of more than normal violence. The passage, if closely examined, exhibits a considerable variety of effects. Lines like—

But pale as fires when master'd by the light

While poor fierce I, that was, am dispossesst

have the authentic ring of serious poetry, while in—

I'll fright my Keeper when I shake my chaine

we have an unexpected image which borders on the comic.

Almanzor's speech of withering invective against Abdalla, at the end of the same scene, derives much of its force and point from the imagery—

Abdalla: Your boldness to your services I give:
Now take it as your full reward to live.
Almanzor: To live!
If from thy hands alone my death can be,
I am immortal; and a god to thee.
If I would kill thee now, thy fate's so low,
That I must stoop 'ere I can give the blow.
But mine is fix'd so far above thy Crown,
That all thy men,
Pil'd on thy back can never pull it down.
But at my ease thy destiny I send,
By ceasing from this hour to be thy friend.
Like Heav'n I need but onely to stand still;
And, not concurring in thy life, I kill.
Thou canst no title to my duty bring:

[10] *Ibid.*, Part I, III.

I'm not thy Subject, and my Soul's thy King.
Farewell, when I am gone,
There's not a starr of thine dare stay with thee:
I'le whistle thy tame fortune after me:
And whirl fate with me wheresoe're I fly,
As winds drive storms before 'em in the sky.[11]

The effect is one of gigantic contrast. While Abdalla is dwarfed and annihilated, Almanzor takes on prodigious stature; he becomes the vehicle of a terrific dynamic power, before which creatures like Abdalla are scattered like chaff before the wind. There is at least one image which is frankly comic, and at least one example of unmistakably "metaphysical" wit. But in its carefully-devised extravagance, the whole passage might justly be said to be in the best metaphysical manner.

It is easy to see how different Dryden's treatment of Almanzor is from, say, Marlowe's treatment of Tamburlaine. For Dryden heroic virtuosity is an idea to be played with; an opportunity for poetry, but also an opportunity for wit. The "power" element in the hero may fill his mind with grandiose conceptions, and so inspire magnificent rhetoric; but it also tempts his essentially plastic mind to indulge in effects of exaggeration or distortion.

It is doubtful whether this dual treatment makes for dramatic success. The intention is probably too subtle to be appreciated by the average playgoer, and it might be difficult to convey in the acting. We have no evidence that it was fully grasped by any of Dryden's contemporaries.

In the character of Almanzor, we see a mixture of the splendid and the grotesque. In some of the minor characters, it is the latter quality which predominates. There were certain types of character which offered themselves as admirable subjects for such treatment—Boabdelin, the wretched king of Granada, whose weakness and vacillation appear doubly contemptible in comparison with Almanzor's superhuman strength; his counterpart, the Emperor in *Aureng-Zebe,* who is as wilful and autocratic as he is impotent; the villainous characters, Abdalla in *The Conquest of Granada,* Morat in *Aureng-Zebe,* and Maximin in *Tyrannic Love*. Dryden makes excellent capital out of the ridiculous figure of the Emperor who, in spite of his decrepit condition, does not consider himself too old for love. The scene in which he quarrels violently with his Empress has been described by Mr. T. S. Eliot as "admirable purple comedy"—

Emperor: 'Tis true, of Marriage-bands I'm weary grown;
Love scorns all ties, but those that are his own.
Chains, that are drag'd, must needs uneasie prove:
For there's a God-like liberty in Love.

[11] *Ibid.*

Nourmahal's reply is exquisitely insulting—

> What's Love to you?
> The bloom of Beauty, other years demands;
> Nor will be gather'd by such wither'd hands;
> You importune it with a false desire:
> Which sparkles out, and makes no solid fire.
> This impudence of Age, whence can it spring?
> All you expect, and yet you nothing bring:
> Eager to ask, when you are past a grant;
> Nice in providing what you cannot want.[12]

In another context, she says of him—

> He only moved and talked, but did not live.

When the Emperor catches one of his courtiers making advances, as he supposes, to the lady he covets, his resentment is expressed with magnificent absurdity—

> Did he my Slave, presume to look so high?
> That crawling Insect, who from Mud began,
> Warm'd by my Beams, and kindl'd into Man?
> Durst he, who does but for my pleasure live,
> Intrench on Love, my great Prerogative? [13]

Dryden is admirable in expressions of gross conceit and self-complacency. Here, his power of creating an effect of spurious plausibility by ingenious argument is frequently brought into play. The scene in which Nourmahal first sees Indamora, the object of her husband's attentions, contains a brilliant example. Nourmahal is struck by her remarkable beauty, and tries to explain to herself how so formidable a rival to her own charms could possibly exist—

> A fairer Creature, did my eyes ne'r see!
> Sure she was form'd by Heav'n, in spite to me!
> Some Angel copi'd, while I slept, each grace,
> And molded ev'ry feature from my face.
> Such Majesty does from her forehead rise,
> Her cheeks such blushes cast, such rays her eyes,
> Nor I, nor Envy, can a blemish find;
> The Palace is, without, too well design'd:
> Conduct me in, for I will view thy mind.

[12] *Aureng-Zebe,* II.
[13] *Ibid.*

Speak, if thou has a Soul, that I may see,
If Heav'n can make throughout, another Me.

Indamora, who has been asleep, wakes, and Nourmahal is reassured by the fear and humility in her manner, that as far as "soul" is concerned, she has nothing to lose by the comparison—

The Palm is, by the Foes confession, mine.
But I disdain what basely you resign.
Heav'n did, by me, the outward model build:
Its inward work, the Soul, with rubbish fill'd.
Yet, Oh! th' imperfect Piece moves more delight;
'Tis gilded o'r with Youth, to catch the sight.
The Gods have poorly robbed my Virgin bloom,
And what I am, by what I was, o'rcome.
Traitress, restore my Beauty and my Charms,
Nor steal my Conquest with my proper Arms.[14]

In the following speech by Morat, Aureng-Zebe's villainous brother who resents his position as a younger son, the imagery is of a peculiar flavor—

for when great Souls are giv'n,
They bear the marks of Sov'reignty from Heav'n.
My Elder Brothers my fore-runners came;
Rough-drafts of Nature, ill-design'd and lame.
Blown off, like Blossoms, never made to bear;
Till I came, finish'd; her last-labour'd care.[15]

The heroic plays and, indeed, the whole of Dryden's work, abound in a kind of imagery, the effect of which is to represent the human species, and processes relating to the creation or generation of the species, as absurd or monstrous. Such imagery corresponds to an habitual mental attitude in Dryden—his delight in thinking ignobly of the soul. It is deliberately used with comic intent.

Here is Aureng-Zebe's description of his brother—

When thou wert form'd, Heav'n did a man begin;
But the brute Soul, by chance, was shuffl'd in.[16]

Nourmahal on Indamora (quoted in full above)—

Heav'n did, by me, the outward model build.
Its inward work, the Soul, with rubbish fill'd.

[14] *Ibid.*, V.
[15] *Ibid.*
[16] *Ibid.*, III.

The Emperor's description of his subjects—

> The Vulgar, a scarce animated Clod,

and

> The little Emmets with the humane Soul.

His definition of children—

> Children the blind effect of Love and Chance.[17]

Dryden enjoys overturning human standards in favor of the sensual self-sufficiency of the brute creation—

> Reason's nice taste does our delights destroy:
> Brutes are more bless'd who grossly feed on joy.[18]

> Or make thy Orders with my reason sute,
> Or let me live by Sense a glorious Brute—[19]

We have already noticed his use of novel and striking imagery as an instrument of characterization. Its effect is usually to distort the character and give it a grotesque quality. In the following lines spoken by Maximin, who expresses resentment because love has come inopportunely into his life, the images have been deliberately chosen to make his emotional condition absurd—

> This Love which never could my youth engage,
> Peeps out his coward head to dare my age.
> Where hast thou been thus long, thou sleeping form,
> That wak'st like drowsie Sea-men in a storm?
> A sullen hour thou chusest for thy birth:
> My Love shoots up in tempests as the earth
> Is stirr'd and loosen'd in a blustring wind,
> Whose blasts to waiting flowers her womb unbind.[20]

There is a touch of oddity in the dying speech of Abdalla—

> *Abdelmelech:* Now ask your Life.
> *Abdalla:* 'Tis gone: that busy thing,
> The Soul, is packing up, and just on wing.
> Like parting Swallows, when they seek the Spring.[21]

[17] *Ibid.*
[18] *Ibid.*, V.
[19] *Ibid.*, III.
[20] *Tyrannic Love,* III.
[21] *The Conquest of Granada,* Part II, IV.

The piquancy of the image is often enhanced by Dryden's splendid powers of statement, his ability to create an impression of weight and importance. For example—a description of a "heavy father"—

> It is a murdering will!
> That whirls along with an impetuous sway;
> And like chain-shot, sweeps all things in its way.[22]

Almanzor on Boabdelin—

> The word that I have giv'n shall stand like Fate;
> Not like the King's, that weathercock of State.
> He stands so high, with so unfixt a mind,
> Two Factions turn him with each blast of wind.[23]

Sometimes an image which is fine in itself becomes absurd in its context—

> Let my Crown go; he never will return;
> I, like a Phœnix, in my Nest will burn.[24]

The speaker is Boabdelin.

More examples may be given of Dryden's witty use of casuistical argument. Some of the best scenes in the heroic plays consist of debates, in which the protagonists—often quarrelling lovers—play a game of skillful wrangling. The scenes between Lyndaraxa and her helplessly amorous victim, Abdelmelech, usually take this form. There is often a mischievous, and sometimes a frankly comic, purpose in Dryden's handling of these debates. The following conversation between Montezuma and the Spaniards, on the subject of the proposed Christianization of Mexico, is typical—

> *Pizarro:* The Soveraign Priest,—
> Who represents on Earth the pow'r of Heaven,
> Has this your Empire to our Monarch given.
> *Montezuma:* Ill does he represent the Powers above,
> Who nourishes debate, not Preaches love;
> Besides, what greater folly can be shown?
> He gives another what is not his own.
> *Vasquez:* His pow'r must needs unquestion'd be below,
> For he in Heaven an Empire can bestow.
> *Montezuma:* Empires in Heaven he with more ease may give,
> And you perhaps would with less thanks receive;
> But Heaven has need of no such Vice-roy here,
> It self bestows the Crowns that Monarchs wear.

[22] *Ibid.*, Part I, V.
[23] *Ibid.*, Part I, III.
[24] *Ibid.*, Part II, I.

Pizarro: You wrong his power as you mistake our end,
Who came thus far Religion to extend.
Montezuma: He, who Religion truely understands,
Knows its extent must be in Men, not Lands.
Odmar: But who are those that truth must propagate
Within the confines of my Father's state?
Vasquez: Religious Men, who hither must be sent
As awful Guides of Heavenly Government;
To teach you Penance, Fasts, and Abstinence,
To punish Bodies for the Soul's offence.
Montezuma: Cheaply you sin, and punish crimes with ease,
Not as th' offended, but th' offenders please.
First injure Heaven and when its wrath is due,
Your selves prescribe it how to punish you.
Odmar: What numbers of these Holy Men must come?
Pizarro: You shall not want, each Village shall have some
Who, though the Royal Dignity they own,
Are equal to it, and depend on none.
Guyomar: Depend on none! You treat them sure in state,
For 'tis their plenty does their pride create.
Montezuma: Those ghostly Kings would parcel out my pow'r,
And all the fatness of my Land devour;
That Monarch sits not safely on his Throne,
Who bears, within, a power that shocks his own.
They teach obedience to Imperial sway,
But think it sin if they themselves obey.[25]

The passage in which Almanzor asserts his claim to Almahide, Boabdelin's betrothed, contains a remarkable mixture of logic-chopping, metaphysical wit, and rhetoric—

Almahide: Alas it is in vain;
Fate for each other did not us ordain.
The chances of this day too clearly show
That Heav'n took care that it should not be so.
Almanzor: Would Heav'n had quite forgot me this one day,
But fate's yet hot—
I'le make it take a bent another way.
(*He walks swiftly and discomposedly, studying.*)
I bring a claim which does his right remove:
You're his by promise, but you're mine by Love.
'Tis all but Ceremony which is past:
The knot's to tie which is to make you fast.

[25] *The Indian Emperor,* I, 2.

Fate gave not to *Boabdelin* that pow'r;
He woo'd you but as my Ambassadour.

Almahide: Our Souls are ty'd by holy Vows above.

Almanzor: He sign'd but his: but I will seal my love.
I love you better, with more Zeale than he.

Almahide: This day—
I gave my faith to him, he his to me.

Almanzor: Good Heav'n thy book of fate before me lay,
But to tear out the journal of this day.
Or, if the order of the world below
Will not the gap of one whole day allow,
Give me that Minute when she made her vow.
"That Minute, ev'n the happy, from their bliss might give;
"And those, who live in griefe, a shorter time would live."
So small a link, if broke, th' eternal chain
Would, like divided waters, joyn again.
It wonnot be; the fugitive is gone,
Prest by the crowd of following Minutes on;
That precious Moment's out of Nature fled,
And on the heap of common rubbish layd,
Of things that once have been, and are decay'd.[26]

There are some admirable examples of audacious and crushing repartee—

Don Arcos: Since thus you have resolv'd, henceforth prepare
For all the last extremities of war:
My King his hope from heavens assistance draws:

Almanzor: The *Moors* have Heav'n, and me, t'assist their cause.[27]

Emperor: You may be pleas'd your Politiques to spare:
I'm old enough, and can my self take care.

Indamora: Advice from me was, I confess, too bold:
Y'are old enough it may be, sir, too old.[28]

Debate and verbal skirmishing are not confined to a few scenes; they dominate the larger part of the heroic plays. The reader of Dryden learns to look to them as a more important source of pleasure than the more dramatic elements in the action.

We are now in a position to sum up our conclusions regarding these plays. It is quite clear from the examples given—and numerous as they

[26] *The Conquest of Granada,* Part I, III.
[27] *Ibid.,* Part I, I.
[28] *Aureng-Zebe,* II.

are, they are merely a selection—that Dryden deliberately used heroic melodrama as a playground for his powers of wit and rhetoric. In choosing this subject-matter he was not going against his nature, as Van Doren suggests. On the contrary, the theme was peculiarly suited to his temperament, and his treatment of it was calculated to the last degree. When he began to write heroic plays, he did not become immediately aware of the possibilities of his material. He was probably attracted to it, in the first instance, merely because it gave him a chance to "let himself go." *The Indian Queen* (in which he collaborated with Sir Robert Howard) contains scarcely any of the elements to which we have referred, though there is a slight tendency towards the comic in Zempoalla. Undercurrents begin to appear in *The Indian Emperor*. Montezuma's tirade against the gods, for example, has some of the flavor of Maximin's much more extravagant outbursts—

> Take, gods, that Soul ye did in spight create,
> And made it great to be unfortunate:
> Ill Fate for me unjustly you provide,
> Great Souls are Sparks of your own Heavenly Pride:
> That lust of power we from your god-heads have,
> You're bound to please those Appetites you gave.[29]

The development is carried further in *Tyrannic Love,* where Maximin is entirely grotesque, and it reaches its height in *The Conquest of Granada* and *Aureng-Zebe*. In the latter play, most of the important characters—the Emperor, Nourmahal, Morat—are comic. Aureng-Zebe, the hero, is a serious figure, an upholder of virtue and loyalty, but his character is modified significantly by frequent expressions of disillusion and resentment against life, all in Dryden's favorite vein.

It is because the heroic plays are completely unreal that it was possible for Dryden to play with his material in this way. The characters, the emotions, the sentiments, are entirely artificial—but in the positive sense of that word. Dryden, as Van Doren points out, had no real insight into human feelings or the springs of human action; he could never have become a dramatist in the Shakespearean manner. But what Van Doren fails to realize is that Dryden was aware of his own limitations, and deliberately chose subject-matter which lent itself to artificial treatment. The theme is so far removed from reality, his version of heroism so cut off from serious values and ideals, that it was possible for him to exploit his material in whatever way suited his fancy.

Dryden composed these plays between 1664 and 1675, and they represent his main poetical output during this period. They have an important place in his development as a poet, because it is in them, especially in

[29] *The Indian Emperor,* II.

The Conquest of Granada and *Aureng-Zebe,* that his great powers are first exercised to the full. The Dryden of the early poems—even *Annus Mirabilis*—was still immature. His individuality had not yet emerged. In the heroic plays he seems to have found a medium in which his personality could develop itself freely. Nearly all the qualities which later made him such a superb satirist were developed at this stage, including the satirical spirit itself. His methods of comic portraiture, for example, were carried over from the plays into the poems, as the imagery in the following lines from *Mac-Flecknoe* clearly demonstrates—

> Some Beams of Wit on other Souls may fall,
> Strike through and make a lucid intervall;
> But Sh—'s genuine night admits no ray,
> His rising Fogs prevail upon The Day:
> Besides, his goodly Fabrick fills the eye
> And seems design'd for thoughtless Majesty:
> Thoughtless as Monarch Oakes that shade the plain,
> And, spread in solemn state, supinely reign.

His powers of debating in verse were exercised in the heroic plays many years before the composition of *The Hind and the Panther.* Critics of Dryden have erred seriously in their failure to trace the continuity between these two phases of his work.

But the Dryden of the heroic plays is different in many ways from the later Dryden: much richer in imagery, much more given to poetical and intellectual exuberance. This is due partly to the difference of subject-matter—the plays gave more scope for free indulgence in fantasy than the satires, which are concerned with topical actualities—and partly to the fact that the plays are earlier work. The metaphysical quality of this earlier style is especially notable. That Dryden was influenced by the metaphysical poets has always been realized, but the examples cited have usually been from those poems in which he was still largely imitative. The examples in the plays, which are much richer and more individual, have been neglected. Dryden differs from the other metaphysical poets in several respects. His images and ideas are not obscure or complicated. On the contrary, the whole effect of his style is to make everything palpable and obvious. While the reader of a poem by Donne is immediately struck by the unusualness of the intellectual content, Dryden's poetry, being essentially rhetorical, makes its first impact on the ear rather than on the mind. Of the two qualities, magniloquence and wit, the former appears to predominate. It is, perhaps, on this account that his metaphysical qualities have been missed.

The Significance of Dryden's *Aureng-Zebe*

by Arthur C. Kirsch

The second decade of the Restoration witnessed two significant changes in the development of serious drama: the advent of sentimental heroes and domestic situations, and the abandonment of rhyme. The changes are particularly interesting because they seem to be related. They can be seen in all the serious plays of the decade, but their relationship is perhaps most clear in Dryden's *Aureng-Zebe* (1676), the play which stands midway between *The Conquest of Granada* (1672) and *All for Love* (1678), the former a rhymed play whose hero exemplifies an aristocratic code of glory and self-aggrandizement, the latter an unrhymed play whose hero is guided by standards of sentiment and self-indulgence.

Sentiment and the Fall of Glory

Aureng-Zebe gathers up many themes and characters long familiar in Dryden's rhymed plays. The Emperor is a variation upon the old Montezuma in *The Indian Emperor,* debasing himself and imperiling his kingdom by a love he cannot control. Nourmahal is a duplicate of the lustful and villainous Zempoalla in *The Indian Queen,* and Arimant, who sues in vain for the heroine's love, is a carbon copy of the equally unsuccessful Acacis of *The Indian Queen*. Indamora is a slightly weaker version of Almahide, the heroine of *The Conquest of Granada;* Melisinda, a considerably more pathetic copy of Valeria, the self-denying mistress of *Tyrannic Love*. Aureng-Zebe and Morat repeat the contrast of virtue and vice embodied by Guyomar and Odmar in *The Indian Emperor*.

But if the characters are old the way in which they are treated is new. Dr. Johnson commented that "The personages [in *Aureng-Zebe*] are imperial; but the dialogue is often domestick, and therefore susceptible of sentiments accommodated to familiar incidents." [1] The clearest verification of his observation is to be found in the character of Melisinda. Melisinda is descended from the unrequited lovers of Dryden's earlier plays,

"The Significance of Dryden's *Aureng-Zebe*." From *ELH,* XXIX (1962), 160-75. Reprinted by permission of Arthur C. Kirsch and of The Johns Hopkins Press.

[1] *Lives of the English Poets,* ed. G. B. Hill (Oxford, 1905), I, 360-61.

but she also anticipates Octavia in *All for Love*. She is a wife and she cannot thrive, as her predecessors had, by meriting the love which her rival possesses. When Morat first reveals his infidelity, Melisinda *"retires, weeping, to the side of the Theatre."* (sig. [G3])[2] Afterwards she tells Morat plaintively of her love for him. Morat replies:

You say you love me; let that love be shown.
'Tis in your power to make my happiness.
Melisinda: Speak quickly: to command me is to bless.
Morat: To *Indamora* you my Suit must move:
You'll sure speak kindly of the man you love.

But Melisinda is not such stuff as the old heroines were made of, though Morat himself, of course, is hardly the hero to inspire her. She answers:

Oh! rather let me perish by your hand,
Than break my heart, by this unkind command . . .
Try, if you please, my Rival's heart to win:
I'll bear the pain, but not promote the sin.

Morat then casts her off, and she weeps again. At this point the Emperor intrudes upon them and notices her tears. Rather than have him think that her marriage has been violated and that her "Lord" is "unkind," she says:

Believe not Rumor, but your self; and see
The kindness 'twixt my plighted Lord and me.
[*Kissing* Morat.
This is our State; thus happily we live;
These are the quarrels which we take and give.
I had no other way to force a Kiss. (*Aside* to Mor.)
Forgive my last Farewel to you, and Bliss.
[*Exit.* (sigs. [H4]-I)

The sentimentality of this farewell is particularly important because the scene is not isolated, as such scenes usually were in Dryden's other plays. The domestic sentimentality with which Melisinda is portrayed pervades the entire play.

The most significant evidence of this domesticity is the contrast between Morat and his brother, Aureng-Zebe. With the partial exception of Guyomar in *The Indian Emperor,* Aureng-Zebe is like no other hero in Dryden's previous plays. Before Aureng-Zebe Dryden's heroes had been distinguished by their capacity for passion, frequently expressed in rant, by their primitivistic if not primitive natures (both Montezuma and

[2] References to Dryden's plays are to the texts of the first editions.

Almanzor are characterized as children of nature), and by their constant desire to prove their worth in love as well as in war. None of them were temperate men: if they denied themselves the physical satisfaction of love they did so, as Almanzor made clear, "because I dare" (*Conquest of Granada,* Part 2, sig. N2). They lived not by virtue, in any conventional sense, but by their pride. They conformed only to their own most extravagant conceptions of individual power, to what Corneille and other French writers termed *la gloire,* and like the Cornélian heroes, they sought not approval but admiration.[3]

To such motives and aspirations Aureng-Zebe is essentially immune. He is described, in contrast to all his brothers, as a man

> . . . by no strong passion sway'd,
> Except his Love, more temp'rate is, and weigh'd: . . .
> He sums their Virtues in himself alone,
> And adds the greatest, of a Loyal Son. (sig. B2v)

The moment he appears on stage he kneels to his father and kisses his hand, exclaiming:

> Once more 'tis given me to behold your face:
> The best of Kings and Fathers to embrace.
> Pardon my tears; 'tis joy which bids 'em flow,
> A joy which never was sincere till now. (sig. C)

Since his love for Indamora is his one "strong passion," he is at first enraged to learn that his father has become his rival, and he threatens to rebel against him to protect Indamora from imprisonment. But she chastens him:

> Lose not the Honour you have early wonn;
> But stand the blameless pattern of a Son. . . .
> My suff'rings for you make your heart my due:
> Be worthy me, as I am worthy you.

Aureng-Zebe rises to the challenge:

> My Virtue was surpris'd into a Crime.
> Strong Virtue, like strong Nature, struggles still:
> Exerts itself, and then throws off the ill.
> I to a Son's and Lover's praise aspire:
> And must fulfil the parts which both require. (sig. C3v)

[3] For a full discussion of these points see my article, "Dryden, Corneille and the Heroic Play," *Modern Philology,* LIX (1962).

For the remainder of the play he does so; he refuses to cede to his father his right to Indamora's love, and at the same time he refuses to sully the "glory"—the word is his—of his name by rebelling against him.

Despite his protestations about the strength of his virtue, Aureng-Zebe is what Indamora calls him, "the blameless pattern of a Son." The enormous capacity for passion of all Dryden's previous heroes—a capacity which Aureng-Zebe is allowed to demonstrate only with the emotion of jealousy—is gone; Aureng-Zebe is a temperate man. Gone too are the roughness which characterized the earlier heroes and the rant which was the emblem of their heroic pride. Aureng-Zebe's failure to embody these qualities would not alone signify Dryden's departure from his earlier conception of heroic drama: Guyomar, for example, had been drawn on similar lines in *The Indian Emperor*. But Guyomar shared the stage with Cortez; Aureng-Zebe is the only hero of the play which bears his name. All the marks of heroic virtue which he lacks are appropriated by Morat, and in Morat the quest for personal glory which had distinguished such characters as Almanzor and Montezuma is stigmatized as unmistakable evidence of villainy. Dryden thus splits the hero, and in the process he irrevocably undermines the heroic *ethos* which had animated his earlier plays.

The change is discernible the moment Morat makes his first appearance. He is a soldier, proud in his power of arms, triumphant in his speech:

> To me, the cries of fighting Fields are Charms:
> Keen be my Sab[r]e, and of proof my Arms.
> I ask no other blessing of my Stars:
> No prize but Fame, nor Mistris but the Wars. (sig. F2)

He also aspires to greatness:

> Me-thinks all pleasure is in greatness found.
> Kings, like Heav'ns Eye, should spread their beams around.
> Pleas'd to be seen while Glory's race they run. (sig. F2v)

But his designs upon the state are unscrupulous; and the maxims by which he proposes to rule are the hallmarks of political villainy. Like his heroic forbears, he is a child of nature, but of a nature which Dryden now makes clear is nasty, solitary and brutish, the reverse of the natural paradise which nourished the virtues of Montezuma and Almanzor. Aureng-Zebe remarks to Morat:

> When thou wert form'd, Heav'n did a Man begin;
> But the brute Soul, by chance, was shuffl'd in.
> In Woods and Wilds thy Monar[c]hy maintain:
> Where valiant Beasts, by force and rapine, reign.

In Life's next Scene, if Transmigration be,
Some Bear or Lion is reserv'd for thee. (sig. F4v)[4]

But this is not the worst of the indignities which Morat's grandeur must suffer. In what is certainly one of the most extraordinary scenes in all of Dryden's heroic drama, Indamora successfully persuades Morat to abandon forever the corrupt code by which he lives. Morat argues that usurpation by force eventually justifies itself:

But who by force a Scepter does obtain,
Shows he can govern that which he could gain.

Indamora replies that such a doctrine is an invitation to an anarchy of power, and Morat begins his retreat:

I without guilt, would mount the Royal Seat;
But yet 'tis necessary to be great.
Indamora: All Greatness is in Virtue understood:
'Tis onely necessary to be good.
Tell me, what is't at which great Spirits aim,
What most your self desire?
Morat: —Renown, and Fame,
And Pow'r, as uncontrol'd as is my will.
Indamora: How you confound desires of good and ill!
For true renown is still with Virtue joyn'd;
But lust of Pow'r lets loose th'unbridl'd mind.
Yours is a Soul irregularly great,
Which wanting temper, yet abounds with heat:
So strong, yet so unequal pulses beat.
A Sun which does, through vapours dimnly shine:
What pity 'tis you are not all Divine! . . .
Dare to be great, without a guilty Crown;
View it, and lay the bright temptation down:
'Tis base to seize on all, because you may;
That's Empire, that which I can give away:
There's joy when to wild Will you Laws prescribe,
When you bid Fortune carry back her Bribe:
A joy, which none but greatest minds can taste;

[4] Aureng-Zebe uses similar language in condemning Nourmahal when he realizes that she is trying to seduce him:

Hence, hence, and to some barbarous Climate fly,
Which onely Brutes in humane form does yield,
And Man grows wild in Nature's common Field. (sigs. H2-H2v)

Cf. Montezuma's account of his wild upbringing (*The Indian Queen,* in Sir Robert Howard, *Four New Plays* [1665], sig. Z2v) and Almanzor's boast of kinship with the "noble Savage" (*The Conquest of Granada,* Part I, sig. [A4]).

A Fame, which will to endless Ages last.
Morat: Renown, and Fame, in vain, I courted long;
And still pursu'd 'em, though directed wrong. . . .
Unjust Dominion I no more pursue;
I quit all other claims, but those to you.
(sigs. K2v-[K3])

Morat does not give up his claims to Indamora, even at his death, but he signifies his reclamation by renouncing his "pleasure to destroy" and by showing generous feelings towards both his brother and Indamora herself (sigs. [K3]-K3v).

There are, of course, many scenes in heroic drama in which the villain converts to virtue on his deathbed. But Morat's capitulation involves far more than himself. With his fall from grandeur, and with Aureng-Zebe's corresponding rise to the virtues of love and piety, Dryden, in effect, recognized the exhaustion of the form of drama which only four years before he had acclaimed as the equal of the tragedies of the last age. *Aureng-Zebe* does not mark a total break with the earlier plays. The peripatetic stage pattern remains, as it was to remain in the drama for years to come; and though the super-hero is clearly repudiated, some of his principles survive. Both Aureng-Zebe and Indamora seek to make themselves worthy of each other, and love and honor are still the principal catch-words. The play closes, in fact, with the Emperor giving Aureng-Zebe Indamora's hand as his "just [reward] of Love and Honour." (sig. M3v) But if the topics are the same—the *"mistaken Topicks of Tragedy,"* Dryden was later to call them—the purposes for which they are used have begun to change. Pity and the capacity for tears have begun to supersede the union of private and public pride as the credentials of heroism, and the focal scenes are those which occasion a display of these sentiments rather than those which demonstrate grandeur and evoke admiration.[5] The virtues which Indamora and Aureng-Zebe insist

[5] This change of focus is evident not only in the scenes and speeches that have been cited, but throughout *Aureng-Zebe*. Compassion is a constant touchstone of virtue in the play. During their first scene together Indamora tells Melisinda that because she is "Distress'd" herself, she "therefore can compassion take, and give," and Melisinda, in return, promises to "pay the charity" which Indamora has "lent [her] grief" (sigs. F, Fv). In a later scene, when their fates seem to have been reversed again, Melisinda remarks:

Madam, the strange reverse of Fate you see:
I piti'd you, now you may pity me. (sig. [G4])

Indamora praises Arimant for his "generous Pity" (sig. C4v) and tells Morat when she pleads for Aureng-Zebe's life:

Had Heav'n the Crown for *Aureng-Zebe* design'd,
Pity, for you, had pierc'd his generous mind.
Pity does with a Noble Nature suit:
A Brother's life had suffer'd no dispute. (sig. [G3])

upon are those of the private life, and there is no corresponding emphasis upon public responsibility. Aureng-Zebe is less the best of subjects than he is the best of sons, one of the first heralds of the paragons of filial devotion that abound in eighteenth-century plays.[6] In Morat's case even the antinomy of love and honor itself begins to be sapped at its roots, for he gives up an honor which, though corrupted, still bears the marks of the old heroic grandeur; and he gives it up *for* love. This is the first time in all of Dryden's drama that love and honor constitute a real antithesis, and the victory of love in this context spells the end of the heroic play. Two years later, Antony also gives up honor, and he does so all for love.

Rhyme and Decorum

The exploitation of sentiment in *Aureng-Zebe* is reflected in the structure of its verse. Saintsbury pointed out that "There is in *Aureng-Zebe* a great tendency towards enjambment; and as soon as this tendency gets

---

Aureng-Zebe confirms Indamora's judgment by taking pity upon Nourmahal, who he thinks is his enemy (sig. E), and upon the Emperor, who he knows has been his rival (sig. I4v).

All the virtuous characters, moreover, demonstrate their compassion by crying. Aureng-Zebe sheds tears when he first sees his father (sig. C), and weeps as a means of earning Indamora's forgiveness after a quarrel (sig. [I4]). Indamora kneels to Nourmahal in tears (sig. Lv), and weeps at Morat's death, as she explains to the jealous Aureng-Zebe, in tribute to her own redemptive powers:

> Those tears you saw, that tenderness I show'd,
> Were just effects of grief and gratitude.
> He di'd my Convert. (sig. M)

Melisinda is described as "bath'd in tears" before the audience ever sees her (sig. E4v), and the moment she does appear, Indamora greets her as a personification of grief:

> When graceful sorrow in her pomp appears,
> Sure she is dress'd in *Melisinda's* tears. (sig. F)

On one occasion Melisinda even delivers a lecture on the beneficence of tears:

> *Indamora:* I'm stupifi'd with sorrow, past relief
> Of tears: parch'd up, and wither'd with my grief.
> *Melisinda:* Dry mourning will decays more deadly bring,
> As a North Wind burns a too forward Spring.
> Give sorrow vent, and let the sluces go. (sig. [K4])

[6] The emphasis upon family relationships throughout *Aureng-Zebe* is notable. For the first time in Dryden's plays, family piety becomes an essential means of differentiating virtue and vice. The virtuous characters in the play are uniformly conscious of their domestic obligations. Aureng-Zebe, as we have seen, is the best of sons; Indamora promises to be the best of daughters-in-law; and Melisinda, as Dryden remarks of her in the dedication, is *"a Woman passionately loving of her husband, patient of injuries and contempt, and constant in her kindness, to the last . . ."* (sig. *a*). On the other hand, the Emperor is loyal neither to his son nor to his wife; Morat is both unconstant and brutal to his wife; and Nourmahal, who boasts that "Love sure's a name that's more Divine than Wife" (Sig. G), entertains desires that are incestuous as well as unfaithful.

the upper hand, a recurrence to blank verse is, in English dramatic writing, tolerably certain." [7] Dryden himself is aware that this is happening, for he complains in the prologue to the play that he

> Grows weary of his long-lov'd Mistris, Rhyme.
> Passion's too fierce to be in Fetters bound,
> And Nature flies him like Enchanted Ground. (sig. [*a*2])

In the dedication he remarks that *"If I must be condemn'd to Rhyme, I should find some ease in my change of punishment. I desire to be no longer the* Sisyphus *of the Stage; to rowl up a Stone with endless labour (which to follow the proverb,* gathers no Mosse) *and which is perpetually falling down again"* (sig. [A4]). At a distance of three centuries we may overlook the importance of these statements, since our own prejudices about the failure of rhymed verse in English drama may lead us to believe that Dryden was simply acknowledging an obvious fact. But in order to understand the significance of what he is saying we must appreciate how central rhyme had been both in his theory and practice of heroic drama.

Dryden's first discussion of rhyme appears as early as 1664 in his dedication of *The Rival Ladies* to the Earl of Orrery. He points out that rhyme is *"not natural"* only *"when the Poet either makes a Vicious choice of Words, or places them for Rhyme (sic) sake so unnaturally, as no Man would in ordinary Speaking . . ."* He states further that

> *the Excellence and Dignity of it, were never fully known till Mr.* Waller *taught it; He first made Writing easily an Art: First shew'd us to conclude the Sense, most commonly, in Distichs; which in the Verse of those before him, runs on for so many Lines together, that the Reader is out of Breath to overtake it. This sweetness of Mr.* Wallers Lyrick *Poesie was afterwards follow'd in the Epick by Sir* John Denham, *in his* Coopers-Hill: *a Poem which your Lordship knows for the Majesty of the Style, is, and ever will be the exact Standard of good Writing. But if we owe the Invention of it to Mr.* Waller, *we are acknowledging for the Noblest use of it to Sir* William D'avenant; *who at once brought it upon the Stage, and made it perfect, in the Siege of* Rhodes. (sig. [A4]; Ker, I, 7)[8]

Having established the literary excellence of this form of verse, and its attendant dignity and majesty, Dryden considers the subjects which are appropriate to it. He acknowledges the common objection that *"Rhyme is only an Embroidery of Sence, to make that which is ordinary in it self pass for excellent with less Examination,"* but he concludes that such a

[7] *Dryden* (London, 1881), p. 57.

[8] With the exception of "A Defence of an Essay of Dramatique Poesie," quotations from Dryden's criticism are from the texts of the first editions, but I have also cited page references from *Essays of John Dryden,* ed. W. P. Ker, 2 vols. (Oxford, 1926). Quotations from "A Defence" are from Ker's text.

defect is caused by an abuse of rhyme: "*. . . as the Best Medicines may lose their Virtue, by being ill applied, so is it with Verse, if a fit Subject be not chosen for it. Neither must the Argument alone, but the Characters, and Persons be great and noble; Otherwise,* (*as* Scaliger *says of* Claudian) *the Poet will be,* Ignobiliore materiâ depressus. *The Scenes, which, in my Opinion, most commend it, are those of Argumentation and Discourse, on the result of which the doing or not doing some considerable action should depend*" (sig. A4v; Ker, I, 8-9). T. S. Eliot has suggested that Dryden defended the rhymed couplet "because it was the form of verse which came most natural to him," [9] and the suggestion is persuasive. The argument of the dedication to *The Rival Ladies* reads suspiciously as if Dryden were trying to parlay his instinct for rhyme into a full-fledged theory of drama; all the salient features of his later theory are present, even the epic analogy, which is implied in the reference to Denham's *Cooper's Hill.* But in any case, the essay stresses the literary perfection of verse which had been practiced by Denham and Waller and ennobled on the stage by Sir William D'avenant, and its argument is controlled throughout by the principle of decorum of style. At its inception, therefore, Dryden's theory of the heroic play constituted a commitment to rhyme and an exploration of the subjects suitable to it.

The following year, in the preface to *Four New Plays,* Sir Robert Howard objected to rhymed plays, arguing that since a play, unlike a poem, "is presented as the present Effect of Accidents not thought of," rhymed verse and rhymed repartee were unnatural, appearing rather as the premeditation of the author than as the natural result of the dialogue and conversation of characters. He added that "the dispute is not which way a Man may write best in, but which is most proper for the Subject he writes upon . . ." [10] In *Of Dramatick Poesie* (1668) Crites reiterates Howard's position, offering a series of arguments terminating in the assertion that since people do not speak in rhyme and since drama must imitate the conversation of people, rhyme has no place in serious drama. Crites recommends that blank verse, which is "nearest Nature," should be preferred. Neander's response is an appeal to decorum: "I answer you . . . by distinguishing betwixt what is nearest to the nature of Comedy, which is the imitation of common persons and ordinary speaking, and what is nearest to the nature of a serious Play: this last is indeed the representation of Nature, but 'tis Nature wrought up to an higher pitch. The Plot, the Characters, the Wit, the Passions, the Descriptions, are all exalted above the level of common converse, as high as the imagination of the Poet can carry them, with proportion to verisimility. Tragedy we know is wont to image to us the minds and fortunes

[9] *John Dryden* (New York, 1932), p. 37.

[10] *Critical Essays of the Seventeenth Century,* ed. J. E. Spingarn (Oxford, 1908), II, 101, 102.

of noble persons, and to portray these exactly, Heroick Rhime is nearest Nature, as being the noblest kind of modern verse" (sigs. I-I2v, Kv; Ker, I, 90-93, 100-01). As in the dedication of *The Rival Ladies* the burden of Dryden's argument lies in his insistence that the style be suited to the purpose of the genre. Thus, a serious play is "nearest Nature" when, in certain respects, it is farthest from it; decorum, not illusion, is the measure of artistic perfection. As Dryden explains, "A Play . . . to be like Nature, is to be set above it; as Statues which are plac'd on high are made greater then the life, that they may descend to the sight in their just proportion" (sig. K2; Ker, I, 102); and the artifice of rhyme, "the noblest kind of modern verse," is the means by which this aesthetic distance can best be achieved.

In "A Defence of an Essay of Dramatique Poesie" Dryden amplifies this position. Howard had repeated his objections to rhyme in the preface to *The Duke of Lerma,* and Dryden replied with a searching exposition of his belief that, above all, "a play is supposed to be the work of the poet" (Ker, I, 114). In support of this conviction he argued that " 'Tis true, that to imitate well is a poet's work; but to affect the soul, and excite the passions, and, above all, to move admiration (which is the delight of serious plays), a bare imitation will not serve. The converse, therefore, which a poet is to imitate, must be heightened with all the arts and ornaments of poesy; and must be such as, strictly considered, could never be supposed spoken by any without premeditation" (Ker. I, 113-14). This passage provides further evidence that in Dryden's mind the heroic play was inseparable from "all the arts and ornaments of poesy," and that rhymed verse was intimately associated with the stipulated end of heroic drama, the creation of epic admiration

In the preface to *The Conquest of Granada* Dryden once again justifies rhyme—this time confident that it was *"already in possession of the Stage."* He remarks that *"it is very clear to all, who understand Poetry, that serious Playes ought not to imitate Conversation too nearly"*; and he adds that *". . . it was onely custome which cozen'd us so long: we thought, because* Shakespear *and* Fletcher *went no farther, that there the Pillars of Poetry were to be erected. That, because they excellently describ'd Passion without Rhyme, therefore Rhyme was not capable of describing it* (sigs. a2-a2v; Ker, I, 148-49). Rhymed heroic verse, *"the last perfection of Art,"* was clearly Dryden's bid for dramatic fame. He wrote in the preface to *Annus Mirabilis* (1667) that he preferred Virgil to Ovid because Virgil, speaking usually in his own person, *"thereby gains more liberty then the other, to express his thoughts with all the graces of elocution, to write more figuratively, and to confess, as well the labour as the force of his imagination"* (sig. A8; Ker, I, 15-16). The self-conscious employment of artifice had a long history in the drama and criticism of Jonson, Fletcher and their followers, including D'avenant. Dryden was an heir to this tradition, and the rhymed heroic play was his attempt to preserve it by perfecting upon the English stage a language of tragedy that would *"confess as well the labour as the force of his imagination."*

But the practice of such a language, as Dryden had repeatedly argued, was contingent upon a conception of tragedy which could justify it. Consequently, his admission in the prologue to *Aureng-Zebe* that he is weary of rhyme and that "Passion's too fierce to be in Fetters bound" is not primarily a confession of impatience with the heroic couplet itself—Dryden continued to use rhyme in other genres—but rather a critical recognition that the purpose of serious drama was changing and that therefore the artifice of rhyme could no longer exercise its proper function in the theatre.[11] The same principle of decorum by which Dryden had justified rhyme for the representation of grandeur and glory compelled him to acknowledge its inappropriateness for the portrayal of sentiment and piety.

In both its form and substance, therefore, *Aureng-Zebe* represents a turning point in Dryden's dramatic career; and the domesticity, sentimental characterizations, and appeals to pity and tears which are evident in *Aureng-Zebe* become increasingly dominant in the plays which immediately follow it: particularly in *All for Love* (1678) and *Troilus and Cressida* (1679).[12] *All for Love* is professedly designed "to work up the pity [of the original story] to a greater heighth . . ." (sig. b). Octavia is introduced as a stock if uninviting symbol of the family and the scene in which she appears *"leading* Antony's *two little Daughters"* (sig. [F3]) is a paradigm of sentimental drama. Cleopatra, who complains that "Nature meant" her to be "A Wife, a silly harmless houshold Dove,/Fond without art; and kind without deceit" (sig. [G4]), is a drastically domesticated version of Shakespeare's heroine; and Antony, who Dryden notes is not "altogether wicked, because he could not then be pitied" (sig. b), is as different from Shakespeare's hero as he is from the heroical hero of Dryden's earlier plays. Indecisive, and the constant prey of conflicting sentiments, Antony is thrown by the successive pleas of Ventidius,

[11] Judging by the stage effects in *Aureng-Zebe* itself, and by the form of heroism the play supports, audiences began to demand a sense of illusion rather than of artifice, domesticated heroes whom they could sympathize with rather than admire. Under such circumstances, as Dryden seems increasingly to have realized, Sir Robert Howard's arguments were valid. Dryden fully disavowed the style of the rhymed heroic play in the preface to *Troilus and Cressida* (1679) and the dedication of *The Spanish Fryar* (1681); see Ker, I, 222-24, 245-47. For a discussion of the aesthetic consequences of this change of taste see Earl R. Wasserman, "The Pleasures of Tragedy," *ELH,* XIV (1947), 283-307.

[12] The material of *Oedipus* (1679), which Dryden wrote in collaboration with Lee, was less amenable to sentimental treatment, although Dryden made the most of his opportunities. Oedipus and Jocasta are reduced to figures of sensational distress, and a new sub-plot is introduced dealing with the pathetic circumstances of the lovers, Euridice and Adrastus.

Octavia, Dolabella and Cleopatra into alternating postures of grief and hope; and his capacity to assume such postures with extravagance and tears becomes the final measure of his heroism. Dryden describes him accurately in the prologue:

> His Heroe, whom you Wits his Bully call,
> Bates of his mettle; and scarce rants at all:
> He's somewhat lewd; but a well-meaning [m]ind;
> Weeps much; fights little; but is wond'rous kind. (sig. χ)

To an extent, the description applies to every major character in the play, all of whom, with the exception of Alexas, an unregenerate villain, demonstrate their worth by fighting little and weeping much.[13]

Troilus and Cressida shows a similar orientation towards sentimental effects. Cressida, like Cleopatra, is made transparently faithful; and Troilus, like Antony, is portrayed in a series of tableaux of grief and hope; Hector, the play's most exemplary character, numbers as a principal heroic virtue his devotion as a husband and a brother. All three characters, but especially the men, are distinguished by their ability to feel compassion for one another. Hector is valiant, but Andromache's highest praise of him is that his "Soul is proof to all things but to kindness" (sig. I2). Troilus, younger and more demonstrative than Hector, shows his mettle by tears and distraction. During their farewell scene he and Cressida *"both weep over each other"* (sig. G), and after Cressida kills herself to prove her fidelity to him, he demonstrates his own love by the extremity of his grief:

> . . . she dy'd for me;
> And like a woman, I lament for her:
> Distraction pulls me several ways at once,
> Here pity calls me to weep out my eyes;
> Despair then turns me back upon my self,
> And bids me seek no more, but finish here.
> [*Sword to his breast.* (sig. K2v)

The play's most celebrated scene, added by Dryden at the suggestion of Betterton, shows Troilus and Hector debating whether to surrender Cressida to the Greeks. The dispute has the same turns and counterturns as

[13] The tears of the men in *All for Love* are especially conspicuous. Antony weeps three times onstage (sigs. C. [F4], I3v-[I4]) and once his "falling tear" is reported (sig. D). Dolabella cries when Antony exiles him, (sigs. I3v-[I4]) and even Ventidius cries twice, once in grief for Antony (sig. C) and once in joy over Antony's family reunion:

> My joy stops at my tongue;
> But it has found two chanels here for one,
> And bubbles out above. (sig. G)

the rhymed debates in Dryden's earlier plays, but the crux of the argument is now plainly the point of pity rather than the point of honor. After Troilus agrees to give Cressida up, Hector tells him, "I pity thee, indeed I pity thee," and Troilus answers:

> Do; for I need it: let me lean my head
> Upon thy bosome; all my peace dwells there;
> Thou art some God, or much much more then man!

In a final turn, Hector offers to fight to keep Cressida in Troy, but Troilus refuses: "That you have pitied me is my reward," and Hector concedes: "The triumph of this kindeness be thy own" (sig. F4v).[14]

The reward of pity and the triumph of kindness in *All for Love* and *Troilus and Cressida* are the natural results of the process which begins in *Aureng-Zebe*. There are specific resemblances between *Aureng-Zebe* and the later plays: the give and take of compassion between Indamora and Melisinda looks forward to the debates between Antony and Ventidius and between Hector and Troilus; Indamora's praise of Aureng-Zebe's capacity for pity anticipates Andromache's praise of Hector's responsiveness to kindness; Melisinda's abandonment is a model for Octavia's. But more important than the particular analogues is the major shift of emphasis in *Aureng-Zebe* which makes the later developments possible. Morat's conversion and the repudiation of his aspirations to personal glory, Aureng-Zebe's temperance and family loyalty, Melisinda's unrelieved distress, and the general disposition of all the exemplary characters to demonstrate their virtue through tears and compassion mark Dryden's distinct departure from his earlier ideals of heroic drama and pave the way for the stress upon domestic piety and compassion that characterizes both his own subsequent plays and the plays of the dramatists who succeeded him.

Dryden, of course, was not alone in creating this orientation, nor did he exploit it as extensively as his younger contemporaries, Lee and Otway, but *Aureng-Zebe* is a testimony to his sensitivity to its dramaturgical consequences. In the history of the late seventeenth-century English theatre *Aureng-Zebe* stands out as an important anticipation of the sentimental drama that flourished in the following century.

[14] In analyzing the aim of tragedy in the preface to *Troilus and Cressida,* Dryden says that "*. . . when we see that the most virtuous, as well as the greatest, are not exempt from . . . misfortunes, that consideration moves pity in us: and insensibly works us to be helpfull to, and tender over the distress'd, which is the noblest and most God-like of moral virtues,*" (sig. a2v; Ker, I, 210) a statement which relates Dryden's growing concern with pity to contemporary benevolist theories. See R. S. Crane, "Suggestions toward a Genealogy of the 'Man of Feeling,'" *ELH,* I (1934), pp. 205-30.

All for Love

by Eugene M. Waith

The comparison of *All for Love* with Shakespeare's *Antony and Cleopatra* has been an exercise for innumerable students, the subject of at least one German dissertation,[1] and of a few sentences in every history of the drama. Here, aside from an occasional reference to Shakespeare, the context will be Dryden's other plays. It is easy to exaggerate the differences between *All for Love* and the two heroic plays already discussed [*The Conquest of Granada* and *Aureng-Zebe.* ED.]. Dryden himself led the way towards putting it in a category apart not only by abandoning couplets to "imitate the divine Shakespeare," [2] but by his comment in the late essay, "A Parallel of Poetry and Painting," that he never wrote anything (presumably meaning any of his plays) for himself but *Antony and Cleopatra* (Ker, II, 152). Since Dryden's time critics have considered it exceptional in having an artistic merit which they deny to *The Conquest of Granada* or *Aureng-Zebe,* and one of the most astute of the recent critics has seen it as an exception in Dryden's thematic development.[3] There can be no doubt that there are differences, but the resemblances which bind *All for Love* to its predecessors, if less obvious, are very strong. The verse is certainly much freer; yet it retains often the antithetical balance common to heroic couplets, as when Cleopatra says of Caesar:

> He first possess'd my person; you, my love:
> Caesar lov'd me; but I lov'd Antony. (II, 353-4)

Though emotion is presented with more immediacy in this play than in *The Conquest of Granada,* the basic concerns from which the emotions arise remain very similar, and the entire framework of feeling and

[1] F. Hannmann, *Dryden's Tragödie "All for Love" und ihr Verhältnis zu Shakespeare's "Antony and Cleopatra"* (Rostock, 1903).

[2] Preface to *All for Love, Essays of John Dryden,* ed. W. P. Ker (2 vols., Oxford, 1926), I, 200.

[3] John Winterbottom, "The Development of the Hero in Dryden's Tragedies," *Journal of English and Germanic Philology,* LII (1953), 162.

thought within which the characters discuss their problems is the same. If the characters of *All for Love* are less stylized in presentation, they are still of the same family as the characters in Dryden's other heroic plays.

One of the family connections is seen in the traits of the Herculean hero which reappear in Antony. Though the title of the play leaves no doubt about the primacy of the theme of love, the hero, like his prototype in Shakespeare's play, is a warrior whose nobility and generosity are combined with strong passion and a contemptuous disregard for the mores of his society. Dryden's Antony manifests these characteristics in ways which relate him even more closely to Almanzor and Morat than to Shakespeare's hero. And Cleopatra is much more closely related to other Dryden heroines than to Shakespeare's Cleopatra. These relationships must now be examined in more detail.

The first extended description of Antony is given by his general, Ventidius, who is known to the Egyptians as one who does not share in Antony's debauches, "but presides/O'er all his cooler hours" (I, 103-4):

> Virtue's his path; but sometimes 'tis too narrow
> For his vast soul; and then he starts out wide,
> And bounds into a vice, that bears him far
> From his first course, and plunges him in ills:
> But, when his danger makes him find his fault,
> Quick to observe, and full of sharp remorse,
> He censures eagerly his own misdeeds,
> Judging himself with malice to himself,
> And not forgiving what as man he did,
> Because his other parts are more than man. (I, 124-33)

Here again is an "irregular greatness" which cannot be quite contained within the bounds of virtue. Antony is farther than Almanzor from being a "pattern of perfect virtue," much farther than Aureng-Zebe, and not so far as Morat. The admiration of Ventidius is apparent, but equally so is his Roman attempt to distinguish neatly between what is to be praised and blamed in Antony. As Aureng-Zebe tries to dissect the paradox of Morat into man and brute, Ventidius divides Antony into erring man and "more than man," but in spite of this logical division the implication of the speech is that virtue and vice are distinctions of secondary importance when discussing so vast a soul. Later in the play, echoing the "taints and honours" speech of Shakespeare's Maecenas, he says:

> And sure the gods, like me, are fond of him:
> His virtues lie so mingled with his crimes,
> As would confound their choice to punish one,
> And not reward the other. (III, 48-51)

The impossibility of confining Antony's spirit is the essence of his heroic individuality. When his fortune has ebbed to its lowest point, he compares his fortitude to a "native spring" which again fills the dried riverbed to overflowing:

> I've still a heart that swells, in scorn of fate,
> And lifts me to its banks. (III, 133-4)

The image recalls Shakespeare's Antony, but echoes Almanzor more closely:

> I cannot breathe within this narrow space;
> My heart's too big, and swells beyond the place.
> (1 *Conquest,* V, 3, 23-4)

In Ventidius' initial description Antony's love is sharply differentiated from his virtue. It is obviously the vice into which the great man has "bounded"—an unruly, excessive infatuation. It may be compared with the "wild deluge" of the opening lines of the play, where Serapion is talking of "portents and prodigies." To stem this disastrous flow is the task which Ventidius has set himself, regardless of the admiration he has for Antony's largeness of spirit.

It is a commonplace of criticism that the first act of Dryden's play is dominated by Ventidius. Never again are we so completely in the warrior's world. From a dramatic point of view the showpiece of this act, and indeed one of the best scenes of the entire play, is the quarrel and reconciliation of Antony and his general. It has always been thought to derive from the famous quarrel and reconcilation of Brutus and Cassius, and Hart and Mohun, who took these parts in Shakespeare's play, distinguished themselves as Antony and Ventidius. Dryden preferred the scene, as he states in the preface, to anything he had written "in this kind." It bears a certain resemblance to the reconciliation of Aureng-Zebe with his father and more to the quarrel and reconciliation of Dorax and Don Sebastian, written many years later. In all of these scenes the generosity of the heroic mind triumphs over *amour propre.*

The significance of Antony's scene with Ventidius, however, is totally different from that of Aureng-Zebe's scene with the Emperor. Not only is the hero in this instance more sinning than sinned against, but the result of the dialogue is to arouse, not to pacify, the party at fault. The Emperor had to be induced to give up the senseless persecution of his son; Antony has to be roused from the torpor of remorse. Antony's change is presented in a highly dramatic contrast. At the beginning of the scene he throws himself on the ground, calling himself the "shadow of an emperor" and thinking of the time when he will be "shrunk to a few cold ashes." At the end, standing with Ventidius, he says:

> O, thou has fir'd me; my soul's up in arms,
> And mans each part about me. (I, 438-9)

The vital spark which makes him great has been restored.

In *All for Love* appears again the contrast between the fiery spirit and the cold one, analogous, as I have suggested, to Dryden's familiar contrast between wit and dullness. Though Antony is cold and torpid at the beginning, he is by nature fiery, and is brought to himself by the force of friendship. Caesar, his opposite, is "the coldest youth," who gives "so tame" an answer to Antony's challenge, has not even warmth enough to die by a fever, and rather than risk death will "crawl upon the utmost verge of life" (II, 113-30).

> O Hercules! Why should a man like this,
> Who dares not trust his fate for one great action,
> Be all the care of heav'n? (II, 131-3)

The task that Ventidius accomplishes in the first act may be looked at in two ways. It is in one sense a curbing and controlling of Antony. This aspect is suggested early by Ventidius' stern disapproval of Cleopatra's lavish plans for celebrating Antony's birthday. But it is also the firing of Antony's soul, and this is the aspect which is emphasized. To Ventidius the enemy is, of course, Cleopatra, but the worst of her effect on Antony is to have made him a "mute sacrifice" and "the blank of what he was." The state of mind which Ventidius has to combat directly is a paralyzing remorse:

> You are too sensible already
> Of what y'have done, too conscious of your failings; (I, 312-13)

> you sleep away your hours
> In desperate sloth, miscall'd philosophy. (I, 336-7)

In fact, Antony is at this time in a state very similar to Samson's when Manoa comes, in the second episode of *Samson Agonistes,* to warn him against being "over-just" with himself. The maintaining of the inner fire is so important a part of Dryden's concept of the heroic that it is stressed even in the depiction of Cleomenes, the nearly perfect hero of Dryden's last tragedy. The words of Cleomenes' mother might be almost as well applied to Antony:

> This melancholy flatters, but unmans you.
> What is it else, but penury of soul,
> A lazy frost, a numbness of the mind,
> That locks up all the vigour to attempt,
> By barely crying,—'tis impossible! (I, SS, VIII, 276)

Only when Cleomenes assures her that his is a grief of fury, not despair, is his mother satisfied. "Desperate sloth," "penury of soul," "a lazy frost" —by the heroic code these are the true sins, beside which other forms of moral deviation pale.

Cleopatra is first seen as the cause of Antony's unmanning. The theatrical strategy of this first unfavorable impression, established only to be radically altered later on, is almost the only similarity between Dryden's treatment of his heroine and Shakespeare's. After exposure to the charms of Shakespeare's Cleopatra, who manages to remain marvellously attractive even at her most hoydenish and deceitful ("holy priests bless her when she is riggish"), one is apt to find the Cleopatra of Dryden shockingly tame and stiff. While it is easy to picture Shakespeare's Cleopatra in anything from Egyptian dress to the bodice and farthingale she probably wore on the Elizabethan stage, Dryden's Cleopatra belongs in late seventeenth-century court dress, complete with train. Passion never quite robs her of dignity. There is no haling of messengers by the hair, no riggishness. To understand this Cleopatra is an essential preliminary to understanding the play.

She dominates the second act as Ventidius does the first. In her initial appearance with Iras and her eunuch, Alexas, she proclaims her love a "noble madness" and a "transcendent passion" which has carried her "quite out of reason's view" till she is "lost above it" (II, 17-22). Force and excessiveness combine here with nobility as they do in Ventidius' first description of Antony. The heroine is no mere temptress to lure the hero from the path of virtue.[4] She is herself carried away by a passion of heroic proportions like his. Serapion's description of the flood, already suggested as an analogue for Antony's love, may be associated even more properly with Cleopatra's:

> Our fruitful Nile
> Flow'd ere the wonted season, with a torrent
> So unexpected, and so wondrous fierce,
> That the wild deluge overtook the haste
> Ev'n of the hinds that watch'd it . . . (I, 2-6)

Dryden has taken over Shakespeare's insistence on the resemblances between the lovers and added another in giving Cleopatra a heroic stature like Antony's. Grandeur and largeness of mind are hers as much as they are his. In fact it is her high-mindedness rather than her sensual attraction which persuades Antony not to leave her. The telling blow is her announcement that she refused a kingdom from Caesar because of her

[4] Largely for this reason I cannot accept in its entirety the interesting parallel between the play and Carracci's "Choice of Hercules" proposed by Jean Hagstrum, *The Sister Arts* (University of Chicago Press, 1958 [pp. 184 ff.]).

loyalty to Antony (in her noble contempt for wealth she resembles the Cleopatra of Fletcher and Massinger's *The False One*). By the end of the act these similar lovers have been brought together to the dismay of Ventidius, but it is to be noticed that Antony's conviction that Cleopatra is worth more than all the world does not alter his heroic determination to fight with Caesar. There is now the additional motive of revenge for Caesar's attempt to corrupt Cleopatra. Love for her is not entirely the effeminizing passion Ventidius thinks it to be, and despite her dignified bearing she is far from tame.

One sentence of self-description has exposed Cleopatra to a great deal of unfriendly laughter:

> Nature meant me
> A wife; a silly, harmless, household dove,
> Fond without art, and kind without deceit. (IV, 91-3)

The comparison is not apt, and it is particularly unfortunate that the incongruity blocks the understanding of a crucial point—Cleopatra's attitude towards being a wife. In Shakespeare's play "Husband I come" owes its brilliance as much to its unexpectedness as to its rightness. It signals a transformation in Cleopatra matching the re-emergence of the heroic Antony. In Dryden's play the change is a much smaller one, and so thoroughly prepared that it is no shock to hear:

> I have not lov'd a Roman, not to know
> What should become his wife; his wife, my Charmion!
> For 'tis to that high title I aspire . . . (V, 412-14)

Her first reference to marriage is contemptuous, as one might expect. Charmion has brought a message that, though Antony is leaving, he will always respect Cleopatra, and she picks up the word with obvious irritation:

> Is that a word
> For Antony to use to Cleopatra?
> O that faint word, *respect!* how I disdain it!
> Disdain myself, for loving after it!
> He should have kept that word for cold Octavia.
> Respect is for a wife: am I that thing,
> That dull, insipid lump, without desires,
> And without pow'r to give 'em? (II, 77-84)

The speech not only expresses Cleopatra's pique but establishes an attitude towards the cold and the dull exactly like that of Antony (the speech precedes Antony's comments on Caesar by only thirty lines). Though Cleopatra in other moods and other circumstances speaks more favorably of being a wife, she retains to the end her scorn of a "dull, insipid lump."

Immediately after vowing to follow the dead Antony as a dutiful wife, she adds:

> Let dull Octavia
> Survive, to mourn him dead: my nobler fate
> Shall knit our spousals with a tie too strong
> For Roman laws to break. (V, 415-18)

The opposition between "spousals" and "Roman laws" provides the necessary clue here. Cleopatra considers her love above and beyond law as it is above and beyond reason, yet she borrows from marriage law the terms which distinguish this love from an infatuation of the senses. Her unfortunate self-comparison to a household dove (the context of which will have to be examined later) is part of this process of distinguishing her feelings both from the dullness of the routine and every-day and from the purely sensual and transient.

A glance back at *The Conquest of Granada* will make the distinction clear. Cleopatra's love (and Antony's too) is the sort that Queen Isabella defines[5]:

> Love's a heroic passion which can find
> No room in any base degenerate mind:
> It kindles all the soul with honor's fire,
> To make the lover worthy his desire.
> (2 *Conquest,* I, 1, 145-8)

The fire and honor of such a love distinguish it from the "lethargy" to which Abdalla succumbs under Lyndaraxa's spell and also from the mere legality of Almahide's relationship to Boabdelin, "When all I knew of love, was to obey!" Almanzor at first takes love for a "lethargy," but by the time of his debate with Lyndaraxa he has learned that though it is not controlled by reason it is both constant and strong:

> 'Tis an enchantment where the reason's bound;
> But Paradise is in th'enchanted ground . . .
> My love's my soul; and that from fate is free;
> 'Tis that unchang'd and deathless part of me.
> (2 *Conquest,* III, 3, 146-7, 179-80)

Similarly, Antony is lethargic at the opening of the play, seemingly unmanned by love. He is "fired" first by Ventidius, though still half unwilling to leave Cleopatra. When she has persuaded him of the nobility of her love, he identifies his passion with his heroism, much as Almanzor does, and prepares with a whole heart for his battle with Caesar. The

[5] See Scott C. Osborn, "Heroical Love in Dryden's Heroic Drama." *Publications of the Modern Language Association,* LXXIII (1958), 480-90.

spectacle of triumph with which the third act opens presents the momentarily successful fusion of warrior and lover.

When Cleopatra compares herself to a household dove she is explaining to Alexas why she does not want to adopt his plan of flirting with Dolabella to arouse Antony's jealousy: she is opposed to all deceit. Repeatedly during the play her plainness is brought out. Though she finally takes the advice of Alexas, she is unable to maintain the counterfeit. Later, when the false news of her death is carried to Antony, she, unlike Shakespeare's heroine, is unaware of the ruse. Antony, too, has a transparent nature, and both of them in this respect resemble Almanzor, who compares his heart to a crystal brook. Antony complains of his "plain, honest heart," and compares himself to "a shallow-forded stream" (IV, 432-40). Plainness is another heroic trait which Dryden has given to Cleopatra; his desire to emphasize it in the scene with Dolabella leads him to force the comparison of his heroine to a wife, who is further compared to a fond and artless dove. If Cleopatra lacks the dullness of a wife, she hopes to prove that she lacks the meretriciousness of a mistress.

The comparison of two kinds of love is best seen in Cleopatra's interview with Antony's legal wife, who is hardly more like a household dove than Cleopatra. Dryden was well aware that the unhistorical introduction of Octavia in Act III was his most daring innovation. I doubt whether it has the effect which Dryden most feared, of dividing the audience's sympathies (and he notes that no critic made this objection), but it has other consequences, very likely unintentional, though by no means damaging to the total effect of the play. Briefly stated, they are the shift from the contrast between Cleopatra and Caesar to the contrast between Cleopatra and Octavia and the resulting transfer of heroic values to the realm of love.

In Shakespeare's play Caesar remains throughout the chief embodiment of the Roman point of view as Cleopatra of the Egyptian. Caesar's ideal of heroic man is a Stoic concept of the warrior, whereas Cleopatra's includes both warrior and lover. The same might be said of the ideals of these two characters in *All for Love,* but from the moment that Octavia appears, she usurps her brother's antipodal position. The confrontation with Cleopatra establishes her firmly as Antony's alternative choice. Even Ventidius, who represents Roman values though qualified by his admiration for Antony, relies on Octavia to make the Roman ideal compelling. Thus, though the issue remains Antony's choice of love or his responsibilities in the world, the stage presents as the dramatic symbols of these alternatives two women, Cleopatra and Octavia, and the choice at the centre of the play becomes one between love and marriage. The turn of the third act which determines Antony for the second time to leave Cleopatra is not, as it was in the first act, the responsibility to fight Caesar in order to show the world who is master, but duty to a wife, through whom he may reach a peaceful understanding with Caesar. Octavia's weapons are her unrequited love and her children. Cleopatra, who was portrayed in the first act as a deterrent to heroic action, now appears as an alternative to domestic love. When the two women meet, they naturally quarrel over which one of them loves Antony more, and Cleopatra stakes her claim on the very extravagance of her love, which has made her give up her good name in order to become Antony's mistress. The fourth act in effect tests the truth of this love in the episode of Dolabella, showing that it is too great to be concealed. Octavia's love, in this same act, is overwhelmed by outrage. When she leaves in the midst of angry (though justifiable) accusations, it is reduced to duty, its basic component all along.

In the fifth act Antony is separated from both women. Octavia has left and he has quarrelled with Cleopatra over her supposed liking for Dolabella. The problems of empire are raised again but only to be reabsorbed in the problems of love. Though the Egyptian fleet has deserted and Caesar is at the gates, Antony is primarily concerned with Cleopatra's feelings towards him. When he thinks that she has fled, his first thought is that she has "fled to her Dolabella"; the accusation that she has turned to Caesar comes second. The idea of a heroic last stand is banished in an instant by the false news of Cleopatra's death, which seems to prove her innocence. The only possible heroic action now is suicide, since

> I was but great for her; my pow'r, my empire,
> Were but my merchandise to buy her love . . . (V, 270-1)

The structure of the play has been called episodic. Noyes says that "like that of *The Conquest of Granada,* it deals with successive adventures in the life of one man, not with one central crisis" (p. xlix). Jean Hagstrum says the play "is not a closely concatenated action that unfolds moral justice. It is a gallery of related heroic poses intended to arouse our sympathy . . . and our admiration . . ." (*The Sister Arts,* p. 196). The second judgment is much the more acceptable, and surely the relatedness which Hagstrum recognizes is provided by the crisis in the love-relationship of Antony and Cleopatra, the concern of each act in the play. It is strange to complain of looseness of structure in a play whose strength resides in concentration upon one problem. In this respect the structure is a refinement upon that of *The Conquest of Granada* and *Aureng-Zebe.* The three plays constitute a series in progressive tightness and simplification.

In *All for Love* the Herculean hero's quest for unbounded power is replaced by a quest for unbounded love. In *The Conquest of Granada* a noble love modifies the masculine drive for power, redirecting it towards a goal acceptable to society. In *Aureng-Zebe* Indamora tries to exert a similar modifying and redirecting influence, but without achieving the same results as Almahide. Aureng-Zebe's love for her is his one unruly passion, and Morat gives up his ambition for "unjust dominion" only to replace it by a love which ignores marital bonds. We never see Antony, as we do Almanzor and Morat, at a time when military conquest is his chief aim. In spite of the efforts of Ventidius, the problems of empire rapidly sink to a position of secondary importance, hardly competing in Antony's mind with his desire for Cleopatra. At the end of the play, instead of the heroic image of him conjured up by Shakespeare's Cleopatra, we are presented with a stage picture of the bodies of the two lovers, regally attired and seated next each other in throne-like chairs. When Serapion finds them he says:

> See, see how the lovers sit in state together,
> As they were giving laws to half mankind! (V, 507-9)[6]

Only in this paradoxical image is the idea of world-conquest restated, and even here it is subordinated to the triumph of love.

It is a curious fact that this play, which is so thoroughly a love-tragedy, is in one important respect closer to the pattern of Herculean plays than either *The Conquest of Granada* or *Aureng-Zebe*. In both of these plays the final emphasis is on a reconciliation of heroic energies with the laws of society. Almanzor remains an invincible hero but in the service of Ferdinand and Isabella. Morat's case is more ambiguous, but at the end death has removed his irregular greatness, and the compelling image of the hero lying at Indamora's feet gives way to tableaux of orderly family relationships. Aureng-Zebe, after a quarrel, is reconciled to Indamora. Melesinda marches in a religious procession to her husband's funeral pyre, where she will commit suttee. Nourmahal, the spirit of restless disorder, dies on the stage. Aureng-Zebe, having succeeded in restoring his father to power, receives the crown from his hands. In *All for Love* the effort to tame or redirect the hero's energies is totally unsuccessful. The love which the play celebrates soars beyond reason and legality, leading the lovers to defiance of the world and a final self-assertion in suicide. In his unrepentant commitment to a highly individualistic ideal Antony is a logical successor to Morat, but far more Herculean than Almanzor or Aureng-Zebe.

For different reasons, the play as a whole is more like the other Herculean plays than is Shakespeare's *Antony and Cleopatra*. There Antony's love is more clearly an alternative to heroic action, however attractively that alternative is presented. In *All for Love* it is not merely that the world is well lost for such a love, but that Dryden, largely through his treatment of Cleopatra, has elevated the love and made its truth and

[6] Noyes, departing from the quarto, prints the first "See" as a separate line.

strength unquestionable, though to attain it the world must be defied. Thus presented, it becomes a suitable enterprise for a hero.

In the preface Dryden makes it clear that the lovers are to be blamed for not controlling their passions and finds the attraction of the story in the "excellency of the moral," but he also states that he has drawn the characters of the hero and the heroine as favorably as his sources would permit him. His emphasis on the greatness and nobility of their love is obviously part of this process. The result is a powerful claim on the sympathy of the audience and perhaps less moral instruction than Dryden liked to think. In fact, the love of Antony and Cleopatra, elevated to the level of a "heroic passion," contains the very sort of contradictions which make a moral judgment of Tamburlaine or Bussy so difficult. The love itself is an extravagant, fiery force, knowing no obligations, and yet ennobling in spite of its extralegality. It is a pattern of loyal commitment. One might say that the moral is not (as Dryden implies) the punishment of lovers who fail to control their passions, but the tragic limitations imposed by human existence on the infinite aspirations of heroic passion.

The Herculean hero seen on the English stage from Marlowe's time to Dryden's was essentially a Renaissance figure—a revival of a heroic concept already very old when it was presented by Sophocles and Euripides. Though firmly based in a morality of its own, it was a concept which challenged orthodox morality and was not widely accepted even in times which prized individualism highly. If it formed the root of the Western idea of heroism, it never became the standard form of the idea. In the Christian era it was a lion in constant danger of being thrown to the faithful. In England at the end of the seventeenth century, Jeremy Collier's famous and ludicrously misnamed "short view" of the stage created an atmosphere still more hostile to moral ambiguity. But Collier's attack was, of course, only one manifestation of a general "shift of sensibility," to use Frederick Pottle's phrase. The growing sense of civic responsibility which found persuasive advocates in Addison and Steele demanded unequivocal self-sacrifice of the hero. Cato, on these grounds, was infinitely preferable to Hercules. Parallel to this development and intimately related to it was the increasingly high regard for pity, already described by Dryden in 1679 as "the noblest and most god-like of moral virtues," [7] and associated by Rowe with "good-nature," [8] that civic virtue so much discussed in the eighteenth century. The Herculean hero, not conspicuously good-natured himself, does not appeal primarily to the good-natured pity of the spectator.

[7] Preface to *Troilus and Cressida* (Ker, I, 210).

[8] Epistle Dedicatory to *The Ambitious Stepmother* (1700).

Admiration for the uncompromisingly individual warrior ceases for a time, to begin again in a somewhat different form in the Romantic movement. Heathcliff and Captain Ahab, different as they both are from Tamburlaine or Morat, are loved and feared for somewhat similar reasons. Their shocking infractions of the code of ordinary decency are similarly accepted as integral parts of their heroism. That the most obvious examples of the type occur in the novel rather than on the stage is one of many indications of the absorption by the novel of themes formerly sacred to epic and tragedy. If the Herculean hero is to be found on the nineteenth-century stage, it is in the drama of Germany and France or in the opera. The drama of England and America has hardly seen his like since the time of Dryden.

George Etherege and the Form of a Comedy

by Jocelyn Powell

George Etherege was a playwright by instinct: he wrote for the pleasure of writing, not to gain a living. The easy and graceful exercise of language, the witty perception of the manners and motives of others, were necessary attributes of a gentleman; they indicated grasp of life. Writing was a leisure occupation through which a man expressed and extended his own personality. The control exercised in molding experience into an artistic form makes that experience more entirely your own, and in a society where the art of living was the highest accomplishment, art was a way of possessing life. It is this ability to bring contemporary life and manners on the stage that is the strength of Etherege's plays. It is not original; Jonson, Middleton and their followers had all used telling observation of the details of daily existence to give their plays a quality of immediacy and reality; but Etherege's realism is more from the inside. In the Jacobeans detail is used critically; the observation holds the characters up to ridicule, because their actions are selected to expose their vices; whereas Etherege's details are primarily atmospheric. They show a subjective understanding and enjoyment of experience for its own sake, rather than a satirical awareness of the absurdity and pretentiousness of man's behavior. This subjectivity is at once the great quality and the great problem of Etherege's writing.

Etherege was a comic writer, and objectivity is built into the neoclassical theories of comedy. The conception that comedy corrects the vices and follies of men by rendering them ridiculous and contemptible presupposes an objective idea of vice and folly; it is essentially critical, and criticism demands a structure based upon a determined morality. What is more, the conventions of such comedy assist this objectivity; for a comedy of the classical tradition does not use a plot to represent life, but to provide a series of images that bring out the moral implications of experience. The comic devices of disguise, mistaken identity, trickery, and triumph in marriage are not literal redactions of experience, but analogies; they are accepted without the need for rational explanation because they give the play a new logic of fantasy. This logic can ignore the structure of material existence, and enable the dramatist to provide heightened images of the experiences about which he is writing, rich poetic analogies for life. The weddings that close the plays are frequently more important as symbols of attainment and unity than as comments upon human relationships. It is the nature of experience, not the nature of existence that is important, and this is true whether the dramatist emphasizes the lyrical content of the conventions, as did Shakespeare, or tries to give them the immediacy of life by realistic detail, as did Jonson. Whether the world of the comedy was given the poetry of a dream or the vigor of city life, it was still basically a world of analogy, and analogy that originally rose from an objective critical perception.

But Etherege does not have that objective perception, and he has a hard struggle with the forms of comic criticism. There is a clear development through his three plays, each one showing an increasing economy of dramatic means and an increasing dissatisfaction with comic conventions. The weddings of *Love in a Tub* are completely emblematic. There are six of them, and in the best Middletonian manner the fools are married to whores and the true men to the ladies of their choice. The weddings act as a resolution of the characters involved, a comment on the sort of beings they are. There is no sense of relationship; it is pure analogy. But when we come to *The Man of Mode* the resolution is studied at a more complex and highly personal level, and the conventional finale has become an impertinence. The relationship of Dorimant and Harriet is left for the audience to resolve. Etherege becomes more preoccupied with the outward forms of existence and the inner realities they conceal, and the form of his last play looks not back, but far forward, to the work of that greatest writer of comedy of manners, Anton Chekhov. The plot is curtailed to a minimum, and the action is disposed so as to give the greatest possible sense of reality. The dramatist is trying to make his audience experience what it is like to be alive in these situations, to communicate the texture of existence. To do this he builds his dramatic interest on the tensions of conversation rather than on the suspense of plot, and the atmosphere is created by a detailed knowledge of the pressures developing between the characters on the stage. The sympathies of the audience are engaged in the realities of a situation, not in a rich image presented so as to appear real. Form has become a means of expressing experience, rather than idea.

If a judgment arises out of such a play it must be intuitive rather than critical. It comes from inside the play, and lies in the individual reaction to the experiences portrayed. Its center is sympathy, not judgment, sympathy in its proper sense of the ability to feel with [others], to understand them and their actions, whether your judgment be for or against them. The objective simplifications of criticism and ridicule are gone; hero and villain have disappeared to be replaced by characters we know so intimately that all such designations must be superfluous. The comedy of judgment gives way to the comedy of experience.

Love in a Tub, Etherege's first play, is a remarkable piece. It contains elements of many forms of dramatic expression, blended together into something quite new; its touches of realism, excursions into the heroic and picaresque, and elaborate sequences of song and dance, combine all the basic ingredients of Restoration play-writing into a form that is all its own.

Above all it is a play of contrasts. Contrasts so great that critics have condemned it out of hand as unwieldy and ill-constructed; but it is not altogether so. It is a highly original conception executed with tremendous vitality and a great sense of fun. Deservedly it was a huge success. If it does not seem so successful to us now, this is partly due to Etherege's failure in one essential part of the drama, and partly due to a misunderstanding of the form in which it is written. When Pepys saw it on 4 January 1664/5, he remarked that it was "very merry, but only so by gesture, not wit at all," and the criticism gives the key to the play;[1] for Etherege holds his plots together by translating the variety of their styles and moods into dramatic energy through the impetus of music and rhythm. A unity of mood is created by extravagance and stylization of gesture, making a dramatic fantasy of sheer exhilaration and enjoyment

Enjoyment is one of the essential qualities of comic writing, for it is the foundation for the best type of laughter, the laughter of sympathy. This laughter is based on a sense of relationship between the man who is laughing and the man with whom he laughs, and through the laughter there is asserted the value and goodness of the experience that causes the laughter. It is the enjoyment by one human being of the life and vitality of another. The spirit of the man who laughs is broadened and stimulated by the energy of the man who makes the laughter; together they share their joy in life. In *Love in a Tub* Etherege constructs images of life in a comedy of analogy, but turns the play into anything but a critical comedy by engaging us wholly in enjoyment of its characters through the vigor with which they are presented. It is not the intellectual interdependence of theme among the plots, grouped as they are like *divertissements* on ideas of love and honor, that catches and holds the audience; the ironies created in this way are actually rather crude; it is rather

[1] Pepys adds: "which methinks is beneath the house." It is extraordinary how often critics insist that the emotional experience of farce is of a lower order than the intellectual experience of high comedy. They are simply two different things. [Quotations of Etherege plays in this chapter are to act, scene, and line in *The Works of Sir George Etherege,* ed. H. F. B. Brett-Smith (2 vols., Oxford, 1927). ED.]

through the spectacle that the experience of the play is grasped. The contrasting plots, with their contrasting values, are presented in different conventions of movement, so that the human impulses behind the various codes of behavior are explored in terms of action; rhythms of thought and plot are translated into equivalent rhythms of movement, and the vitality of these rhythms draws one into the play, integrating it as a spectacle. It is a flamboyant exercise in pure theatre.

There are four main divisions of plot, each with its particular variation on the central themes, and its particular convention for the expression of it. In the complicated courtly difficulties of Beaufort's love for Graciana we get a conventionally idealized view of the problems of love and personal honor; the emphasis is on a perfection of conduct and is expressed in language and gesture suitable to its ideals. The characters speak in formal couplets, and act with the broad and stylized movements associated with grand passions:

> *Graciana:* Sir, you mistake; 'tis not my Love I blame,
> But my Discretion; ★Here the active flame
> (★*Pointing to her breast.*
> Shou'd yet a longer time have been conceal'd;
> Too soon, too soon I fear it was reveal'd. (II, ii, 5)

It is this part of the play that fails: Etherege dallies half-heartedly with conventional problems of "platonic" love that neither his imagination nor his technique are fitted to handle; but in spite of the lack of success the intention of the scenes is clear. They provide a lyrical handling of the central emotion and form part of a pattern of mood and movement.

This idealism is counteracted by a plot of Middletonian realism in which two cheats, Wheadle and Palmer, trick a foolish Puritan knight out of his money. The two cheats turn the concepts of honor used in the "ideal" plot to their own nefarious ends, and engineer Sir Nicholas Cully into a duel in which he displays his cowardice and loses his cash. This duel, the climax of this plot, forms an ironical parallel with the climax of the ideal plot, also a duel. The details are the same in both: the seconds strip, leaving the principal protagonist dawdling and arguing the case; but where Sir Nicholas is fumbling with his doublet out of cowardice, Colonel Bruce delays on a nice point of honor. The flamboyant movements of the tricksters' mock duel make a comment on the vigor of the real duels of Colonel Bruce and Lovis. The duel of dishonor and the duel of honor complement each other.

This element of burlesque is continued when the cheats and Sir Nicholas disguise themselves as characters from the other plots. Palmer and Grace appear as Lord Bevill and the Widow, and behave in marked contrast to their garments:

Palmer: What a rogue is that *Wheadle,* to have kept such a Treasure to himself, without communicating a little to his Friends! *(Offers to kiss her.*
Grace: Forbear; you'l be out in your Part, my Lord, when Sir *Nich'las* comes.
Palmer: The truth is, my Lady, I am better prepar'd at this time to act a Lover then a Relation.
Grace: That grave dress is very amorous indeed. (IV, iii, 3)

Their whole plot comes to a fine climax when Sir Nicholas takes it upon him to imitate one of Sir Frederick's frolics:

Enter Cully Drunk, with a blind Fellow led before him playing on a Cymbal, follow'd by a number of boys hollowing, and persecuting him. (V, ii)

It is the frolics, parodied here, from which Sir Frederick Frolick, the play's central figure, takes his name, that give the piece its energy and consistency. The two opposed worlds, the ideal and the earthy, are drawn together in a network of song and dance which unifies the extremes through its own extravagance and fantasy. Sir Frederick and his disguised fiddlers provide a vigorous and graceful series of masquerades, which are in turn complemented by the contrastingly grotesque escapades of the French valet, Dufoy. The lewd scene of the servants dancing round the sweat-tub into which Dufoy has been locked as a punishment for pretending his peakiness was due to love when it was due to the pox, forms an anti-masque to Sir Frederick's masquerades;[2] the war of the sexes which is the basis of the play finds its expression in the opposition of crude and elegant dances.

The handling of Sir Frederick's scenes is brilliant. In them Etherege finds a way of suggesting in spectacle the ironies of experience, and involving the audience in the experience by catching them up in the excitement of movement. Sir Frederick himself is a magnificent blend of freedom and ceremony, elegance and animal spirits, and this tension between the controlled and the abandoned is particularly suited to expression in the dance. By centering the scenes of his wooing of the Widow Rich round a series of midnight masquerades and musical disguises Etherege makes full use of these possibilities. He gives his hero a band of fiddlers that accompany him upon his escapades, ready to give the impetus of music wherever it is needed. They are almost always about him, either as link-boys, bailiffs, or pall-bearers *"with their Instruments tuck'd under their Cloaks,"* moving at his pleasure, so that they become

[2] The justice of this punishment derives from its reference to the method of treating venereal disease by the suffumigation of the patient with cinnabar in a tub or vat normally used for pickling meat; cf. *Measure for Measure,* III. ii.
Lucio: How does my dear morsel thy mistress? Procures she still, ha?
Pompey: Troth, sir, she hath eaten up all her beef, and she is herself in the tub.

extensions of their master, and spread his vigorous personality all over the stage. But while the spectacle does create an element of fantasy Etherege also uses it to point the details of the reality involved in the situation. It is not merely the energy, but also the complexity of the relationship with the Widow that is expressed in the movement. The Widow is rich and lusty and wants a man; Sir Frederick is young and extravagant and could do with a rich widow; the tension between them arises from the inevitable insecurity in both of them, produced by their awareness of the other's possible motivations. Sir Frederick wishes to show he is unengaged and doing the Widow a favor in return for ready cash; the Widow wishes to prove there is more to the relationship.

The struggle is handled with splendid frankness, which builds up a genuine sympathy between the two characters. As the conflict within and between them of sex, love, and money develops it becomes impossible to discern the dominant motive. But the sympathy is not without its darker side. It is a very real relationship, and in their mutual attempts to make each other ridiculous and so preserve their own independence and self-respect Etherege anticipates one of the main themes of *The Man of Mode.* Their malice is both exuberant and cruel. When Sir Frederick tries to trick the Widow into mourning over his supposed corpse he is unmasked and mocked unmercifully in his turn:

Sir Frederick: Laugh but one minute longer I will forswear thy company, kill thy Tabby Cat, and make thee weep for ever after.

Widow: Farewell, Sir . . .

Sir Frederick: Hark you, hark you, Widow: by all those Devils that have hitherto possess'd thy Sex—

Widow: No swearing, good Sir *Fred'rick.*

Sir Frederick: Set thy face then; let me not see the remains of one poor smile. So, now I will kiss thee, and be friends. *(Widow falls out a laughing.* Not all thy wealth shall hire me to come within smell of thy breath again. Jealousie, and, which will be worse for thee, Widow, Impotence light upon me, if I stay one moment longer with thee. *(Offers to go.*

Widow: Do you hear, Sir; can you be so angry with one that loves you so passionately she cannot survive you?

Sir Frederick: Widow, May the desire of a man keep thee waking till thou art as mad as I am. *(Exit Sir Frederick.*

Widow: How lucky was this accident! How he wou'd have insulted over my weakness else! (IV, vii)

And indeed he does so later, when the Widow mistakes his disguised fiddlers for bailiffs come to arrest him and gives them money to release him. The insults, as before, are very near the mark, and his brutality could easily lose our sympathy. The scene brilliantly exploits this ambivalence in the audience by turning the tensions of the situation into action. The fiddlers take their instruments from under their coats and play; Dufoy, who came to rescue his master and revealed the trick, dances a jig in triumph round the stage; the Widow storms, and Sir Frederick mocks her, shaking his pockets at her to make her guineas ring. "I shall not trouble thee much," he says, "till this is spent." It is a cruel moment and its cruelty is emphasized, and at the same time made acceptable by the crude energy of the stage picture—the music, the malicious gestures of the man, the angry woman, and the absurdly triumphant figure *"with a Helmet on his head, and a great Sword in his hand"* jigging in and out between them.

Such scenes as this, in which the grotesque and farcical is brought into direct contact with the elegant and witty, provide, by this juxtaposition of effects, what is apparently a commentary by one set of actions upon another; but though there is a thematic connection, the way that the scenes are handled in movement ensures that the modification of one by another has not the objectivity of comment. The images of the play are complementary in that they provide different facets of the same subject, but because they are danced rather than enacted one finds oneself simply experiencing the same idea in different ways, rather than appreciating different attitudes to it. Dance is a very subjective medium. It draws you inside an experience through the compulsive effect of rhythm working directly upon the emotions. The intellect is occupied only with the aesthetic forms of movement and the experience is apprehended without it. By his use of dance Etherege gives what is fundamentally a critical structure a new dimension. The ironies set up by the juxtapositions of the plot are crude intellectually, but they are presented so as to create a physical response. The play is a tremendous extravaganza that builds up a sense of exhilaration sufficient to enable us to take its crudities in our stride. The diversity of moods is fused and the ugly and vulgar made to take their part in a pattern of experience. They are almost exorcised by being given qualities of even greater vitality, for the greater the vitality, the greater the sympathy and enjoyment. It is the exaggeration that creates the sympathy. *Love in a Tub* should not be read as a comedy of manners that has failed, but as a comedy-ballet.

The analogies of *Love in a Tub* take us to the heart of experiences in much the same way as that employed by Molière and the Italian comedians. Molière learned much from the Commedia troupe with whom he shared a theatre, and it is possible that Etherege may have developed his instinct for the emotional significance of movement from the same source.[3] The manner of Italian comedy was to subordinate all intrigue

[3] The influence of France on the Restoration dramatists is under constant argument, but it seems likely that Etherege had spent some time there (Cibber, *Lives of the Poets* [1753], III. 33). The Italian comedians first played in London in 1673 (A. Nicoll, *Masks, Mimes and Miracles* [1931], p. 344).

and dialogue to the expression of feeling through movement. Plot and speech there were; but the center of interest was the spectacle. In this they combined a realistic observation of natural movement with a stylized execution that created aesthetic poise out of the clumsy manifestations of ordinary life. All that was extraneous was pared away, leaving clear the motive and meaning of gesture. The disarray of passion was presented with perfect control. In *Love in a Tub* Etherege discovered and explored the possibilities of this type of drama, and it became a central motif in his comedy of experience, a mechanism for drawing his audience into his play.

His awareness of the character and rhythm given to action by movement comes out very clearly in his stage directions, full as they are of strong verbs and descriptive adverbs. In *Love in a Tub* we find *"Enter . . . Sir* Nicholas, *kicking a Tavern boy before him,"* Palmer *"with a bag of Money under his arm, and flings it upon the Table"*; in *She Wou'd if She Cou'd: "Enter* Ariana *and* Gatty *with Vizards, and pass nimbly over the stage"* and *"Enter the Musick playing, Sir* Oliver *strutting, and swaggering, Sir* Joslin *singing and dancing"*; in *The Man of Mode* Dorimant *"coming up gently, and bowing"* to Harriet, who *"Starts, and looks grave."* All these show an eye for the significance of gesture that is extremely perceptive, for the movements do not simply suggest character or situation; they can be used to express it. His directions do not show merely the sort of things a character might be seen doing; they show what he is by the way he does it.

Etherege's art is subtle and successful. He is placing realistic actions in a pattern that visualizes for the audience the tensions of the scene. Recognition of natural movement gives the scene immediacy and reality, while the selection and patterning of the movements give it form. In the first scene of *The Man of Mode* Dorimant rebukes Handy for fiddling about him; on Harriet's first entrance she is rebuking Busy for the same fault. The repetition provides an immediate and illuminating connection between the two characters. The device has made the play more natural, more formal, and given an added significance. Etherege has the gift of the choreographer: an understanding of the meaning and aesthetic content of natural behavior.

Here Etherege has found a thread on which to hang his new comedy of experience. In the two later plays the mood is more intimate, the texture of the action barer, the external impetus of song and dance more rarely employed. The outward forms of experience are becoming of greater importance. In his next play, *She Wou'd if She Cou'd,* they come into sharp conflict with the exuberance of his comic analogies.

In general structure *She Wou'd if She Cou'd* is a comedy of judgment. It uses most of the well-known devices of comic analogy to create an action that will focus satirical attention on the follies of the characters. The play opens and closes with technically accomplished scenes of comic intrigue, in which various persons who would be in some embarrassment to explain their presences to new arrivals on the stage are stowed away in closets, wood-piles, or under tables, to avoid discovery. Much play is made of this sort of comic coincidence. The wrong person is always coming along at the right time: while Lady Cockwood's maid is talking to Ned Courtall, Sir Oliver arrives; when Sir Oliver and Sir Joslin go to the Bear Tavern for a little relaxation with good wine and Madame Rampant, her ladyship turns out to be in the next room; when Courtall and Freeman accompany Sir Joslin home to meet his nieces they find them to be the girls they picked up in the park that afternoon, "Gatty *and* Ariana *seeing* Courtall *and* Freeman *shriek and . . . Exeunt.*" It is all a good-humored demonstration of the way men are trapped by their deceits.

Properly this method ought to render the characters involved completely ridiculous. The audience in the theatre is always ready to laugh out of contempt for a person whose designs miscarry; there is no surer way to alienate sympathy than to fail. One of the chief devices of critical comedy is the continual frustration of plans, the contradiction of one mind by another; the passive complement to this is embarrassment, or the potential contradiction of one mind by another; frustration and embarrassment both have the effect of allying the audience with the winning mind against the absurd loser. People in these circumstances become puppets, and so lose their independence; they are, therefore, ridiculous.

But in *She Wou'd if She Cou'd* they somehow refuse to become so, despite these attempts. Etherege is basically too sympathetic to his characters. Ostensibly he has a main theme ideal for a critical comedy; but apparently instinctively he turns it into something quite different. Sir Oliver and Lady Cockwood are both prime hypocrites. The one pretends to instincts he no longer has, the other tries to conceal instincts all too strong; Sir Oliver is only too anxious to be thought a libertine; Lady Cockwood to be a whore without anyone thinking so. As the play develops we see them alternately frustrating each other's designs by being in the same place, for the same purpose, at the same time; or else at home trying to give two contrary impressions of their married life, Lady Cockwood that she is the best of wives, Sir Oliver that he is the worst of husbands. The situation is piquant, but the laughter it provokes quite uncritical.

To start with, Etherege presents them in the form of parody. The effects are all heightened so that the comedy is of the grotesque. The boisterousness with which they handle the situations in which they find themselves turns condemnation into amusement. It is the extravagance of their behavior, not the falsity, that strikes us, and we delight in it.

When Sir Oliver returns home drunk, for example, we have a situation that could be treated with satirical distaste. His mock-heroics have quite another effect.

> *Sir Oliver:* Dan, Dan, Da ra, Dan, &c. (*Strutting.*
> Avoid my presence, the very sight of that face makes me more impotent than an Eunuch.
> *Lady Cockwood:* Dear Sir *Oliver!* (*Offering to embrace him.*
> *Sir Oliver:* Forbear your conjugal clippings, I will have a Wench, thou shalt fetch me a Wench, *Sentry.*
> *Sentry:* Can you be so inhumane to my dear Lady? (II, ii, 141)

The whole thing is dynamic. One is swept along with it, involved in the comic contrast of movement, Lady Cockwood's advances, Sir Oliver's repulses. There is simply not time to stand back and be critical, not a moment to notice the pretence or the hypocrisy. The laughter is the laughter of sympathy.

The reason for this is that again the intellect is entirely uninvolved; the audience, the characters, and the author are all responding to the situation intuitively and emotionally. Their minds are as far in the background of the experience as can be. Now where there is no mind there is no morality, for morality is an invention of reason. Where the characters on the stage operate by instinct the audience will react by instinct also, leaving the critical faculty in abeyance.

It is certainly instinct that is at work in the Cockwoods. They get themselves both into and out of every situation by the inspiration of the moment. The spontaneity of Lady Cockwood's double-thinking is breathtaking. With plans in her head for getting Sir Oliver out of the way while she spends the day with Courtall, she says, of his drunkenness.

> These are insupportable injuries, but I will bear 'em with an invincible patience, and to morrow make him dearly sensible how unworthy he has been. (II. ii. 215)

There is a new contradiction in every phrase.

The next day she arrives with Courtall at a tavern where she discovers Sir Oliver and Sir Joslin have engaged a room "to solace themselves with a fresh girl or two," as the Waiter confides. The confusion of her response is wonderful:

> *Lady Cockwood:* Oh *Sentry!* Sir *Oliver* disloyal! My misfortunes come too thick upon me.
> *Courtall:* (aside): Now is she afraid of being disappointed on all hands.
> *Lady Cockwood:* I know not what to do, Mr. *Courtall,* I would not be surpriz'd here my self, and yet I would prevent Sir *Oliver* from prosecuting his wicked and perfidious intentions. (III, iii, 39)

My own feeling towards one who can contrive such a state of mind in such a situation is not of criticism but of envy. It is so ingenuous. "Misfortunes" as a blanket term to cover the discovery of a husband's infidelity, and fear of that husband's discovering her own, is stunning! In such scenes as these Lady Cockwood may be said to be pure instinct, and as such she is in a state of innocence. She simply does not possess the knowledge of good and evil.

This innocence is elaborated in the characterization of Sir Joslin Jolley. He is imported directly from *Love in a Tub,* and brings all Sir Frederick's animal spirits with him, as well as Sir Frederick's apparatus of music, song, and dance. His lewd ballads provide the answer of instinct to the play's title, *She Wou'd if She Cou'd:*

> I gave my Love a Green-gown
> I'th' merry month of May,
> And down she fell as wantonly,
> As a Tumbler does at Play. (V, i, 632)

If we were to cast a critical eye upon him he would be the tempter of the play, the country knight showing his friend the wicked pleasures of the town; but the response to him cannot be this. The scene where he coaxes Sir Oliver to go out on the town, even in his penitential suit, displays in both of them a similar innocence to that of Lady Cockwood:

> *Sir Oliver:* I vow thou hast such a bewitching way with thee!
> *Sir Joslin:* How lovely will the Ladies look when they have a Beer-glass in their hands!
> *Sir Oliver:* I now have a huge mind to venture; but if this should come to my Lady's knowledge! . . .
> *Sir Joslin:* A Pox upon these Qualms.
> *Sir Oliver:* Well, thou hast seduc'd me; but I shall look so untowardly.
> *Sir Joslin:* Again art thou at it? in, in, and make all the haste that may be, *Rake-hell* and the Ladies will be there before us else.
> *Sir Oliver:* Well, thou art an errant Devil—hey—for the Lady's, Brother *Jolly.*
> *Sir Joslin:* Hey for the Lady's, Brother *Cockwood.*
> (*Exit singing.* (II, ii, 47)

It would be possible here to give the impression of ridiculous, elderly vicariousness; but this is not done. There is too much extravagance and enjoyment, so their absurdity becomes sympathetic, not contemptible. One would be disappointed if they were to reform. Good humor is the key-note of their sinning, and their desire is good company. Their world is of instinct, without reason, and so without morals. And so, also, it is an entirely fictional world. Men in reality possess reason, so the antics of Sir Joslin have no literal reference to reality. In spite of the close observation of life in the characters, the irrationality of response moves them to a different world. But it is only in literal reference that their world is unreal. The instinct they represent is a part of everyone watching. Its energy is released in the comic analogy. The experience of the comedy is a real experience, though the life it presents is merely an image. To deny it reality is not to deny it meaning.

But, *She Wou'd if She Cou'd* is more complicated than this, for as well as this exploitation of comic analogy it contains an attempt towards comedy of experience too, which seriously disturbs the play. The Cockwoods and Sir Joslin are characters of humor; but the lovers are characters of wit. Whereas humor does without the intellect, wit depends upon it; the alternation of the two here confuses the response, the more so since Etherege begins to give his lovers a quality of naturalness and intimacy that makes them very much a part of life. The wit in their speeches is simpler and more spontaneous than those of the later dramatists; one feels it to be an accurate representation of a certain type of conversation, rather than a heightened image of polite talk; and this reality gives a quite new dimension to the operations of the comedy. It creates a confusion between the comic pattern and life as it is lived. When Gatty says of Sir Oliver "I dare say he counterfeited his sin, and is real in his Repentance" (III. iii. 375), or Courtall suggests to Lady Cockwood, on her promising to keep out of the great business of the town for the future, "'tis a very pious resolution, Madam, and the better to confirm you in it, pray entertain an able Chaplain" (V, i, 603), the enjoyment of the emotions is arrested by the penetration of the intellect. The analogy of experience becomes a representation of life. Through the wit of the lovers, and their characterization as real men of the town, this confusion becomes constant.

The play opens with Courtall, just risen, discussing the coming day with his friend. There is a servant "brushing him" to give the texture of life to the scene. It is all very much routine, the start of another day. The way they start gives an effect of normality and boredom quite out of keeping with the comic coincidences that are to follow:

> *Courtall:* Well, *Franck,* what is to be done to day?
> *Freeman:* Faith, I think we must e'ne follow the old trade; eat well, and prepare our selves with a Bottle or two of good *Burgundy,* that our old acquaintance may look lovely in our Eyes; for, for ought as I see, there is no hopes of new. (I, i, 3)

The men are hunting after occupation; they have nothing to do; and this places the coincidences of the comedy in a new relation to actual life. For their attitude to everything is based upon just this sense of casual acquaintanceship. They take up with people always on the same grounds: the possibility of temporary amusement. Freeman says of Courtall's ripening affair with Lady Cockwood:

> 'Slid, I know not how proud you are, but I have thought my self very spruce e're now in an old Suit, that has been brush'd and laid up a while. (I, i, 223)

The same frivolous level of relationship with other people is continued in Courtall's regrets when he discovers the lady he met in the park is the same as that to whom he was to have been later introduced. She is, at the play's end, to become his future wife:

> *Courtall:* . . . that which troubles me most, is, we lost the hopes of variety, and a single intrigue in Love is as dull as a single Plot in a Play, and will tire a Lover worse, than t' other does an Audience.
>
> *Freeman:* We cannot be long without some under-plots in this Town; let this be our main design, and if we are any thing fortunate in our contrivance, we shall make it a pleasant Comedy. (III, i, 105)

The comic intrigues become like life because it is the way the characters see life. And their games are made more real because they are as possessive about them as children with their toys. The life of the young men becomes a telling comment upon a leisured society. There is so little to do that it is necessary to create obstacles and involvements to give life some zest. It is one of the chief needs of life to give it the suspense of a play, and this need involves a basic pretence in all human relationships, since once a thing is known it loses the suspense of mystery and becomes dull. This leads us round to a motive for hypocrisy quite different from that suggested in our response to Lady Cockwood's humorous endeavors, but which lies underneath the actions of all the ladies. In a song Gatty sings in the last act, while the two lovers lie concealed in the closet, the dilemma of the piece is stated:

> My passion shall kill me before I will show it,
> And yet I wou'd give all the world he did know it;
> But oh how I sigh, when I think shou'd he woo me,
> I cannot deny what I know wou'd undo me! (V, i, 320)

The temper of the time is such that the truth of almost any relationship must be concealed. Intercourse is carried on in paraphrase. In the relationships of the lovers in *She Wou'd if She Cou'd* this insecurity is explored, and explored not by analogy but with an attempt to give the real feeling of the situation. In the big ensembles, in the Exchange, or at the Bear, Etherege creates scenes that set the situation of the lovers against the life they live. The confusion of pretence and motive is excellently suggested in the counterpoints of plot and dialogue. Courtall at

Sir Oliver's house, joking with his friend, and intriguing with his friend's wife and niece, creates a life-like ambiguity in the audience's attitude towards him. They are too involved to condemn, as in the Comedy of Judgment, but at the same time too disturbed to enjoy. The play does not succeed because it suspends the audience between the humor of the Cockwoods who have no sense of what they are about but respond by instinct, and the realism of the lovers, who know about good and evil and manage their lives with the mixture of the two that characterizes human morality. In *The Man of Mode,* his last play, written eight years after *She Wou'd if She Cou'd,* Etherege discovers the way to exploit this ambiguity: he finds a comic form that can fully express his individual response to life. The nature of this response, which prompted the stylistic experiments of the earlier plays, can be seen from a study of the third.

At the very opening of *The Man of Mode* we become intimately involved with the quality of life. The first scene—it is curious how Etherege always opens with his hero's awakening to a new day—is a delicate exploration of the personalities of the chief characters entirely in terms of business and conversation. Almost nothing happens in it, but we are kept awake and interested throughout and move into the main action of the play with both an intimate acquaintance with the characters and an acute feeling for their situation and way of life. It is mood drama, but brilliantly handled so that the apparent random realism of the conversation puts us in possession of all the important elements of the ensuing action. Etherege utilizes the dramatic techniques explored in the earlier plays and provides a solution to the problem of creating an aesthetically satisfactory sequence which preserves the casual appearances of life that is similar to that of Chekhov. He, too, unifies his scene by counterpointing physical action and narrative promise. The scene is held together by stage business that embodies the mood of the passage, while the attention of the audience is held by recurring hints of impending situations. This creates a drama of inaction, or more properly a drama that explores the tensions in the moments of inaction that precede action. The conversation is given at the same time intellectual direction and emotional and physical reality.

The first entrance of Dorimant with his letter for Loveit gives promise of an impending situation, his breaking with his mistress. During the scene friends and servants accumulate with endless matter for conversation, some atmospheric, some relating to later developments of the plot, but throughout the casual discussion, which gives the exact impression of "the talk of the town," recurs the name of Loveit, and with the name the implications of the opening speech are developed and held out to us. As a further unity, Etherege, with his eye for significant and aesthetic detail, hinges the structure of the scene on the procedure of Dorimant's levée. His friends chat to him while he dresses, the Orange Woman brings him fruit and the latest news of ladies newly come to town; the shoemaker rounds it all off, pulling on his boots, parodying in his personality the libertinism of the young gentlemen. The dressing provides the narrative framework of action, and the detail of it gives reality and atmosphere. It also is carefully selected to enable the actor to express the impulses of his character in the combination of speech and action already discussed:

> *Orange Woman* . . . here, bid your Man give me an Angel.
> (*Sets down the Fruit.*
>
> *Dorimant:* Give the Bawd her Fruit again.
>
> *Orange Woman:* Well, on my Conscience, there never was the like of you. God's my life, I had almost forgot to tell you, there is a young Gentlewoman lately come to Town with her Mother, that is so taken with you.
>
> *Dorimant:* Is she handsome?
>
> *Orange Woman:* Nay, Gad, there are few finer Women, I tell you but so, and a hugeous fortune they say. Here, eat this Peach, it comes from the Stone, 'tis better than any *Newington* y'have tasted.
>
> *Dorimant:* This fine Woman, I'le lay my life, is some awkward ill fashion'd
> (*taking the Peach.*
> Country Toad, who not having about Four Dozen of black hairs on her head, has adorn'd her baldness with a large white Fruz, that she may look sparkishly in the Fore Front of the Kings Box, at an old Play. (I, i, 39)

Dorimant is speaking of his future wife, and the irony is beautifully caught in the business, while the characterization of the Orange Woman, as she stalls about giving the information for which she is really paid, and plays her game about the fruit, gives an air of routine reality while introducing the central event of the play. We learn how Dorimant gets his pleasure, his attitude to it, and of the arrival of Harriet, and the sense of all this is expressed in one sequence of action.

This naturalism in the detail of the staging creates an effect of intimacy. The characters quickly become our acquaintances and our interest and sympathy is with them; but it is with all of them, for the naturalism engages us with them all. Since we are made to understand the way each mind is working the possibilities of comic analogy are lost, for our understanding of all the characters modifies our approval of each of them, and the sympathy we have for them prevents the dissociation necessary for ridicule and contempt. We are seeing them in human, not in moral terms. In a critical comedy when a fool is gulled we allow it to be justice for his foolery, but when we know him as a person not as a fool he assumes the rights of a person, and the man gulling him the limitations of humanity. In terms of critical comedy Loveit's ill-controlled and possessive passion deserves a rebuke; but in terms of humanity where is Dorimant's right to administer that rebuke? The essential difference between the comedy of criticism and the comedy of experience is that in the former, though a good character may be given faults and a bad character virtues, there is never any serious doubt as to the category to which the character belongs; whereas in the latter there are no categories. Criticism sees characters from one angle, but experience is constantly modifying the angle from which a character is seen, so that, like a shot silk, his color changes with the light.

This exploration of the texture of experience gives Etherege the form he needs for his analysis of the tensions of boredom, politeness, and passion towards which he was feeling in *She Wou'd if She Cou'd*. It avoids the identification of the characters with moral qualities, and explores their personal predicaments realistically; experience is presented in terms of itself. Our own sympathy and understanding for the characters helps us to perceive their own lack of sympathy for each other, our connection with them, their lack of connection with each other. The absence on the stage of the human contact that exists between it and the audience throws into strong relief the emptiness of the relationships there presented. This provides a comment on the play; but it has been apprehended through the experience in the theatre. It is implication, not judgment.

Love and friendship in *The Man of Mode* arise out of and return to the self. The friendship of Dorimant and Medley exists because they find each other entertaining as companions, but they are as willing to be amused at each other's expense as in each other's company. They look upon each other, as upon everyone else, as cogs to the wheel of pleasure; the acquaintance helps in one way or other to make life go round

> 'Tis good to have an universal taste; we should love Wit, but for Variety be able to divert ourselves with the Extravagancies of those who want it:
>
> (III, ii, 131)

Lady Townley speaks of passing acquaintances, but one feels that the sentiment is applied by and large to all human contact. Other human beings exist, not even simply for one's entertainment—that is to put it too passively—but for one's use.

The malignant aspect of this can be seen from Dorimant's relationship with young Bellair. Bellair is presented as a frank, good-natured young man who instantly acquires our sympathy, as does Emilia, the girl he wants to marry. They are both simple, unaffected people, and our interest in them is considerable, as it should be in two persons whose plans and difficulties form a central intrigue of the play. Dorimant's first scene with Bellair bears out this impression. It is jovial, intimate, and apparently open-hearted. But no sooner has the young man gone than we are presented with a very different view of the relationship:

> He's Handsome [says Dorimant], well bred, and by much the most tolerable of all the young men that do not abound in wit. (I, i, 424)

There is a complacency in the judgment which is displeasing, and the displeasure is increased by Dorimant's later remarks to the effect that he is interested in the young man's marriage largely because he thinks it will make possible attempts upon the lady that are ineffective while she is a virgin. The combination of real intention and libertine bravado gives a new perspective to what appeared to be frank and open relationship. The apparent sympathy does not exist.

The emptiness of this life of isolation is given full expression in the exploration of Dorimant's relations with women. The three main affairs, of Loveit, Bellinda, and Harriet, are cleverly contrasted and build up a ruthless picture of lovelessness and boredom. Dorimant is the typical erotic, spending most of his wit on retaining his independence and achieving his pleasure. He considers his affairs to be a mutual indulgence between himself and the lady, and considers there should be no obligation incurred upon either side. Each party is responsible for his own person and his own pleasure; nothing is shared. The resulting associations are scarcely worthy of the name relationship, they are casual, and quite meaningless.

The seduction of Bellinda is obviously a typical episode in the life of Dorimant, and the tone in which it is drawn scarcely gives the impression that it has been very satisfactory. Bellinda's attitude to the affair is complicated and ambiguous. She continually hesitates to give herself, wishing to make sure the performance is one of love. She demands Dorimant should throw off Loveit to prove his feeling, but though he does so she never altogether believes him. She comes to him out of a desire she has not the power to resist. When she has finally yielded, she makes all the conventional demands on him, but apparently with little expectation of success. Her very coyness is half-hearted:

> *Bellinda:* Were it to do again——
> *Dorimant:* We should do it, should we not?
> *Bellinda:* I think we should: the wickeder man you to make me love so well—will you be discreet now?
> *Dorimant:* I will——
> *Bellinda:* You cannot.
> *Dorimant:* Never doubt it.
> *Bellinda:* I will not expect it.
> *Dorimant:* You do me wrong.

Bellinda: You have no more power to keep the secret, than I had not to trust you with it. (IV, ii, 11)

There is nothing between them but a momentary sensual gratification, the casualness of which is neatly stressed by a visual detail. As they come out of the bedroom we are to see "Handy, *tying up Linnen.*" The touch is unsavory, and by its suggestion of the usual, the stream of such acquaintances before and after, robs the situation of any glamor. The work of the household goes on; Handy, doubtless, continues to do the laundry throughout the little passage quoted above. When the lady has gone Dorimant's friends arrive, and sum up the position on sight:

Medley: You have had an irregular fit, *Dorimant.*
Dorimant: I have.
Young Bellair: And is it off already?
Dorimant: Nature has done her part, Gentlemen; when she falls kindly to work, great Cures are effected in little time, you know. (IV, ii, 69)

The whole business is sordid and without hope. The almost complete lack of resistance on Bellinda's part removes the comedy that would arise from a conflict of wills, and does, indeed, do so in the case of Loveit. Bellinda has no will: simply a cynical wavering between what she would like to think love is and what she thinks she knows it to be. The disillusionment that comes to her hurts, but it was expected, and is accepted. The negatives that litter her speeches characterise her attitude, and establish the isolated nihilism of herself and her lover. It all finds expression in her injunction to him at parting:

Take no notice of me, and I shall not hate you. (V, ii, 303)

Bellinda accepts isolation and independence, but her lack of resistance is so depressing that it sets up a curious tension with Mrs. Loveit's comic and selfish passion. We laugh at this, we find her dramatics, her pretensions, her possessiveness quite ridiculous; but at least it is positive, and at least it has something to give. Mrs. Loveit is comic because she allows Dorimant to manipulate her. She is worked on so that the effects of her actions are the contrary of those she intended. The discrepancy between her will and its effect renders her ridiculous. But this arises out of an opposition of motive. Dorimant can manage her because he is completely indifferent; he does not care what comes of the interview, and she does. She wishes to give herself to him, and the desire to submit destroys the desire to hurt. The comedy this creates is complex. We laugh with Dorimant at Loveit, because he controls her and makes her ridiculous. When she tears her fan we laugh at the impotence of the gesture to express the feeling, and her helplessness before him. But though she is selfishly clinging, she is also genuinely passionate; there is a sense of sincerity in her actions which shows well against the frivolity of his, a warmth which reflects upon his cold destructiveness. The sympathy in the laughter is undermined as it asserts itself, for we find ourselves laughing at something to which we are emotionally sympathetic, with someone whose actions deny our sympathy. We are deriding something we feel to be ultimately of value. This creates a deep sense of insecurity that is at once comic and profound.

This insecurity, arising from a sense of the value of something we are mocking, finds its complement in the relation of Dorimant and Harriet, which, partly through its contrast with the affairs of Loveit and Bellinda, and partly from within itself, continually suggests that what we find brilliant and sympathetic is actually hollow. The selfishness of Dorimant's previous relationships give one the impression that he is unable and unwilling to give himself to anyone, and this leaves the prospect of his marriage on a high level of difficulty. There is no doubt of the physical attraction, and of a certain sympathy arising from their equality in wit and will. The relationship is genuinely exciting: in Harriet Dorimant has met his match; but through the play we see him struggling to keep his independence, and the end shows no definitive sign that he has resigned it. The feeling is reinforced by Harriet's own doubts on the subject.

But there are also deeper grounds for disquiet. The libertine's own independence of person has, as a necessary corollary, the desire to possess others. In all Dorimant's relations with Loveit this is uppermost in his mind. He asserts his independence through her dependence; his power over her is the mark of his superiority. He tries to show this power by maneuvering her into making a fool of herself for his sake with Sir Fopling; but Loveit turns the tables by entertaining Sir Fopling at Dorimant's expense. Each is trying to prove their power over the other. And the same is true of Dorimant and Harriet:

> *Harriet:* I was inform'd you use to laugh at Love, and not make it.
>
> *Dorimant:* The time has been, but now I must speak——
>
> *Harriet:* If it be on that Idle subject, I will put on my serious look, turn my head carelessly from you, drop my lip, let my Eyelids fall and hang half o're my Eyes—Thus—while you buz a speech of an hour long in my ear, and I answer never a word! why do you not begin?
>
> *Dorimant:* That the company may take notice how passionately I make advances of Love! and how disdainfully you receive 'em.
>
> *Harriet:* When your Love's grown strong enough to make you bear being laugh'd at, I'll give you leave to trouble me with it. 'Till when pray forbear, Sir. (IV, i, 169)

This is the iron hand in the velvet glove, right enough. Harriet, with her conscious posing, is playing a game at her lover's expense. There is no equality or balance; she simply wishes to subdue. The nearest they get to sharing an experience is their joint effort to enrage Loveit and offend Sir Fopling at the end of the play; Dorimant acting out of a natural desire to revenge his own frustration, and Harriet out of one equally natural, that of displaying her triumph. It is true; it is very funny; and it is distinctly unpleasant. Their last exchange does nothing to resolve the difficulty: they are both still struggling for the last word. Harriet paints a picture of life in the country and asks if this does not stagger his resolution to ask for her:

> *Dorimant:* Not at all, Madam! The first time I saw you, you left me with the pangs of Love upon me, and this day my soul has quite given up her liberty.
> *Harriet:* This is more dismal than the Country! *Emilia!* pitty me, who am going to that sad place. Methinks I hear the hateful noise of Rooks already—Kaw, Kaw, Kaw—— (V, ii, 427)

One cannot help asking oneself who is the fool. Dorimant's line is one we have seen him at before; Loveit and Bellinda are not so easily forgotten; and Harriet's retort shows a steady persistence in demanding her pound of flesh. Their marriage is ideal in Restoration terms, being between a young wit and a fine woman with "a hugeous fortune"; but the two personalities, with their determined independence and overt possessiveness, make one question its future. The best comment upon it is perhaps Etherege's own letter written many years later to congratulate the Earl of Arran on just such an auspicious marriage:

> It is one of the boldest actions of a man's life to marry. Whoever passes that Rubicon has need of the fortune of Caesar to make him happy; but you have made so prudent a choice that you have secured to yourself all the joy I can wish you. The charms my Lady Anne has in her own person are sufficient for this work, were they not joined with that of being so nearly related to my Lord President. In this alliance you seem to have had an equal regard to your love and your ambition. The daughter is the most beautiful object that you can sigh for, and the father is the best appui this can desire. But to be less serious with your Lordship, I have had the honour of your confidence and you have told me of mighty deeds you have performed. I should be glad to be satisfied whether you are as great a hero now you fight in a good cause as when you drew your sword in a querelle d'allemande; the truth is that sort of courage is a little too violent for the present purpose. The business you have now on your hands is to be spun out in length and not to be ended at once.[4]

The Earl of Arran was killed in 1712 in a duel with Lord Mohun. They fought over a matter arising out of a Chancery case concerning some property he believed should have been left to his wife.

[4] *The Letterbook of Sir George Etherege,* ed. Sybil Rosenfeld (London, 1928), p. 327. [ED.]

The particular quality of Etherege's Comedy of Manners is achieved not through a superficial, but through an actual realism. It comes from our taking his characters as real human beings and experiencing the implications of their conduct in terms of actual life.

Dorimant is a portrait of Rochester, and the mood in which he is portrayed communicates that combination of glamor and viciousness which burns so much more fiercely in Rochester's satires. The form of the play, in which one mood or attitude continually reveals the flaws in another, while our sympathies are engaged to comprehend the nature of both, creates in Dorimant a figure in which tremendous life and energy generate a sympathy which is continually frustrated by the realization that all the energy turns back upon itself. It is useless; it becomes atrophied. The whole is a tremendous display of brilliance which has no aim. Powers of expression are called forth, but there is nothing to express. The wit, the forms and manners, the pleasure that has no end beyond itself, are almost desperate means to express an energy that has nowhere to go. The end of it all is increasing isolation and emptiness.

When Dryden, in his Epilogue to *The Man of Mode,* wrote:

> Yet none Sir *Fopling* him, or him can call;
> He's Knight o' th' Shire, and represents ye all

he gave us a clue to the mood and method of the play. The fault of Dorimant is the personal equivalent of the fault of his whole society: form has become a substitute for feeling.

Sir Fopling is a comic embodiment of this idea. In him the elements of lyrical and musical life and energy that lifted *She Wou'd if She Cou'd* and *Love in a Tub* off the ground have been pared away to a rhythmic precision conveyed through the words. He is the successor of Sir Frederick and Sir Joslin, picking up the realism of the play and turning it into a dance; he occurs as they do to give a rhythmic finish to important scenes; but, with the exception of the Masquerade, he does so without any help. The whole effect comes from his own personality unaided by music or song. He creates his own accompaniment, and the effect is at once drier, and more real: exactly suited to the texture of the play. Like Sir Frederick, too, he is not one man but eight. His "equipage," like Sir Frederick's masquers, spreads his personality over the stage: the exquisite with the fatal flaw. The whole tension of this personality goes with them as they follow him about, a page, five Frenchmen, and an Englishman, like the famous centipede with the wooden leg. Each exquisite ripple of movement initiated by Sir Fopling collapsing in the final and inadequate execution of the ill-fated John Trott. It is a brilliant comic device, and translates into pure spectacle the empty emotionless forms of the rest of the play. Life, for Sir Fopling, is a continual pose, as it was, or had to be, for Ariana and Gatty, and as it is with Harriet with her accurate observations of behavior designed to deceive; and, since it is so, the whole energy of his personality goes into the pastime.

The feeling is given perfectly in a little Pamphlet entitled *News From Covent Garden or The Town Gallant's Vindication.* It appeared in 1675, but it might almost have been written as a portrait of Etherege's hero. The Gallant is describing the difficulties of his way of life:

> To know how to discar'd the Goloshooes in due season in their proper place: to tie the knot of one's Muff Ribbon, to the best advantage: to walk with such pleasing Gate that your Swinging Arm may keep true time with your Feet, which must dance to the Musick of the Points, Ratling on your Pantaloons, and especially to provide that the Foot-Boy be observant in his distances, that he never stand just behind, but bearing a respectful point *East* or *West* from his Master. You know full well Gentlemen! tis no such easie business to discern how much of the *Handkerchief* ought to hang out of the Right Pocket, and how to Poise it Mathematically, with the Tortoise shell comb on the left: to apprehend what a boon Grace there is in some notable words keenly pronounced, with a neat shrug and a becoming lisp, to avoid the horrible absurdity of sitting both feet flat on the Ground, when one should always stand tottering on the toe, as waiting in readiness for a *Congee*!

It is all form and no meaning; manners have become a contradiction of themselves, for manners are really the means by which men and women, wishing to know each other, can express themselves and yet not impose upon the identity of those to whom they are speaking. They are the means of communicating one's deepest feelings and preserving at the same time a respect for the feelings of others. They arise out of consideration and respect for other people. But in the society Etherege portrays manners have become not a means to an end, but an end in themselves, and an end which denies their original purpose; that which was intended to express feeling, now dictates to it, and manners prevent the intercourse they were designed to aid. Instead of ensuring you do not impose yourself upon another, they ensure that others do not impose themselves on you. They have become a means of personal isolation rather than a means of personal communication, and what was designed as a medicine has become a weapon. To shame Loveit, Dorimant determines to pluck off her "mask" and show "the passion that lies panting under." Feeling has become ridiculous, the mask important; the real has given place to the trivial.

The energy of love and of living is expressed in the communication between human beings; but the Restoration reaction against the repression of the Puritan conscience produced a repression as, if not more, disastrous; for licence of action was accompanied by restriction of feeling. Throughout *The Man of Mode* one is kept constantly aware that the brilliance is suppressing and vitiating the reality of life and passion. What is serious and important is being destroyed by what is brittle and frivolous. Manners no longer express but contradict reality. The secret of the form and the drama of Etherege's last play lies in the tension he creates between the lightness and elegance of fashion on the surface and the underlying reality of passion it conceals. The energy and wit of the former creates in the audience a sympathy, which is questioned by the intimacy and humanity with which the characters are drawn. All the devices of comedy, charm, cleverness, and wit encourage one to laugh with Dorimant at his victims, but the sympathy with which those victims are themselves described make us aware that the approval we have been giving through our laughter is of what we hate. We are given a double view of the situation, a view of the pretence, and of the truth, and before it we are helpless, aware that our intellectual and emotional responses form a devastating contradiction. The laughter and the experience attack each other with the ambiguity of life.

This ambiguity explains the curious contradictions that have arisen in comments upon the play. St. Evremont said that in Dorimant Etherege gave us Rochester with his vices "burnished to shine like perfections." [5] Sir Richard Steele said:

> To speak plainly of this whole work, I think nothing but being lost to a sense of innocence and virtue, can make any one see this comedy, without observing more frequent occasion to move sorrow and indignation than mirth and laughter. (*Spectator,* No. 65)

Each has taken one aspect of the play and made it into the whole. Dorimant's charm does "burnish" his vices, but only for a moment, the next our sympathy with one of his fellows is showing us more matter for sorrow in what we laughed at before. This ambivalence, this floating between laughter and indignation, is the essence of Etherege's comedy. He knew these emotions did not exclude but reinforce each other, and that the sense of this was one of the most common experiences of life. It is this experience his plays explore. As Congreve put it: "The two Famous Philosophers of *Ephesus* and *Abdera* have their different Sects at this day. Some Weep and others Laugh at one and the same thing." [6] This ambiguity of response is the essence of the comedy of experience.

[5] *A Memoir of the Life of John Wilmot, Earl of Rochester . . .* in *The Works of the Right Honourable Earls of Rochester & Roscannon* (1707).

[6] *Concerning Humour in Comedy:* Letter to John Dennis (1695); reprinted in J. E. Spingarn, ed., *Critical Essays of the Seventeenth Century* (3 vols.; Bloomington, 1957), III, 249.

The Comic Language

by Dale Underwood

The language of Etherege's plays and of the Restoration comedy of manners as a whole divides with peculiar clarity into two distinct sets of literary characteristics. Provisionally we may label these the metaphoric and the nonmetaphoric. This is not to say merely that the language has its "logical" and its "poetic" components of meaning. In such terms, both aspects of the language are "poetic." Indeed, we shall find that they organize the experience of the plays at much the same level of awareness, with much the same meaning, and fundamentally in much the same manner. But their precise rhetorical characters are distinct, and they complicate the logical surfaces of the language in somewhat different ways.

If, for the moment, we view the "nonmetaphoric" language as constituting a distinct mode of expression, we can see at once that it has several salient characteristics. We may briefly summarize them here before investigating them in detail.[1] The language is, first of all, prevailingly "substantive" in nature. The verbs, even when they are not merely connective or "copulative," seldom carry the weight of the meaning. The weight is consistently in the nouns or in adjectives derivative from them. As a result, the language at its surface does not characteristically seem to express movement or change. The components of experience seem fixed and discrete. The sense of experience expressed by the language appears to be more a matter of "being" than "becoming." Second, it is not a sensuous language. It is only sporadically interested in projecting the immediate and concrete surfaces of experience. As a rule it deliberately abstracts that level of experience into generalized classes and categories.[2]

[1] It is perhaps necessary to stress that the following statements are generalizations based upon predominant characteristics in the plays. For most of the generalizations here and elsewhere in this chapter, one can find, of course, specific exceptions. But careful inspection of the language will reveal, I believe, the justness of the observations made.

[2] Among the exceptions to this generalization are a few passages often cited as Etheregean language at its "best"—usually with the implication that the passages are

It is concerned, that is, to express directly and explicitly the generalized attitudes and values of the comic worlds which we have already examined: Nature, love, honor, wit, malice, passion, good humor, impertinence, and so on through a long list of constantly recurring terms with which we are familiar. Third, therefore, the language must be primarily concerned with establishing relationships among those terms. The tone and rhetorical structure thus become assertive, "indicative" in "mood." And since the realities and values of the comic world are pervasively schematized, both the words and the rhetorical patterns by which their relationships are expressed also assume a schematic and oppositional character. Wit and fool, gentleman and fop, reason and passion, good nature and malice, virtue and vice are, at the level of diction, the immediately expressed "raw stuff" of experience. And the shape and mold of the experience projected is the sum of their relationships. These relationships being schematic and oppositional, the whole movement of the language becomes one of persistent parallelism or balance: "He knows so much of virtue as makes him well accomplished for all manner of vice" (7). Or, with a double balance, "Blockheads are as malicious to witty men as ugly women are to the handsome" (211). Or, again, in a more elaborate and less precise balance, one of Dorimant's speeches to Loveit: "Good nature and good manners corrupt me. I am honest in my inclinations, and would not, were't not to avoid offence, make a lady a little in years believe I think her young, wilfully mistake art for nature, and seem as fond of a thing I am weary of as when I doted on't in earnest" (216). The parallelism is not at all times, of course, so pronounced.[3] But a continuous preoccupation with the generalized and schematized level of experience here noted results in a pervasive parallelism throughout Etheregean comedy. This characteristic, indeed, becomes more prominent with each successive play.

It is not to our purpose to anatomize the precise rhetorical nature of this parallelism or to examine the kinds of variation which the language manifests within this general characteristic. The point here is simply that the movement of the language, like the diction, is not concerned with the immediate and sensory world of experience. It is part of an impersonalized and highly formalized ordering of general classes and abstractions. And its chief business is to establish relationships in non-

---

somehow typical. Conspicuous here is Medley's extended description of Harriet in *The Man of Mode* (p. 193). [In this chapter, quotations are cited by reference to pages in *The Works of Sir George Etherege*, ed. H. F. B. Brett-Smith (2 vols.; Oxford, 1927). Ed.] But in its degree of particularity and "sensuousness" the passage is not only exceptional but unique in Etherege's play.

[3] It is less pronounced in Etherege than in any other major comic dramatist of the Restoration.

sensuous and rational terms.[4] At the same time, the direct and relatively uninvolved form of the parallelism, together with a highly normalized syntax and general word order, establishes an insistent, repetitive movement in the language. We may note this even in a passage having less marked parallelism and balance than most. (The passage is from the opening scene of *The Man of Mode.*)

> *Medley:* He is like many others, beholding to his education for making him so eminent a coxcomb; many a fool had been lost to the world had their indulgent parents wisely bestowed neither learning nor good breeding on 'em.
>
> *Bellinda:* He has been, as the sparkish word is, brisk upon the ladies already; he was yesterday at my Aunt Townley's, and gave Mrs. Loveit a catalogue of his good qualities under the character of a complete gentleman, who, according to Sir Fopling, ought to dress well, dance well, fence well, have a genius for love-letters, an agreeable voice for a chamber, be very amorous, something discreet, but not over-constant. (200-1)

We shall later see that the character of this general movement contributes in a particularly important way to the comic expressiveness of the language. What we need here to note is that in this and the other verbal characteristics mentioned we have what are usually considered classic nonmetaphoric qualities of prose. But in that case we must ask how the prose is "literary"—or, more to the immediate point, how it is dramatically expressive. To answer the question we shall need to drop the term "prose" and take up the distinction between the language of logic and the language of literature. The distinction is sufficiently commonplace not to require elaboration. But the emphases we shall wish to make prompt one observation.

It is the peculiar characteristic of literary language, not so much to displace words from their established and referential frames of meaning —since it is in the nature of words that their referential meanings persist—as to "disturb" the conventional frames of reference through new or more extended signification. It is in these terms that the language of metaphor is considered the language *par excellence* of literature, though the fact raises the question as to whether all literary language—and therefore literature—is not finally "metaphoric." At any rate our present concern is to note that while the "nonmetaphoric" language of Etheregean comedy is ordering the comic experience of the plays in a fashion which at its surface seems to be, and to an extent is, that of logical discourse, it

[4] It is important to note how this abstracting quality of the language works in projecting the presumably personal emotions of the characters. Thus Loveit's rage when Dorimant proves "unfaithful": "Faithless, inhuman, barbarous man"; "Without sense of love, of honour, or of gratitude," etc. (214).

is also ordering it in a distinctly literary way. More precisely, while the terms of the language, together with surface line and texture, are establishing what seems to be a clear and logically coherent order of experience, the language at another level is consistently confusing that order by "disturbing" the ordinary referential frames of meaning. Out of this situation comes a new and final order of meaning which at the verbal level is the play. It has emerged from the interplay between the logical surfaces of the language and forces working across it. And this general situation corresponds to the dramatic structure and meaning of the play, since, we have seen, Etheregean comedy as a whole is concerned with disturbing and reordering the apparently logical order of its comic world. We shall return to this situation in more detail. For purposes of clarification, however, we may note here a relatively simple case.

In the opening scene of *The Man of Mode,* Dorimant tells his friend, Medley, "Next to the coming to a good understanding with a new mistress, I love a quarrel with an old one" (195). At the surface of the language the statement seems in its clear, assertive balance, to contribute in an explicit and logical way to the portraying of the "honest-man" world of the comic hero. It announces, for example, the libertine's "variety" in love as an aspect of the pursuit of pleasure. It also establishes, as twin aspects of that pursuit, the pleasure of the senses and the pleasure of "warfare." But in the context of the play the full meaning of "good understanding," apart from a possible phallic pun, is highly equivocal. It cuts across the logical order of the statement in such a way as to undermine the surface relationships and schematic distinctions of the terms "new mistress" and "old one," "good understanding" and "quarrel." And out of this disordering emerges a new and final order at the level of the play's comic meaning.

By "good understanding" Dorimant means, of course, that the new mistress—like the old one previously—yields to his persuasions. The first equivocation concerns the terms on which the "good understanding" is reached: whether, for example, they are libertine ("follow nature," "appetite," gratification of the senses, liberty, the philosophy of "use," etc.) or whether they are "courtly" ("honour," "passion," "soul," constancy, obligation, gratitude). In either event, however, the fact of Dorimant's libertine convictions and actions within a double-standard society makes clear that there can be no good understanding on the part of the lady if she is foolish enough to yield on either set of terms. The play's exposition, in fact, has already made sufficiently clear that the good understanding in Dorimant's winning a new mistress must be as much a quarrel as his breaking off with an old one. We are accordingly prepared for the "witty sex battles" which will ensue in the play's development. Dorimant's three "mistresses" in the play exhaustively explore the implications of these equivocalities. Loveit's "good understanding" on courtly terms proves to be ignorance. Belinda's yielding proves not to be a matter of coming to an understanding at all, but the weakness of reason yielding to passion. Harriet's wiser understanding, together with her control, produces a situation of at least temporary if not permanent stalemate. But further, and as a part of all this, the play's exposition before Dorimant's speech has prepared us to ask whether, on the part of the hero himself as well as his mistresses, there is not bad rather than good understanding. Working across the apparently logical surfaces of the statement, in other words, is a set of questions concerning not only the fashionable "mode" but man: the question of true understanding, the relationship of reason to passion, of nature to social and moral order. The reordering and final comic meaning which emerges from these equivocalities relates not only to the "honest-man" world of the hero but to the comic world of man. It suggests, for example, that true understanding and true fulfillment are incompatible with unrestrained liberty and "warfare."

To an extent in the preceding chapters, we have seen this verbal tug-of-war in progress in the plays; and the instances of verbal irony and ambiguity which we have inspected make clear its chief structural source. The alleged realities and values in the "honest-man" world of the comic heroes are expressed in large part by terms which draw upon other realities and values very different from those of the libertine "honest man." Consequently these other frames of meaning—the traditional honest man, the courtly, the heroic, the Christian and classical humanist—provide, in effect, a constant reservoir of ambiguities upon which any of a vast number of words may draw, but the precise meaning of which will be conditioned by the particular verbal and dramatic context. Nature, art, reason, passion, love, honour, wit are a few of the more central terms in which we have seen something of this operation. Thus the equivocalities of this nonmetaphoric language create a literary situation which has certain properties resembling the metaphor. A chief difference is that, though the "vehicles" (the nonlibertine references) are never overtly expressed, there may be as many as four or five brought simultaneously into relationship with the "tenor" (the surface libertine assertion). Consequently the tensions among the several frames of reference and the synthesis which resolves them frequently become highly complicated and charged with comic meaning. The result in a general way, of course, is an emerging definition of the libertine "honest-man" world in terms of its relationship to all the other worlds which the language juxtaposes with it. But this means of definition has a peculiarly comic value. For the characters in the play, it provides repeatedly a kind of comic reversal—the strong, direct, assertive movement of the parallelism and balance, broken by the disruptive intrusion of the meaning in depth. For the play, the final effect is a synthesis of meaning which has something of the order, clarity, and logic of one and the density and complexity of the other.

To illustrate more fully this thus far largely abstract account, we may briefly return to Dorimant's speech, quoted above: "Good nature and good manners corrupt me. I am honest in my inclinations, and would not, were't not to avoid offence, make a lady a little in years believe I think her young, wilfully mistake art for nature, and seem as fond of a thing I am weary of as when I doted on't in earnest" (216). The speech is typical of the language of the play, though the extent to which the particular character and situation add their influence will be apparent. For example, Dorimant has himself, of course, consciously inverted some of the terms. He asserts that he is "corrupted" into being too kind, though he knows—and wishes Loveit to know—that in asserting his kindness, he is actually asserting his malice. Consequently, in the surface sense, he is not corrupt. But beneath the surface inversions lies a network of further implications. Though they still have distinctive meaning for Dorimant as a particular character, they involve his entire "honest-man" world in a series of searching equivocalities. At one level "Good nature and good manners corrupt me" remains a simple inversion for that world. It could never be "kind," as Dorimant is here pretending he is. Further, the whole speech, like Dorimant's general treatment of Loveit, is sufficiently malicious to make clear that he and his world have no real good nature and good manners by which to be corrupted. Yet the very skilled expression of the speech itself provides ample evidence that Dorimant, and his world, have an abundance of "good manners," but carefully corrupted in use. The traditional and the modish honest man are here illuminating each other; and in doing so, they define at a new level of meaning the modish world of the play.

The speech also raises the whole involved question of nature and manners, so central to Dorimant, the play, and Restoration comedy. Since there are at least two very different "natures" in the play, their diverse relationships to manners play upon the equivocalities of Dorimant's general assertion and upon the question of corruption. And this, in turn, leads to "I am honest in my inclinations." He isn't honest, of course, in the traditional sense; he is only "honest." Yet—though here Dorimant and his world have less of a case than the earlier Etheregean "heroes"—he might assert that he *is* the most honest man in acknowledging that the world is made up of "villains and fools" and in acting accordingly. The play's entire set of value oppositions, based upon opposing postulates concerning nature, comes here into focus.

But now "inclinations" comes into the picture. The term reminds us that from one point of view Dorimant is by real inclination honest neither in the traditional nor the modish sense. Even in his own "world" he must conceal his natural inclination to malice beneath the modish surface of "honesty" in order to give the malice outlet. Thus his surface civility is the result of restraint acting as stratagem—not direct inclination. At the same time the term focuses upon the inconsistency of surface good nature as a modish requisite in this world. For we have seen that the insistence on good nature was not entirely a Machiavellian device. It looked to a set of values curiously at odds with the libertine-Machiavel assumptions concerning nature. This in turn reminds us that Dorimant's "wilfully mistake art for nature" is a final summing up not only of the problem of art and nature, but of all the other questions raised by the earlier terms of the speech. Dorimant confidently assumes, beneath his own conscious irony, that he has not mistaken art for nature—with respect either to Loveit's beauty or to his own ideas of reality and value—but that his own art is so skillful that others will. Thus he has at least willfully divorced art from nature, if not mistaken one for the other. He has used art, that is, to conceal nature.[5] The play, however, has long before this made clear that Dorimant in doing so has in a fundamental sense mistaken art for nature also. Good manners and good nature are a *part* of nature when the inclination is truly honest.

The intricate verbal situation in Dorimant's speech does not, of course, prevail at every point in Etherege's plays.[6] But in kind, if not in degree, it typifies the most conspicuous "literary" characteristic of the nonmetaphoric language. And there are throughout the plays passages at least as involved as the excerpt which we have examined. In the simplest cases the situation frequently appears to be nothing more than an inversion. The constant reference to the "good-natured town," for example, seems simply an assertion that the "town" is really malicious. Yet the town *is* "good-natured" at its surfaces, partly as a Machiavellian device but partly because it does, paradoxically, consider good nature to be an absolute value—even though, in effect, its demands stop at surface requirements only. What, therefore, appears at first glance to be a simple verbal inversion actually sustains and defines many of the central concerns of the play—among them, of course, the comedy of appearance and reality.

Beyond this simplest type of situation the degrees of involvement vary. But the verbal comedy at some level of intricacy repeatedly cuts across what at first glance appears to be the clear and logical order of the language. Thus Dorimant's laconic "Kind," when he has finally won

[5] In the particular case considered here, he has also in a sense used art to reveal nature. That is, he has wished to let his natural malice "shine through" the polished surfaces of his "good manners." But except with Loveit, to whom his nature is already known, this is seldom the use to which Dorimant puts his art. Its general function, we have already seen, is to conceal.

[6] It is least prevalent in *The Comical Revenge* and most prevalent in *She Wou'd if She Cou'd*. In *The Man of Mode,* the comic irony and ambiguity in the characters' speeches depend to a larger extent than in the earlier plays upon the dramatic situation.

Bellinda's consent, brings the "mode," the traditional honest man, and courtly love into an elaborate interplay of comic meaning (227). An extended set of terms draw in a similar manner upon these three frames of reference and frequently upon the less specialized ones of general Christian and classical values as well—"obliging," "goodwill," "gratitude," and so on. But there are other terms which relate to virtually all the major frames of reference and which can repeatedly create, therefore, a still greater density than that in the speech of Dorimant just examined. Perhaps the most persistent and central of those terms is "honour." In *She Wou'd If She Cou'd,* we have seen that this word is thematically the central one. It reticulates throughout the play in verbal situations of the type we have considered. The following example of its use will indicate how a single word in dramatic context can acquire the subtlety, counterpoint, and overtones of an extended "conceit."

In the second act of *She Wou'd If She Cou'd,* Lady Cockwood awaits impatiently the arrival of Courtal. Through his stratagem of "flight-in-pursuit" he has been obliged to make an appointment with her—at which, it is her intention, he shall have the opportunity of cuckolding her husband, who is also Courtal's professed friend. Courtal's failure to arrive at the appointed hour gives rise to Lady Cockwood's fear of disappointment and to her "courtly" conviction that her "servant" is "ungrateful," "insensible," "perfidious." A knock, however, revives her hopes, and she sends Sentry to the door with "Peace, he may yet redeem his honour" (110).

The ambiguities of the word "honour" reflect in epitome here again certain ironies and oppositions that are fundamental to the play as a whole, to Etheregean comedy, and to the Restoration comedy of manners. What appears at first glance to be merely an inversion ("dishonour" would seem the proper word) must actually be taken as at once inverted and not inverted. And in each position the word brings into significant relationship a variety of conflicting references. In the "courtly" pose of Lady Cockwood, Courtal has avowedly confessed himself her "servant," so that an entire set of specialized values and assumptions—"gratitude," "constancy," "devotion," etc.—do indeed oblige him in "honour" to fulfill his "lady's" expectations. But these considerations are tangentially related to a less specialized set of values. Courtal has made an explicit commitment, and the honour simply of his "word," of fulfilling an assumed obligation, is also at stake. This consideration, in turn, extends into the specialized honour of the modish "honest man." "Barbarousness," as a matter of purely expedient policy, of efficacious "reputation," is to be avoided. Fidelity to a commitment is even in this frame of reference a necessary point of "honour."

But the word, of course, looks the other way, too—not only in the obvious and conventional senses, but in terms of the inverted "heroic" and "honest-man" values in the world of the play. For if Lady Cockwood's stratagem succeeds, not only will Courtal's fail, but those discriminations of appetite and taste by which the hero and the dupe are distinguished will have been violated. In both instances the hero-dupe relationship will, in fact, be reversed, with an obvious destruction of "honour" for the hero. Thus once more the implications of a single word reflect microcosmically a central insight and a fundamental aspect of structure for the play as a whole. Beneath a superficial opposition and equivocality, the word establishes a paradoxical similarity in reality and value. Implied as a "synthesis" of the terms, in other words, is the inescapable necessity of honour, of obligation, whatever the particular "world" may be. The implications propose that in any context of values sheer individualism, unencumbered by duty or obligation, is a social impossibility. The practical necessity of restraint for fulfillment—at whatever level—is asserted. Some of the basic inconsistencies of the "honest-man" mode are accordingly projected through a verbal complexity in depth. The logical surface of the language has been disturbed by a set of ambiguities which resolve into a kind of comic synthesis.

II

The prominence of certain types of imagery in the Restoration comedy of manners has been customarily noted by students of the plays. But the contributions of that imagery to the comic expressiveness of this body of drama has not been much explored. We may begin such an exploration by noting in the world of Etherege's plays, as in the Restoration society which it reflects, the fashion of the "comparison" or "similitude." As employed in both the drama and its age, the term included types of comparisons which are not commonly considered to be strictly metaphoric: fools are to wits as ugly women to handsome. This type of comparison accounts for much of the persistent balance and parallelism in the general structure of the language, and is a principal means of constructing at the verbal level the play's comic world of logically schematized and abstract terms. We should note, however, that while this particular class of similitudes is not strictly and overtly metaphoric, it frequently involves by the nature of its terms a metaphoric process which cuts across the logical surfaces of the comparison.[7] In Harriet's statement —"Women then [when they are ugly] ought to be no more fond of dressing than fools should be of talking" (219)—the explicit comparison involves merely two examples of violating "decorum" or "degree." But

[7] This situation will, of course, exist to some extent in any comparison where the terms are at all susceptible to such a process. The point here is that Etherege's plays and the Restoration comedy of manners deliberately employ comparisons whose terms can so interact.

there is an implied relationship between the terms which brings them together in a metaphoric synthesis. The dressing in one case becomes a kind of talking, the talking a kind of dressing; and the fools and the women are brought together in a way which enlarges and particularizes the general relationship explicitly asserted.

Most frequently the type of comparison or similitude which is not overtly or entirely metaphoric in nature serves one of two general functions. First, for a variety of comic purposes, it may compare aspects of the world of the play to other "worlds" outside the general milieu of the comedy—as, for example, in Gatty's similitude, "I perceive he [Freeman] runs in thy head as much as a new gown uses to do in the country the night before 'tis expected from London" (168). Explicitly, the comparison twits Ariana for a "country-like" enthusiasm for her "gallant." But the most trenchant comparison lies outside the explicit logic of the statement, and implies, of course, that gallants are like gowns, with a host of significances for the characters and the play which are too obvious to require elucidation. Frequently the metaphoric process is more apparent: Courtal is aware that Lady Cockwood's promoting the acquaintance of the heroes and heroines is as unlikely as "that an old rook should bring a young snap acquainted with his bubble" (104-5). Here, of course, the function in part is to suggest the comic "value" to Lady Cockwood of her "gallant." But, like many of the comparisons which relate outside worlds to those of the play, the function is more extended. It establishes the conniving and trickery which are part of the world of the play; but it also suggests that these are only aspects of man and society at large—not merely of a specialized world. The character and import of the play's world tends thus to be generalized into larger areas of experience. The conniving within the play becomes one aspect of the larger reality of "rooks" and "snaps."

The second common employment of the similitude which is not strictly metaphoric in form is to define aspects of the comic world's general milieu which cannot be or are not objectified in the play: "Beauty runs as great a risk exposed at Court as wit does on the stage, where the ugly and the foolish all are free to censure" (249). At the logical level the addition of Court and stage to the comic world is important, together, of course, with the emphasis upon malice. But the metaphoric implication which cuts across the logical surface is that the Court is like a stage, with consequent suggestions which support major images and concerns of the play: the "game," appearance and reality, and so on. In point of number, these types of comparisons are conspicuous among the metaphoric or quasi-metaphoric aspects of the language. But their main task is to assist in constructing the comic worlds of the plays at the logical level of meaning. Their contribution to the "disturbing" or complicating of that level is relatively slight.

When we come to the fully metaphoric language, we find that it brings directly into the play all the traditional frames of thought and value in terms of which the "honest-man" world is formed. It accomplishes overtly what the "nonmetaphoric" language accomplishes by implication. Like that language, too, but again overtly rather than by implication, it defines the character of the comic world by bringing two or more frames of reference into ironic juxtaposition. The logical surfaces of the language are thus once more "disturbed," but now the complicating process is "lineal" as well as in "depth," since the metaphoric relationships tend to be rhetorically extended rather than compact. And the imagery tends, in its extension, to assume much the same marked balance and direct, repetitive movement as the nonmetaphoric. In this movement it provides concreteness for the abstract terms at the other level of expression; and here again a comic irony is likely to be established between the suggested "realities" of the abstract language and the specific body given to them by the imagery. For example, the "passion" proposed at the abstract level characteristically becomes mere animal appetite at the level of metaphor. Or "honour," in its suggestion of the "heroic," becomes a matter of the hero's marching "bravely at the rear of an army of link-boys" (6). Some of these general characteristics of the imagery require further comment.

One of the most frequent types of image in Etheregean comedy expresses naturalistic attitudes toward love, women, marriage. This, of course, is part of the libertine's postulates concerning nature. But the naturalistic imagery of the plays persistently makes clear that libertine nature has also become Hobbesian or "Machiavellian"—of however comic variety:[8] "Since we know the bush, why do we not start the game" (104); "These deer cannot herd" (106); "Who the devil that has common sense will go a-birding with a clack in his cap" (155). The lover is a kite hovering about a "backside, watching an opportunity to catch up the poultry" (154). Or the two lovers may "fall to and love, as gamecocks fight" (224). In general, the first and most obvious comic incongruity in such images lies merely in their violation of conventional expectations. And their comic expressiveness in this respect would be much the same with or without the specific context of the plays. Within that context, however, the incongruity becomes important as an expressed awareness of conventional ideals violated by reality. And it takes in this respect an extra turn, since it consciously expresses the fact that the sensual pursuit of pleasure by the libertine is no naturalistic state of bliss, but a very

[8] The naturalistic sex imagery is, as one might expect, considerably less common in *The Man of Mode* than in the earlier plays. Sex, as we have seen, is in Etherege's final comedy more a matter of power than of sensual gratification; and the imagery reflects the fact. Further, Dorimant's more persistent posture and guile as a courtly lover tend to keep the libertine's naturalistic convictions concerning sex submerged beneath the verbal surfaces of the play. Finally, the presence of three nonnaturalistic "worlds" conditions, of course, the total imagery of the play.

Hobbesian state of war. While the imagery, then, expresses the revolt of the modish "honest man" from conventional ideals, it makes clear his awareness that his own espoused "reality" is also far from ideal. The imagery can, therefore, at once deprecate conventional assumptions and the assumptions of the libertine "honest man."

Much the same situation exists for the "heroic" imagery. We have seen that the comic "undertaking" is given an inverted heroic or mock-heroic caste. This aspect of the play in terms of character and action is supported by the imagery: Sir Frederick "vanquishes" the constable and "massacres" the windows—"most honourable achievements, such as will be registered to your eternal fame by the most learned historians of Hick's Hall" (6). In the heroic battles the "trumpet sound[s] a charge to this dreadful foe" (16); the heroes become "men-of-war . . . cruising . . . for prizes" (106); or, in completely stock images, they lay "sieges," storm "cities," and send and receive "challenges" which "must not in honour" be ignored (156). The consistent stress here, of course, is upon the "heroic" in "warfare." And the conscious irony by which the plays' "honest men" at once deprecate their own and the traditionally heroic values modulates into the ironies of the Hobbesian-Machiavellian natural state of war. Consequently at the nonmetaphoric level of the language, the abstractions which define the character of the comic world in terms of the heroic are further complicated by the intrusion of the "nature" of the beast. Such terms as "courage," "valor," "defiance," and above all, "honour" become not only mock-heroic aspects of the "undertaking," but inverted terms for Hobbesian warfare and Machiavellian intrigue.

In the Christian imagery of the plays the same general situations prevail. Most commonly at the overtly metaphoric level, the Christian imagery assumes implications also of the courtly in defining the character of the "honest-man" world.[9] To Harriet's question, "Could you keep a Lent for a mistress?" Dorimant replies, "In expectation of a happy Easter" (236). In some respects the imagery in this particular instance is not typical of the general metaphoric language of the plays. "Lent" and "Easter" have a density which is more like the abstractions of the nonmetaphoric language. In terms of comic meaning, the force of the images operates in precisely the same way. But as in the less intricate Christian imagery also, they support and give specific body to a large set of ambiguously charged abstractions operating throughout the plays: "heaven," "hell," "sin," "grace," "fall," "faith," "fanatic," "atheist," "devout." The Lent-Easter witticism embodies, in fact, the whole ironic grace-fall-

[9] Generically speaking, the use of Christian imagery to express courtly love attitudes and values had, of course, been traditional since the Middle Ages. Much of the Christian-courtly imagery in the Restoration comedy of manners reveals this traditionalism. But the dramatic contexts serve to specialize the significance of the juxtaposition in ways which are here explored.

regeneration archetype which characterizes the total comic structure of the plays. And the comment it makes upon the world of the play summarizes the general import of both the Christian abstractions and the Christian imagery. It summarizes, indeed, the central import of Etheregean comedy. It deserves, therefore, to be considered in more detail.

At the surface of the image is, of course, a set of courtly assumptions with Christian overtones: the devoutness of the lover, the self-sacrifice, the final and transcendent fulfillment. But combined with these are a set of distinctly Christian assumptions which also have courtly applications: repentance, atonement, and rebirth. At these levels alone, the point is obvious. The application of either courtly or Christian values to the world of Dorimant makes a sufficient comment in itself. But the customary inversions are again in the imagery. Harriet is obliged, like the earlier heroines, to qualify expectation and desire with libertine reality. And Dorimant's "Easter" is scarcely, at this stage at least, either courtly or Christian. The disparity underlines with greater firmness than in the earlier plays the unquestionable deficiencies of the comic world projected. And it catches the central ironies of character, action, and values in the play: the definition of the comic world by traditional frames of value which reveal not only its character but its inconsistencies and its deficiencies; the ambiguity of the curve of action (from grace to fall, or from fall to grace); the comic uncertainty of man as to either his own nature or his own desires.

III

It is apparent that what we have here been discussing as a "literary" use of language in Etherege's plays is a matter of wit. The language, in other words, is most conspicuously literary by virtue of being witty. From Aristotle to Freud, wit has been considered as the perception of similarities in things dissimilar.[10] What is implied in such a definition is that the dissimilarities are superficially much more marked than the similarities (Dr. Johnson's "occult" resemblances), so that a distinct sense of incongruity exists in the comparison. Consequently the force of the wit may lie merely in the marked differences of the objects. But better still, it may lie in the extent to which both likeness and difference are insisted upon at once. Thus the question of wit impinges upon the question of metaphor.[11] And the two become merged points of interest in the poetry of such a writer as Donne.

As the term "wit" is most currently used today, however, and as it has

[10] Or of dissimilarities in things similar. See "Spectator #62," *The Works of . . . Joseph Addison,* ed. Henry G. Bohn (London, 1856), II, 357-62.

[11] See I. A. Richards' discussion of the metaphor, *The Philosophy of Rhetoric* (Oxford, 1936), p. 125.

been generally applied to the Restoration comedy of manners, it means essentially comic wit. And that in turn would seem to mean that in the wit, as in comedy at large, the incongruities involve a minification which operates upon one or both of the objects compared.[12] The point will help to distinguish comic wit from wit that is not comic. The peculiar power of much of Donne's wit, for example, lies to a considerable extent in the fact that a comparison which by conventional associations and values would be expected to minify the "tenor," serves instead to enlarge it. One should not, presumably, have much trouble in being comically witty about a pair of lovers and a pair of compasses. But Donne has established by his comparison a kind of sublimity in the realm of the potentially ludicrous. The wit is not comic because the poet has kept the minifying power of the "vehicle" suppressed or, as it were, just beneath the surface. Had he permitted some of the potentially ludicrous to materialize, he might then have had comic wit of some complexity.

For, again as with comedy in general, the simpler forms of comic wit merely diminish the object of the witticism. But a more complex form will establish an ambivalence which derives from a simultaneous movement toward diminishment and augmentation. In the field of comedy at large, the distinction will mark a central difference, for example, between Jonson's most characteristic comedy and that of Shakespeare. In terms of character it separates in one essential way Bobadil and Falstaff. Indeed, it is quite apparent that those comic characters whom we instinctively choose as greatest possess almost invariably a marked ambivalence—Falstaff, Don Quixote, Alceste, Parson Adams, Emma, and so on through the list. It is an essential of the comic hero (or comic heroine), in fact, that he have this ambivalence. His attitudes and actions serve, on the one hand, to criticize his society; but they serve on the other to criticize himself. If they do only the former, the character is not comic; if they do only the latter, he is no hero. As an aspect of his ambivalence of character his wit, if he has any, will also be ambivalent. It may sometimes operate to minify his society—and then we laugh with him. Or it may sometimes serve to minify him—and then we laugh at him. But it may simultaneously do both, and then the comic complexity and force of both character

[12] This minifying factor seems implicit in much theorizing about the nature of comedy. One may, for example, interpret Aristotle's definition in the *Poetics* (the "Ridiculous" as "a species of the Ugly") as based essentially upon the element of minification in the comic object or situation. (*The Art of Poetry,* trans. Ingram Bywater [Oxford, 1920], p. 33.) Again Bergson's concept of the "mechanical" in *Le Rire* might be interpreted as proposing—though the author's emphases are elsewhere—a special type or "area" of minification as the essential element in comedy. In these and other familiar theories of the comic, however, minification, to the extent that it seems implied, is entirely one directional. The concepts do not take adequate account of the situation discussed in the following observations.

and language are at their peak. Most of Falstaff's wit is of this variety (for example, the "honour" speeches in the last act of *Henry IV,* Part I). Without in any way proposing, of course, an equality of literary merit, we may note the similarity in these respects to the Etheregean comic hero.[13]

But along with the general similarities, the comparison of Falstaff with the Etheregean hero serves also to mark essential differences. We need not here investigate the comparison in detail. But it is clear that one of the easiest and most obvious distinctions—the highly individualized character of one, the severely typical character of the other—points to a fundamental distinction in every aspect of comic structure. The Etheregean hero is the explicit and direct embodiment of an abstract and generalized system of attitudes and values. The sum of his characteristics, therefore, is little more than the sum of the abstract system which he embodies. In this respect he is essentially like all the other members of his comic world. And it is precisely therein that the characters most fully serve their comic roles. For the immediate as well as ultimate comedy of Etherege's plays is the comedy of one set of assumptions concerning reality and value playing out its merits, defects, inconsistencies, and equivocalities within a frame of other conflicting sets of assumptions.

The first purpose of the wit, then, is to project the nature, conflict, and relative values of these several sets of assumptions. And it is precisely therein that its comic complexity lies. For at a single instant and with a single word it characteristically serves both to minify and enhance not merely one object but several opposing ones. Lady Cockwood's "Peace, he may yet redeem his honour," is not a witticism on the part of Lady Cockwood. But it is comic wit on the part of the play, and from two points of view: First, it univocally diminishes Lady Cockwood by exposing her comic confusion and inconsistency. To this extent it diminishes also the entire world of conventional hypocrisy which she represents. But, second, it at once comically diminishes and enlarges, though in different ways and to different degrees, the unspecialized Christian and Christian humanist traditions, as well as the courtly, the heroic, and the specialized "honest-man" worlds by placing them in comically illuminating positions vis-à-vis each other. The same essential situation prevails for Dorimant's "art" and "nature," Gatty's "challenge," and so on through the comic wit of the play. When the wit of the play is also the wit of the speaker—normally hero or heroine—the situation, of course, takes on a special complexity. But in any event, the final comic meaning

[13] As with the Etheregean hero, Falstaff's wit—like his general comic nature—has still an additional dimension through his ironic awareness of his own ambivalence. As "comic hero," then, he—and the Restoration comedy of manners heroes—are to be generically distinguished as at a more involved level of comic form from, say, Don Quixote, Alceste, and Parson Adams.

of the wit, like that of the total play, is to express the confusion, uncertainty, and ambiguity of human life.

IV

The characteristics of language which we have here discussed suggest, like the total comic structure of the plays, relationships with certain general characteristics of the age. It is not part of our intent to pursue these suggestions in detail. But it is relatively easy to see what the salient connections might be. In the abstract, generalized, logically schematized structure of the comedy, one may see reflected the so-called "rationalism" of the age, or even the Cartesian and scientific preoccupation with "primary qualities." In the abstracting of human experience into the set frames of various traditions of thought, one may perhaps see the intellectualizing force and consciousness of an aristocratic society. Or in the pervasive opposition between two broadly opposing sets of thought concerning nature and man—Hobbes, Machiavelli, the libertine, versus Christian and classical, the courtly, and the traditional honest man—one may see the age's consciousness of an increasing conflict between an older orthodoxy and an emerging individualism which looks to our own age. These and other factors may very well have exercised an influence on Etherege's plays. If they did, so, too, did the comic awareness which—as comic awareness has a way of doing—confounded them. For we have seen in sufficient detail that the plays set up their own and their comic worlds' traditions, rational order, and primary classifications largely for the purpose of violating them at every turn. The hero and the dupe have their relationships blurred; the libertine-Machiavel is threatened, at least, with something approaching a Christian-classical—if not quite courtly—heart; the refinement of a quasi-aristocratic society becomes a maze; a state of grace may prove to be a fall, or a fall a state of grace.

The result of all this, we may once more remark, is not, at the level of the plays' meaning, simply confusion or cynicism or despair. Particularly with *The Man of Mode,* Etheregean comedy proposes its own order—its own set of realities and values. But as with all thoughtful comedy, the order emerges from the comic fact and form of man's inveterate disorder. The disorder is surely not confined to that of a specialized society. On the contrary, the wit by which that society most clearly announces its own special character becomes the principal vehicle for universalizing the comic ritual which the plays project. For the comedy, finally, is one in which not merely libertine but Christian, classical, "heroic," courtly, and honest-man postulates concerning the nature of man are brought to the test of human experience. And from this point of multiple vision, the comic ritual of the plays is primarily one in which man in the pride and assertiveness of his wit progressively reveals its and his own general insufficiency and confusion.

Even from this view, however, the wit is equivocal. In terms of the play we can, on the one hand, see the comic and ritualistic formalism as distancing experience in order to look at it more closely.[14] Yet, on the other, the insistent, repetitive balance and parallelism, both of language and general structure—although highly expressive in their comic tensions between order and disorder—suggest a certain inflexibility. One eventually comes to feel that the persistent irony is somewhat overbrittle, even for the type and level of experience with which the plays deal. But one feels, with whatever difference of degree, something of the same quality in the sterner and more searching irony of Swift, or in the broader and more flexible wit of Pope. The sense of insufficiency derives in part, perhaps, from the Restoration and Augustan refusal, as Herbert Davis has noted concerning Swift, of "the happiness of being well deceived." [15] "I hope," said Swift, in his "Letter to a very young Lady on her Marriage," "you do not still dream of charms and raptures, which marriage ever did, and ever will, put a sudden end to." [16] Etheregean comedy takes a somewhat less categorical view of the matter; but the unyielding intellectualism of its surfaces seems to reflect something of the same disenchantment. To this extent it reflects also something of the ambivalence in the ritual of wit which characterizes its comic world. For if that ritual for hero and heroine took away too much, it also guarded against the expectation of too much and the realization of too little. The comic vision and expression of Etherege's plays keeps, in a generic sense, something of the same middle ground.

[14] Dobrée has suggested that aspects of structure and comic texture in Etherege's plays are like a ballet: "It is all a dance; the couples bow, set to partners, perform their evolutions, and bow again." (*Restoration Comedy 1660-1720* [Oxford, 1924], p. 63.) There is some justness in the observation if one avoids the idea that the comedy is, therefore, merely "gay," "uncritical," "artificial." Certainly the persistent elements of music, dance, song add to the highly formalized structure and suggest an abstraction something like the dance. The comedy is, indeed, a kind of dance, but a ritualistic dance—an ironic and ambiguous version of the dance of life.

[15] Herbert Davis, *Stella. A Gentlewoman of the Eighteenth Century* (Macmillan, 1942), p. 24.

[16] See *ibid.*, p. 47.

William Wycherley

by Anne Righter

Wycherley's first play, *Love in a Wood,* was produced in 1671, just three years after Etherege had charted the basic dimensions of Restoration comedy in *She Wou'd if She Cou'd* (1668). Later, Wycherley was to claim that he had written this initial and, as the Restoration thought, triumphantly successful play in 1659, when he was only nineteen. His second comedy, *The Gentleman Dancing Master,* seems to have been staged in the summer of 1672, although here again Wycherley tried to push the date of composition back to the beginning of Charles's reign. He was not the only well-born writer of comedy who affected to have earned his fame negligently, as the result of a precocious whim and idle hours. The pretence is no more true in his case than in that of most of his contemporaries. Unmistakable topicalities in the two comedies themselves belie their author, suggesting a date close to that of their actual production, at which time Wycherley was hardly an unfledged youth. Even more important, it is clear that both plays build upon the foundation already provided by Etherege, that they are aware both of the experiment represented by *Love in a Tub* (1664) and of the resolution achieved in *She Wou'd if She Cou'd.* It is to Etherege, with some help from Dryden, that the credit belongs of having established those formal principles which were to be the inheritance of Congreve.

That Wycherley should have served a limited apprenticeship to Etherege, in particular to that second and more important of the two comedies which preceded *The Man of Mode* (1676), is scarcely surprising. The initial reception of *She Wou'd if She Cou'd* seems to have been somewhat cool; Pepys records that he thought it very silly and insipid and so did everyone sitting around him. Yet it was afterwards claimed that even on that first, doubtful occasion, the men of wit and sense in the audience recognized the importance of Etherege's achievement. Certainly, by 1671, Shadwell was describing it confidently as "the best Comedy that has been written since the Restauration of the Stage." Wycherley could hardly have failed to take notice. Yet his own nature and predilections were essentially very different from those of Etherege. When, with *The Country Wife* (?1674) and *The Plain-Dealer* (1676), he created his own best comedies, he departed markedly from that Etheregean type of play which he had begun by imitating. Norman Holland has suggested, in *The First Modern Comedies,* that it is precisely in these two plays, magnificent as they are, that the sentimental triumph of the end of the century is first adumbrated. Harcourt, Manly and Fidelia are, he asserts, a-social idealists; the dramatist has divorced cleverness from goodness, evil from folly, as Etherege never did. In these comedies, the innately good man or woman who is a deviant from society triumphs at the end in an increasingly improbable way. This implausible triumph reflects a sense of schism and contains the seeds of the movement from realism to sentimentalism.

Holland's point of view is an interesting one. He is right, surely, to insist upon the originality of Wycherley's final plays, the sense in which they strike off in new directions. However, it is a point of view which perhaps needs qualification. More fundamental, even, than the split between intellectual and moral qualities which he discerns is Wycherley's covert sympathy with excess, both emotional and otherwise. It is a sympathy which effectively destroys the balance of Etheregean comedy. Nor do the emotions suggested seem to resemble the comfortable, self-indulgent sentimentalism of Cibber or of Steele; they are far more astringent, harsh, even nihilistic. From the abandonment of the Etheregean model came not only sentimentalism but also, and more immediately, a kind of "dark comedy" in which the genius of Wycherley was joined by the less certain but even more disturbing talents of Otway, Crowne, and Lee.

There is not much which needs to be said about *Love in a Wood.* It is a confusing and basically centerless play, full of invention, but as tangled and obscure as any of the walks and thickets of the park in which so much of the action occurs. As Holland has seen, it resembles Etherege's *Love in a Tub* in its use of a high and a low plot, although it profits from the seven years which had elapsed since the production of that play by reducing the distance between them. The intrigues of Ranger, Lydia, Valentine and Christina on the one hand, and of Dapperwit, Gripe, Sir Simon Addleplot, Lucy, Martha and Lady Flippant on the other belong recognizably to the same world. The play does not fall apart into two halves, one of them embodying the attitudes of comedy, the other those of tragedy, like *Love in a Tub,* or Dryden's *Secret Love* (1667). Instead, there is a clear scale of success, of relative competence at the social game (combined with certain worldly and natural assets), which establishes the characters of the high plot in a position superior to those of the low. This is an enormously acquisitive society; everybody is out to get something or somebody, preferably somebody possessed of something. In the process they tend to return helplessly, like snow-blind travellers, to the point from which they started out. As if in answer to some inexorable physical law, like matches in the end with exactly that like it had originally sought to leave behind. The foolish, fortune-hunting widow ends up with the foolish, fortune-hunting knight, the would-be wit and man of fashion with the alderman's daughter pregnant by someone else, the hypocritical Puritan with the falsely innocent cast mistress. On a higher level, the rake accepts the girl he tried to deceive; the high-minded but jealous Valentine returns to his original estimate of Christina. The whole comedy presents an ironic view of characters desperately rushing forward who nevertheless remain, despite their efforts, in exactly the place to which their own value assigns them. In their actual working-out, these plots and counter-plots are ingenious but mechanical. The various pieces of the comedy never quite fit together into a whole which is any richer or more satisfying than a diagram of positions on a ladder.

The Gentleman Dancing Master is a much better play. Here, as if in conscious reaction against the overcrowded canvas of his first comedy, Wycherley has reduced some thirteen characters of almost equal importance to five. Essentially, this is a play about a young man of wit and sense and a girl possessed of equivalent qualities who succeed in obtaining one another despite the precautions of a fanatical father, a foolish fiancé and an Argus-eyed old woman. Furthermore, it is a comedy which in its attitudes and construction echoes *She Wou'd if She Cou'd.* Like Etherege's Ariana and Gatty, Courtall and Freeman, Wycherley's young lovers stand at the center of everything, as touchstones. It is against Hippolita and Gerrard that all the other characters, young and old, are measured and found wanting. So basic is their affinity, their likeness in a world which shades off into progressive degrees of coarseness and absurdity as it departs from their standard, that Hippolita's wild ruse (by which she lures Gerrard into her acquaintance the night before her arranged marriage to a fool) loses much of its implausibility, becoming as necessary as the operation of a magnet upon steel. On the level of plot, the lovers must outwit Don Diego, M. de Paris and Mrs. Caution if they are to win through to marriage. The requirements of intrigue force Gerrard into his clumsy impersonation of a dancing master, an impersonation which clearly derives from Calderón's comedy *El Maestro de Danzar,* although Wycherley might also have gotten hints for it closer to home in the sub-plot of *The Taming of the Shrew.* A formidable series of external obstacles threatens, through almost five acts, to separate the lovers forever. These obstacles are not, however, the only ones. Running parallel with them, and even more important, are those bars to marriage and consummation which exist only in the minds of Hippolita and Gerrard. Here, Wycherley takes up the central issues of Restoration comedy:

the problems of communication and the language of love, of fruition and time. The manner in which he deals with these issues associates *The Gentleman Dancing Master* firmly with comedy of the Etheregean type.

Hippolita and Gerrard do not meet until the second act of the comedy. The situation when they do is unusual, to say the least. By chicanery, Hippolita has discovered from her impossible husband-to-be the name of the man generally considered to be the finest gallant in town; through a piece of even more outrageous trickery she has contrived to summon this gallant to her, employing her own fiancé as agent. Suspicious but curious, Gerrard obeys instructions, breaks into the house, and finds himself alone with Hippolita and her maid. It is at this point, when the first stage of Hippolita's scheme has succeeded perfectly, the truewit has been found and smuggled past the guards, that the emotional difficulties begin. Gerrard is enormously attracted by the beauty and charm of the girl he sees before him, but understandably perplexed by the whole affair. As for Hippolita, she has found the man she wants, but she can scarcely explain this fact to him in cold blood. An impasse on a psychological level results from the first enfranchisement on the level of plot. Rather helplessly, Hippolita takes refuge in a pretence of extreme innocence and naïveté quite alien to her own nature. Gerrard, for his part, addresses her in an inflated, cliché-ridden language which he clearly deems appropriate for the seduction of a beautiful but completely guileless young heiress.

> My Soul, my Life, 'tis you have Charms powerful as numberless, especially those of your innocency irresistable, and do surprise the wary'st Heart; such mine was, while I cou'd call it mine, but now 'tis yours for ever.[1] (II, ii; vol. I, p. 177)

Divided from one another as they are by mutual misapprehension and pretence, Hippolita and Gerrard nevertheless prepare to steal away together. They are prevented by the sudden arrival of Hippolita's father, Don Diego, and her aunt Mrs. Caution. This interruption, placing a considerable impediment in the way of any actual elopement, turns Gerrard into a not very convincing dancing master. It also permits Wycherley to continue his account of the changing relationship of the lovers, of their progress towards genuine understanding.

Towards the end of this same scene, Don Diego and his sister withdraw temporarily, leaving the road to freedom open once more. Gerrard is eager to seize the opportunity; Hippolita, rather surprisingly, refuses.

[1] In this chapter, act and scene divisions are those of the Mermaid edition, ed. W. C. Ward (London, 1893 *et seq.*); the quotations themselves are from *The Complete Works of William Wycherley*, ed. Montague Summers (4 vols.; London, 1924), with volume and page references to this edition. Shadwell is quoted from *Thomas Shadwell*, ed. Montague Summers (5 vols.; London, 1927). [Ed.]

For this abrupt turnabout, critics of the play have tended to abuse her in terms far stronger than any of those employed by Gerrard himself. Yet her motivations are clear, and by no means either trivial or unreasonable. She has simply been overcome by doubt.

> I am afraid, to know your heart, would require a great deal of time; and my Father intends to marry me, very suddenly, to my Cousin who sent you hither. (II, ii; vol. I, p. 183)

This is Hippolita's dilemma, a dilemma upon which she meditates for the remainder of the scene. "But what has love to do with you?" she asks Gerrard, more seriously than he suspects. Somewhat pompously, he expatiates upon the well-known power of Love to transform his servants, but receives only a doubtful, hesitating reply: "If he were your Master." Hippolita's next move, a move that is maddening, perverse and on the surface totally irrational, has now been prepared for. She agrees to elope with Gerrard at a specific time, sends him off to make all the arrangements, and then when the moment has come, not only refuses to go but announces that she has lied to him all the while and possesses no fortune whatsoever. To this double blow Gerrard reacts in two ways, both of them, as it turns out, right. First of all, he consents to make a fool of himself by marrying her even without a portion; secondly, when she continues to refuse, he displays such unmistakably genuine signs of passion and jealousy that Hippolita can no longer suspect his sincerity. She rewards him both with her hand and with the twelve hundred pounds a year which she really has.

This idea of the testing of the lover, the demand that he act in a fashion foolish by any standards except those of love, is of course medieval in its origins. It goes back to the courts of love, to distinctions like that which Chrétien de Troyes makes in his account of Launcelot as Guinevere's Knight of the Cart. From Launcelot to the Restoration gallant may seem a far cry, yet there were special reasons why this device of the love-trial should become so important to Etherege and his contemporaries. Restoration comedy in general is obsessed with the idea that passion is ephemeral, that love cannot last. Basically, the truewits and their ladies are romantics cursed with an inconveniently powerful strain of rationalism; they wish to believe in the permanence of something which they know to be transitory. The men possess far more freedom than the women, and this freedom permits them (for a time) to avoid the contradiction. Sooner or later, however, despite their libertine principles, they are caught. They try to turn away from their customary imagery of appetite and the chase in speaking to their love, to make promises and swear a fidelity which the wiser self knows time may not let them keep. At this point, however, the woman imposes the trial. In two of Dryden's early comedies, *Secret Love* (1667) and *An Evening's*

Love (1668), the gallant fails it. The lady accepts him anyway, since she cannot really restrain her own inclination, but prognostications for the future are admittedly dark. Etherege, in both *She Wou'd if She Cou'd* and *The Man of Mode,* does what Shakespeare had already done in a not dissimilar situation in *Love's Labour's Lost.* He allows the women to formulate the terms of the trial in the closing moments of the play: Courtall and Freeman's month of constancy, Dorimant's journey into Hampshire, and then closes the comedy with the outcome of the test still unresolved.

Wycherley, on the other hand, like Congreve after him, preferred to delineate the trial within the action itself. He makes it part of that process by which Hippolita and Gerrard come to understand both their own emotions and each other. At the end of the play, they are addressing one another in terms far removed from that false naïveté matched with an equally false language of eternal passion with which their acquaintance began. There can be no guarantee for the future, but at least Gerrard's actions have assured Hippolita that this marriage begins with sincerity and love, however bitterly it may end. "Let us have a good understanding betwixt one another at first, that we may be long Friends," as she says. Their agreements and stipulations are by no means so elaborate as those which Millamant and Mirabell will exact from each other, but they belong in the same line. With the help of the trial device, two intelligent people have succeeded in establishing an equilibrium of realism and romanticism in their relationship. It is an equilibrium that is temporary, no doubt: sweet, yet not necessarily lasting. But this is the way of the world.

There is nothing in *The Gentleman Dancing Master* that runs counter to the comedy of Etherege. *The Country Wife,* however, is another matter. Its construction seems, at first sight, similar to that of Wycherley's preceding play. Again, two young lovers (Alithea and Harcourt) stand in the center of the play. With two other figures, Horner and the shadowy Dorilant, they represent the truewits as opposed to the fools. At the beginning of the comedy, Alithea is about to deny her own intrinsic value by marrying Mr. Sparkish, a would-be wit who imitates the ways of the truewits extremely badly. Horner describes him as "one of those nauseous offerers at wit, who, like the worst Fidlers, run themselves into all Companies" (I, i). He follows his betters everywhere, like Dapperwit in *Love in a Wood,* and his attentions are almost impossible to discourage. As Dorilant says: "He can no more think the Men laugh at him than Women jilt him; his opinion of himself is so good" (I, i). Alithea is painfully aware of the shortcomings of her future husband, but even after she has met and fallen in love with the truewit Harcourt, she refuses to betray Sparkish for him. Her reasons for remaining faithful are, as the play points out, wrong. She feels that it would be disloyal to jilt

Sparkish on the eve of their marriage because his frankness in permitting her to know Harcourt argues a sincere love founded on trust. Actually, it means nothing of the kind. Sparkish is simply so busy thinking about himself, and about his attempts to pass for a gentleman of wit and fashion, that he has no time to think about anyone else, even the woman with whom he is supposed to be in love. Harcourt, genuinely in love with Alithea, keeps telling her this, as does her own realistic waiting-woman, Lucy. Alithea, however, remains stubborn: " 'tis *Sparkish's* confidence in my truth that obliges me to be so faithful to him." She is saved from the consequences of her romantic blindness only by accident. As the result of the complications and misunderstandings of another intrigue in the play, a love-trial of the familiar sort is imposed upon her two lovers. Sparkish, once he suspects her virtue, flies into a paroxysm of jealousy and injured self-love; he insults her and casts her off without even inquiring into the accusation made against her. When Alithea tries to clear herself, the evidence seems to point even more strongly against her. It is at this moment that Harcourt steps forward and makes that romantic, knowingly foolish gesture which always wins the lady in Restoration comedy: "I will not only believe your innocence my self, but make all the World believe it" (V, iv). As far as Alithea is concerned, the testing of her lovers has been involuntary, but she does not hesitate to act upon its result. She and Harcourt join hands, her realistic appraisal of his worth and Sparkish's folly joining with the romanticism of Harcourt's gesture to create the equilibrium characteristic of Etheregean comedy.

Essentially, this is the story of Hippolita and Gerrard, or of Dorimant and Harriet. The surprising thing about it here, of course, is that it is not the part of *The Country Wife* that one remembers. Alithea and Harcourt stand formally at the center of the play; it is by their standard that Wycherley intends the other characters, including Horner, to be judged. Nevertheless, the interest of the play no longer lies with them. In fact, there is something a little mechanical, a little weary, about the handling of this plot as it works towards its inevitable end. Unlike Etherege, Wycherley is not really interested in his young lovers. What he is interested in is that savage vision of society which is being revealed all the time on the outskirts of the play by the activities of a renegade from the center: Harcourt's friend, Horner.

Horner is the most memorable figure in *The Country Wife,* even as the Vice, with his energy, his realism, his cynicism about love, had been the memorable character in late medieval drama. Like the Vice, Horner stands completely alone in the play. Harcourt and Dorilant are his good friends; when it seems that Alithea will marry Sparkish after all, Horner has enough feeling to say to himself in an aside: "Poor *Harcourt,* I am sorry thou hast mist her" (IV, iii). Yet these friends are never allowed to share the secret behind Horner's supposed impotence. Horner accepts their diffident sympathy, watches them trying to suppress the cruel jokes of Sparkish, and says nothing. Even at the end of the comedy, the nature of his pretence is clear only to people he despises: the quack, the three hypocritical ladies and (rather dimly) to Mrs. Pinchwife. Horner is a solitary, a man who has cut himself off from everyone except those female pretenders to honor who, thanks to his ruse, can sin with him joyously and still keep their reputations immaculate. For these women, Horner has profound scorn; they are devices, impersonal instruments of pleasure. Yet his purely sensual relationship with them is the only honest one he maintains.

Curiously enough, the only other character in the comedy who is at all like Horner is the country wife herself. Margery Pinchwife is hopelessly naïve and foolish; she is quite unaware of what the moral issues are. Like Horner, however, she acts purely and straightforwardly to gratify her desires. She is so much a product of the country that she has not learned that it is necessary to conceal these appetites, or to call them by other names, as Lady Fidget and her friends have learned to do so fulsomely. Mr. Horner's love is more satisfactory than that of her jealous, old "musty husband"; she sees no reason why she should not exchange the one for the other, permanently. In fact, her public insistence upon this preference almost wrecks Horner's pretence. Mrs. Pinchwife is an amusing simpleton; Horner is both sophisticated and almost diabolically clever. Yet they have both arrived at exactly the same place, though by different roads. Their attitudes towards love are the same, Margery's because it is all she knows in the first place, Horner's because he has deliberately excluded all other possibilities. This association of Horner with the country wife makes it doubly clear that Wycherley does not intend him as the hero of the comedy. His purely behaviorist point of view is limited and distorting; like Jonson's Volpone, he is a monomaniac who pays too great a price for his undeniable success.

The trouble with *The Country Wife* is, that although the center of the comedy clearly lies with Alithea and Harcourt, Wycherley cannot really bring himself to believe in them. It is in their love that the conflicting claims of romanticism and the realism of a Horner are reconciled, that marriage fulfils a symbolic role. The dramatist's attention remains fixed, however, upon the negative side of the picture, upon Horner the agent of destruction, the man who flays romantic and social ideals. His behavior scarcely accords with the truewit's standard of natural elegance and decorum; it is grotesque, one-sided and excessive, yet it dominates the comedy just the same. In its overall effect, *The Country Wife* is nihilistic. Horner is a kind of rival touchstone to that represented at the center by Harcourt and Alithea, wholly negative as it is positive. Purely animal motives are revealed in the people Horner contacts: the unvarnished, crude desire of the women behind their virtuous façades, the stupidity of their husbands, the falsity and imperceptiveness of would-be wits like Sparkish. Before Horner, women who customarily proclaim that it is an unspeakable sin for a lady of quality to neglect her honor, begin to talk in another and more honest vein:

> Our Reputation, Lord! Why should you not think, that we women make use of our Reputation, as you men of yours, only to deceive the world with less suspicion; our Virtue is like the State-man's Religion, the Quaker's Word, the Gamester's Oath, and the Great Man's Honour, but to cheat those that trust us. (V. ii; vol. II, p. 80)

All the characters of the comedy reveal their true selves in front of Horner and, with the exception of Alithea, Harcourt, and Dorimant, who actually are what they seem, he profits from them all. The state of society which Horner reveals is not only somewhat frightening, its emotional weight pulls against the meaning inherent in the structure of the comedy. By the end, the young lovers are in danger of standing in almost the same relationship to the Horner plot as the love and honor heroes of Restoration tragi-comedy do to the superior reality of the comic characters.

At one point in *The Country Wife,* Horner asserts: "I am a Machiavel in love, Madam." It is a remark which suggests a comparison with Machiavelli's own brilliant comedy *Mandragola,* a play written in 1518 which has had an even longer and stormier history than Wycherley's. In the Italian play, a young Florentine determined to possess the beautiful, virtuous wife of an old fool, succeeds in making his way to her bed with the strenuous help of her husband, her mother, and her confessor. The girl herself struggles to resist their blandishments and preserve her honor, but the combined greed and folly of those who should support chastity is finally too much for her. She accepts the young man, not merely for the night, but in a permanent liaison. Machiavelli is as implacable about stripping the mask away from the true face of society as Wycherley; he too attacks the clergy, snobbery—when the husband boggles slightly at pimping for his own wife, the conspirators assure him that the king of France does it—self-interest and hypocrisy. What really separates *Mandragola* from the satire of *The Country Wife,* however, is that in Machiavelli's comedy, quite characteristically, the end justifies the means. The young Florentine is really in love with the girl; she is not an anonymous object of desire, as Lady Fidget and her friends are for Horner. At the end of the play, she is saying to her lover:

> Since your cunning, the folly of my husband, my mother's lack of scruple and the wickedness of my confessor have combined to make me do what I would never have done on my own, I can only believe that some divine influence has willed this, and, as it is not for me to resist what heaven

> decrees, I surrender. And so I take you for my lord, and master, and guide. You must be everything to me . . . the sole source of all my happiness. (V, iv)

Here, at the center of his play, Machiavelli permits a genuine value to exist. Beyond the framework of society which has been proved so frail and corruptible, the honesty of love itself still stands, and in it, realism and romanticism come together.

Whether or not Wycherley was aware of the total effect of *The Country Wife,* in his next and last play, *The Plain-Dealer,* he radically altered the structure of his comedy. Like Machiavelli, he made the lover and the man who investigates the ills of society the same person: Harcourt and Horner in one. Yet *The Plain-Dealer* remains a truly disturbing play, far more so than *The Country Wife.* When it was first published, in 1677, Wycherley provided it with a bitter mock-dedication to a London procuress, the savage spirit of which seems to inform the play as a whole. As everyone knows, *The Plain-Dealer* is modelled upon Molière's *Misanthrope;* whether it simply misunderstands and degrades its French original, or whether it represents an inspired reworking of Molière, is, however, a point upon which critics find it hard to agree. One thing certainly seems clear. Voltaire's famous comparison of the two comedies:

> All Wycherley's strokes are stronger and bolder than those of our *Misanthrope,* but then they are less delicate, and the Rules of Decorum are not so well observed in this play

is, if anything, an understatement. Manly, the plain-dealer of the title, is an Alceste who has many of the features of Horner. His extravagance, his uncontrolled sensuality and violence set him apart not only from his French prototype, but also from the ideal of wit and judgment established in comedy by Etherege. Manly is a malcontent on a grand and emotional scale, and while there is a bitter truth in much of what he says, there is also a good deal of absurdity and false judgment. He too is a monomaniac. Certainly, he represents a curious departure from the ordinary Restoration comic treatment of the man or woman who rails against society and the age.

Generally, in Restoration comedy, such characters are highly suspect. They are either old, hypocrites, or cranks, and thus disqualified from membership among the truewits. Harriet's mother Lady Woodvil in *The Man of Mode* complains that "Lewdness is the business now; Love was the bus'ness in my Time" (IV, i, 17), and goes on to deplore what she calls "the deprav'd appetite of this Vicious Age." The audience knows what to think of these remarks not only from the comments of the people standing around, but from the fact that they are addressed in all innocence to Dorimant himself, the blackest devil in Lady Woodvil's hierarchy, whom she has clumsily mistaken for a sober, quiet-spoken young man called Mr. Courtage. Lady Woodvil is old, and hates it; her prejudices spring quite clearly from this fact. Shadwell's *The Virtuoso,* a comedy produced in the same year as *The Plain-Dealer,* presents another elderly hater of the age, one Snarl. The wits of the play agree with many of his strictures against the fops and the gay young fools, but not with all. They realize that in him envy and malice, the lusts of age, have replaced a longing for wine and women. "The last Age was the Age of Modesty," Snarl begins, but he is interrupted by the gallant:

> I believe there was the same Wenching then: only they dissembled it. They added Hypocrasie to Fornication, and so made two Sins of what we make but one. (II; vol. III, pp. 131-2)

And his companion clarifies the situation further by his whispered comment: "After all his virtue, this old Fellow keeps a Whore." Younger malcontents were less frequent, but no more kindly treated. Certainly, Shadwell mocks the two misanthropes of *The Sullen Lovers* (1668) without mercy, allowing more reasonable characters to score off them at will. "Why dost thou abuse this Age so?" one character inquires. "Methinks, it's as pretty an Honest, Drinking, Whoring Age as a Man wou'd wish to live in" (I; vol. I, p. 18).

The hypocrisy of aged railers like Snarl and Lady Woodvil is identical with that delineated by Wycherley in the figure of Mrs. Caution. Hippolita made short shrift of her aunt's invidious judgments in *The Gentleman Dancing Master:*

> By what I've heard 'tis a pleasant-well-bred-complacent-free-frolick-good-natur'd-pretty-Age; and if you do not like it, leave it to us that do.
> (I, i; vol. I, p. 163)

This is essentially the Etheregean attitude, an attitude adopted by Congreve in his treatment of Heartwell in *The Old Bachelor* (1693). Wycherley does not abandon it entirely in *The Plain-Dealer;* certainly, it governs his contrast between the false rigor of Olivia's views and the innocent frankness of Eliza's. Olivia has captured the plain-dealer's heart by affecting to despise the age, a pretence which everyone can see through, except Manly himself. She is Wycherley's version of Molière's Célimène, but a Célimène grown vicious and positively evil, not merely injudicious and silly. Eliza, who corresponds to Molière's Éliante, constantly shows Olivia up for what she is.

> *Olivia:* O hideous! you cannot be in earnest sure, when you say you like the filthy World.
> *Eliza:* You cannot be in earnest sure, when you say you dislike it.
> (II, i; vol. II, p. 119)

As for the plain-dealer himself, it is clear that he does not go uncriticized by his creator. Much of the invective which Manly bestows upon his friends, upon casual fops, fools and passers-by (as well as upon the perfidious Olivia) is brilliant; all of it is passionate, and scarcely any aspect of social life or of the relationships of human beings with each other goes untouched. Yet Manly's attitudes are excessive. Wycherley may have been secretly drawn to excess, but it was still in 1676 too great a sin in Restoration comedy to escape without castigation. Manly's misanthropy is a distorted attitude; it is imperceptive and even a little affected. As such, it is criticized by Freeman, Eliza, even by the rough seamen who have accompanied Manly to London. Most revealing of all is the plain-dealer's tendency to trust precisely those people who are most hypocritical and false. Olivia says of him, shrewdly:

> he that distrusts most the World, trusts most to himself, and is but the more easily deceiv'd, because he thinks he can't be deceiv'd: his cunning is like the Coward's Sword, by which he is oftner worsted, than defended . . . I knew he loved his own singular moroseness so well, as to dote upon any Copy of it; wherefore I feign'd an hatred to the World too, that he might love me in earnest. (IV, ii; vol. II, p. 171)

Self-love, one of the blackest sins in Manly's list, governs his own attitude towards society.

Unlike Snarl, Lady Woodvil, Heartwell or Shadwell's sullen lovers, however, Manly is in no sense a comic character. His behavior, while not to be imitated, is not ridiculous either. Here, Wycherley does depart radically from the conventions of contemporary comedy. At his worst, Manly expresses himself in terms which remind one of Othello at his most frantic:

> Her Love!—a Whore's, a Witches Love!—But, what, did she not kiss well, Sir? I'm sure I thought her Lips—but must not think of 'em more —but yet they are such I cou'd still kiss—grow to—and then tear off with my teeth, grind 'em into mammocks, and spit 'em into her Cuckolds face. (Iv, i; vol. II, p. 160)

Frenzy of this kind outgoes even the hell-and-furies rhetoric of Etherege's Mrs. Loveit in *The Man of Mode*. The interesting thing about Manly's outburst is that it does not ask for laughter. Mrs. Loveit, whatever certain tender-hearted modern critics may feel, was meant to be absurd. When Dorimant mocked her rage with a rhyming couplet, or suggested that her fan would be more useful to her whole than torn in pieces, he embodied both sense and a horror of emotional excess central to Etheregean comedy. It was this ideal of balance, of aristocratic restraint and self-control which gave the whole device of the love-trial such force and poignancy. Dorimant, Gerrard, Harcourt, or Congreve's Valentine all depart suddenly, under the pressure of their passion, from a standard of rational behavior, of realism and social judgment which they have hitherto represented. It is a unique, startling reaction and one which gains its effect by sheer contrast with the worldly wisdom of previous responses. In *The Plain-Dealer,* on the other hand, the love-trial (while present) is overwhelmed and lost in the extravagance of the plot as a whole. Its distinctiveness, both structural and emotional, vanishes. It is part of this new indulgence in emotion for its own sake that Manly's violence on the subject of Olivia's infidelity should be met, not with the corrective ridicule of a Dorimant, but with the uncritical sympathy of Fidelia:

> Poor Man, how uneasy is he! I have hardly the heart to give him so much pain, tho' withall I give him a cure; and to my self new life.
> (IV, i; vol. II, p. 160)

Fidelia herself, the Beaumont and Fletcher heroine strayed into a world nastier than anything a pastoral Sicily could produce, accentuates the imbalance of the comedy as a whole. She, of course, is a character for which there is no analogue in the *Misanthrope.* By introducing her, Wycherley not only destroyed Molière's subtle but perfectly comprehensible equilibrium between criticism and admiration of Alceste, he created a genuine confusion in his own comedy. Fidelia is a character who must be accepted entirely uncritically, or not at all, like the heroines of Restoration tragedy. It is no good trying to regard her disguise and the situation in which it involves her as representing the education of a romantic. She is a fixed pole in the comedy, a character who remains unchanged from beginning to end. Moreover, she triumphs and, by involving Manly in her triumph, effectively negates all serious criticism of the plain-dealer and his attitudes. At the end, Fidelia's devotion restores the misanthrope's faith in human nature. Unlike Alceste, Manly marries at the end of the comedy. The trouble with this resolution, as Holland has pointed out, is that neither Manly nor Fidelia has really come to terms with the world as it is; their agreement is extra-social, romantic, artificial, and almost impossible to believe in. Even more important, it is the victory of excess.

The presence of Fidelia has an important effect upon Wycherley's treatment of two other characters besides Manly. Freeman and Eliza are clearly the equivalents of Molière's Philinte and Éliante: reasonable, intelligent, sympathetic to plain-dealing up to a point, but convinced that some measure of hypocrisy is necessary for life in society. Their destinies, however, are very different from those of Molière's characters. Éliante, in the *Misanthrope,* loves Alceste. Nevertheless, she is forced in the end to reject the extremes of conduct and emotion which he represents, turning instead to Philinte. Her decision is important, because it guides the reactions of the audience. Loneliness and despair are the rewards of

Alceste; he goes his way at the end of the comedy as a splendid fool, but a fool all the same, defeated. Philinte and Éliante stand quite clearly at the center of the *Misanthrope.* They are the characters who marry, and who embody that rational and demanding ideal of the *honnête homme* which Molière is continually advancing in one form or another. There is complexity of judgment here, but no confusion. In *The Plain-Dealer,* on the other hand, something very curious has happened to Freeman and Eliza. They do not marry, in fact they scarcely seem aware of one another. Eliza is used only as a foil to Olivia, after which she is simply dropped. Freeman is more important. Throughout the comedy, he is shown forced by poverty to try either to marry or else simply to swindle a rich, ridiculous old widow with a passion for the law courts worthy of any of the victims of Jarndyce and Jarndyce. Freeman succeeds in securing the money without the old woman, in the end, by cleverly turning the widow's foolish son against her. There is much fun in all of this; the widow is a glorious absurdity and, by the standards of comedy, fair game. But it scarcely adds dignity to Freeman, in any sense that Molière—or Etherege—would understand. What it does do is to show him dealing successfully with the world by stooping to the world's own level, using hypocrisy, deceit and the most unrelenting realism to gain his own, purely materialistic ends.

In its final effect, *The Plain-Dealer* is even more nihilistic than *The Country Wife.* Manly, like Horner, is an agent of destruction. Some criticism of his attitudes is built into the comedy, but Wycherley's insistence that he should triumph at the end effectively overrides it. By minimizing the role of Eliza, and degrading Freeman, Wycherley prevents them from establishing a positive value at the center of the play. It is Manly, negative, savage, wholly self-absorbed, who dominates the action. When one considers the total implausibility of his final agreement with Fidelia, perfunctory in a way that goes beyond even the normal resolutions of romance, there is little that is left standing. Brilliant as it is, *The Plain-Dealer* is a somewhat alarming comedy. Romanticism has lost touch with realism completely; the emotional force of the play denies the artificial solution offered by the plot. Wycherley's juggling with the standard structure of Restoration comedy has resulted in a chaos only rescued by the fertility of the invention and the strength of the language from being recognizably a disaster.

Wycherley is an immensely individual writer, yet at the same time it is hard not to see in *The Plain-Dealer* the reflection of a more general current beginning to appear in the age. Etherege's character Dorimant, the model gallant and man of wit, was an incarnation of Rochester at his happiest. It was a portrait filled with energy and with delight in experience, with a corruscating play of intelligence: all of it kept in balance, under control. Rochester's last years, however, and the last years of the society which he adorned, were not like this. Rochester died of syphilis in 1680, four years after the appearance of *The Plain-Dealer*. He was thirty-three. During the last four years of his life, he was troubled not only by acute physical suffering, but by a conflict in his own mind between his libertine principles and an attraction towards a kind of mystical Christianity. Throughout these last years, he struggled towards that recantation which he eventually made, trying to believe, arguing against his own rationalism. These are the years during which he wrote most of his satires, poems which display the other side of the libertine's coin: the vitality and the former sense of power turned to ashes in the mouth, a loathing of society and of man himself which comes finally to a denial that he is in any way superior to the other members of the animal kingdom.

> Be Judge your self, I'le bring it to the test,
> Which is the basest *Creature Man,* or *Beast*?
> *Birds,* feed on *Birds, Beasts,* on each other prey,
> But Savage *Man* alone, does *Man,* betray:
> Prest by necessity, they Kill for Food,
> *Man,* undoes *Man,* to do himself no good.
> With Teeth, and Claws by Nature arm'd they hunt,
> Natures allowances, to supply their want.
> But *Man,* with smiles, embraces, Friendships, praise,
> Unhumanely his Fellows life betrays;
> With voluntary pains, works his distress,
> Not through necessity, but wantoness.
>
> ("A Satyr Against Mankind," II, 127ff).

Even more extreme is the poem "Upon Nothing." Here is the frank statement of that nihilism which troubles Wycherley's final comedies: a hatred of light as opposed to merciful darkness, of substance as opposed to non-being. In a strange inversion of the passage from Genesis, Rochester sees the tearing of light and matter from the void as a rape, a monstrous, unspeakable act:

> Matter, the wicked'st off-spring of thy Race,
> By Form assisted, flew from thy Embrace,
> And Rebel Light obscur'd thy reverend dusky Face.

The Negative is best; "something" only returns to it stained and corrupted. Between Rochester as Dorimant (the libertine and wit) and Rochester as Manly (the author of the satires) there is an enormous difference in attitude, but almost none of time. *The Man of Mode* and

The Plain-Dealer were, after all, both produced in the same year. Taken together, these two comedies create the Janus-face of the Restoration's apogee.

The Plain-Dealer was Wycherley's last play. In 1682, he was imprisoned for debt; he languished in Newgate prison for almost seven years. After his release, he seems to have remained poor and dispirited, encumbered with law-suits and basically at odds with the world around him. It was a world which had changed markedly from that of the early Restoration, in ways which were by no means favorable to the theatre. Not many new comedies were written during the troubled decade of the 1680's. Dramatists tended to be otherwise occupied and, in any case, there was now only one theatre in London instead of two. Those that did appear, however, declared an affinity with Wycherley rather than with Etherege. They tended to be harsh, bitter and convinced that some profound malaise lurked at the heart of all human experience. In the hands of Otway, Crowne, Lee, and Southerne—all of them, significantly, men better known for their tragedy than their comedy—the tendencies of *The Plain-Dealer* were carried still further. Disgust with society, railing against the age, becomes the inevitable mark of any man of wit and sense. As one of Otway's characters says, more or less in the tone of a man reciting the trivial news of the day,

> Iniquity in general has not lost much ground. There's Cheating and Hypocrisie still in the City; Riot and Murder in the Suburbs; Grinning, Lying, Fawning, Flattery, and False-Promising at Court; Assignations at *Covent-Garden* Church; Cuckolds, Whores, Pimps, Panders, Bawds, and their Diseases, all over the Town. (*The Atheist* [1683], I, i)

It is a world of animal warfare, in which the game is won by only the slightly less dishonorable beasts.

Not surprisingly, the few stable values which had been left standing in *The Plain-Dealer* were swept away altogether in the comedies which derived from it. It had been axiomatic in Etheregean comedy that the truewit never betrayed his friend. This loyalty, in fact, was one of the features which distinguished a member of the inner circle from the Dapperwit who tried to imitate him. Even in the later Wycherley, relations between Horner and Harcourt, Manly and Freeman, though less than ideal, were nevertheless honest. In the comedies of Otway and the later Crowne, however, and in Lee's *Princess of Cleves* (1681), those characters who must be regarded as the heroes lie, cheat, and cuckold each other without compunction. In every case, the dramatist is clearly aware that he is breaking a rule, shattering a convention. A positive desire to shock pervades Otway's *Friendship in Fashion* (1678), guides the treachery of Beaugard in *The Atheist,* of Chartres and Nemours in *The Princess of Cleves.* This is the comedy of complete disillusion.

Wycherley had lost interest in the love-trial in *The Country Wife,* and submerged it in *The Plain-Dealer*. His successors tended either to do away with it completely, or else to pervert its meaning. Towards the end of Otway's *The Soldier's Fortune* (1680), Sylvia decides to test her lover. "A true Lover," she tells her maid, "is to be found out like a true saint, by the Trial of his patience." This sounds familiar enough. When it comes, however, the trial is simply brutal farce. The girl persuades her lover to scale her balcony, and then contrives that he should remain entangled in the ropes all night on the outside of the building, as a figure of fun. It is an idea that reveals more about the character of Sylvia than about her unfortunate lover—and more about Otway than either. This is the same man who, at the conclusion of *Friendship in Fashion,* had insisted upon bringing in two silly but essentially harmless fops with the stage direction: *"their Hands ty'd behind 'em, Fools Caps on their Heads.* CAPER *with one Leg ty'd up, and* SAUNTER *gagg'd."* One cannot imagine Etherege finding it necessary to punish Sir Fopling Flutter in this manner, or introducing so grotesque and excessive an image into *The Man of Mode*. Wycherley's fools had also escaped relatively lightly, but there is a quality in Manly's revenge at the end of *The Plain-Dealer*—the public exposure of Olivia's lust to a gathering of the fashionable world assembled for the purpose, the jewels offered her as the price of a prostitute's hire—which points forward to the comedies of the later Restoration.

Wycherley's emotionalism, those violent extremes of feeling condoned in *The Plain-Dealer,* proved an even more dangerous legacy to the future. Hand in hand with the general feeling of disgust which characterizes comedy after 1676, the nihilism which gradually destroyed the balance of Etherege, went a new attitude towards emotion. Undisciplined passion began to find general approval, sweeping away the restraint of earlier comedy. In some plays it became recognizable as sentimentalism, although it is advisable to be careful about affixing this label at too early a date. Certainly the tears and languishing of the future can be descried, however, in the emotional excesses of Lee's *Princess of Cleves,* of Crowne's *Town Sparks* (1689), or of the later comedies of Mrs. Behn. The handsome but rather frightening rake, dowered explicitly in more than one play with an active case of the pox, is adored despite (or perhaps because of) his disadvantages by a series of women who resort to all kinds of violence, including attempted suicide, to win him. A race of Mrs. Loveits, in short, except that they are no longer despised by their creator, or by the other characters of the comedy. Violent emotion has become a sign of sincerity and depth, not merely of incompetence and lack of self-control. Only one of these women can actually marry the libertine. Yet her defeated rivals tend to stand about in the last moments of the play, their hands resting apathetically in those of more honorable husbands, their eyes fixed longingly upon the blemished, but magnetic figure of the rake.

Many of these plays also reveal how powerful an influence was constituted by Wycherley's anti-heroes, Horner and Manly. Lee's Nemours, in *The Princess of Cleves,* carries their sensuality and ruthlessness one step further. Nemours is a rake whose character has been deliberately coarsened; Lee states flatly in his dedication that he set out to create "a ruffian," a hero who would outdo in lechery and insouciance the worst of his dramatic predecessors. Nemours is a man of indiscriminate libido; he makes no distinction whatsoever between the sexes, and not very much between individuals. Yet he is irresistibly attractive to every woman in the play, including the virtuous Mme. de Cleves, and indefatigable in his pursuit. In fact, as one of his friends remarks, with more truth than delicacy, if he goes on like this he will shortly be nicknamed "the town-bull." On the one hand, Lee insists that Nemours is a character to be admired. Certainly, he represents a standard of wit and accomplishment which the other men in the comedy envy and fail to achieve. Also, there is a sense in which his straightforwardness is refreshing in a world of cant. Yet his position is bewilderingly undercut throughout the play by the presence of two rival standards. One of them is the memory of Rochester, that ghost from the early Restoration which haunts the action under the name of Rosidore; the other, and more important, is that represented by the honorable, blank-verse-speaking, tearful Mme. de Cleves and her husband. From this welter of disparate material not much sense can be made. Certainly, Nemours' sudden reformation in the final moments of the play is implausible in a way which goes beyond even the extra-social agreement of Manly and Fidelia. *The Princess of Cleves* as a whole, with its wild mixture of verse and prose, of nihilism and strict morality, lasciviousness and prudery, brutality and sentiment is a far more disjointed work than *The Plain-Dealer.*

Nevertheless, it is clear that Wycherley was at least partly responsible for the new directions taken by comedy in the later Restoration. Even without him, it is hard to see how the restraint and intellectuality of Etherege could have survived the death and dispersal of the wits, the Popish Plot, and the decline of theatre attendance. Yet there can be no doubt of the influence of *The Plain-Dealer* on subsequent comedy. Not only was it extravagantly admired from the very first, its bitter railing, its passion, and its abandonment to excess all prefigured a change in the temper of the age sensed by Wycherley in the moment before it became universally apparent. These were the qualities which audiences of the 1680's and even 1690's would value. And against which Congreve, looking back deliberately to Etherege, would fight his splendid but losing battle.

The Satiric Design in *The Plain Dealer*

by Rose A. Zimbardo

Criticism of the comedy of the Restoration period is unique in that throughout its history it has centered upon an extra-literary question. The history of this criticism is one long contention between those critics who have dismissed the plays as immoral and those who have devised ever more complex justifications to clear them of that charge. This approach has had very unfortunate consequences. Admirers of the plays, in trying to prove them harmless, have often rendered them trivial. The "manners" [1] school has insisted that the plays are unmoral, "a holiday from the sublime and the beautiful, the coarse and the real." [2] The sociological school,[3] under the guise of rescuing the plays from Cloud-Cuckoo land, has created a no less unreal scene of Restoration life, a carnival of rakes and wenches, which the plays are thought to reflect "with photographic realism." [4]

The peculiar deviation which criticism has taken in this area has resulted in making us think of the comedies as special and therefore unamenable to the treatment which we afford to other areas of literature. The Restoration is looked upon as a cul-de-sac in the literary tradition. And the comedy of the Restoration period is considered so great an aberration that it is usually not even studied in relation to other genres of late seventeenth-century literature.

Cutting the comedy off from the rest of English literature has caused us to view it as homogeneous, to yoke together writers of such markedly different sensibility as Etherege, Congreve, and Wycherley. But the term "Restoration Comedy" used in any but a chronological sense is not merely useless, but destructive to a proper understanding of the comedy

"The Satiric Design in *The Plain Dealer*." From *Studies in English Literature*, I (1961), 1-18. Reprinted by permission of Rose A. Zimbardo and *Studies in English Literature*.

[1] John Palmer, Bonamy Dobrée, and others.

[2] John Palmer, *Comedy* (New York, 1914), p. 33.

[3] Kathleen Lynch, Thomas Fujimura, and others.

[4] Thomas Fujimura, *The Restoration Comedy of Wit* (Princeton, 1952), pp. 52, 53.

of these three writers. Their works differ in central concern and method. Even the traditions in which each wrote are different and, indeed, Etherege and Congreve wrote in traditions inimical to each other. Etherege's sceptical questioning grows out of the temper of his times. Congreve, for all his wit, is at heart sentimental, and his comedy prepares for the tradition of eighteenth-century sentimentalism. Wycherley is a satirist, and his best work bridges the two great periods in English satire, the Elizabethan and the Augustan ages.

The characterization of Wycherley's satiric spokesmen, Horner and Manly, grows out of a long tradition in English satire which has its origin in the Anglo-Saxon period and comes to its full flowering in the Elizabethan satyr-satirist.[5] But while Wycherley leans upon the Elizabethans in the characterization of his spokesmen, his satiric structure departs from the Elizabethan notion of satiric decorum, which demanded that the form of satire be irregular and primitive. Rather, the structure of Wycherley's last two plays reflects the rediscovery in the Restoration period of the form of classical Roman satire. This rediscovery of classical form is part of a larger movement, a whole approach to literary composition that emphasizes style and "correctness," and that comes to its fullest development in the eighteenth-century English Augustan style.

Wycherley's last two plays show the direct influence of Roman satire, particularly that of Juvenal. The limitations of a paper of this kind forbid showing instances of direct imitation. My purpose here will be to show that Wycherley's structure is based upon the structure of Roman verse satire, that, indeed, *The Plain Dealer* is a perfect rendition of formal satire in the dramatic mode.

We must first consider what the classical satiric form is. Reduced to its simplest terms, classical satire is bipartite in structure. It breaks into two markedly disproportionate divisions, the thesis, which consists of an attack upon some specific vice or folly, and the antithesis, which recommends the opposing virtue. In the thesis the vice under consideration is turned on all sides and attacked from as many different angles as possible, "in something of the way the premises are turned about in the octave of a sonnet." [6] The antithesis, always the weaker of the two arguments, is usually presented as struggling hopelessly against the forces described in the thesis. "Often the admonition to virtue . . . is only implied . . . . But it is there, it must be there if the piece is to be more than mere virulence and fleeting invective." [7] The thesis and antithesis are the minimal essentials in satire. The usual form that this essential assumes is this: an outer framework encloses thesis and antithesis. In this

[5] Cf. Alvin Kernan, *The Cankered Muse* (New Haven, 1959).

[6] M. C. Randolph, "The Structural Design of Formal Verse Satire," *Philological Quarterly*, XXI (1942), 369.

[7] Randolph, p. 369.

framework are the satirist and the adversarius, a kind of combative hollow man. The adversarius may be simply "you" understood, a shadowy figure, or he may be an annoyingly persistent member of the group under attack, who detaches himself from them and draws near the satirist. The function of the adversarius is to draw the satirist's fire. He either baits the satirist with questions or barbed rejoinders, or cautions him about being too outspoken. Both devices are used to draw fresh comment and explanation from the satirist upon the vice in question.

These two figures, the satirist and the adversarius, talk against a background; not infrequently it is a moving background—a street, a royal court, Westminster Hall. The setting must be such that it will allow a stream of figures to pass by upon whom the satirist can comment, and who will serve as proof of the satirist's contention that human nature is corrupt. In addition, the satirist uses miniature dramas, vignettes, portraits, or "characters" to push his argument forward, so that there occurs a background within a background. The three pillars of the satiric design, then, are the satirist, the adversarius, and a background of sorts. Given these, the thesis may be argued. The argument is always an indictment of human nature, for the satirist exaggerates downward to achieve his effects. Man is seen at his most gross and beastly.

Wycherley's *The Plain Dealer* fulfills in every detail the structure outlined above. In addition to the basic, tri-elemental structure of satirist, adversarius, and background, it contains a parody substructure, so that it is at once a satire and a satiric questioning of satire itself. With beautiful irony, the questioning of satire is framed in perfect formal satiric design.

The play begins, as formal satire must, with a crashing declaration of the theme. The vice under consideration is hypocrisy. It is ubiquitous, and even a plain-dealer, who attacks, or tries to flee from it, is in danger of being overtaken. The thesis is declared both in the spoken rebuke of Lord Plausible made by Manly, and dramatically—that is, Manly, a plain-dealer, is pursued by Lord Plausible, a personification of hypocrisy. The former figure lashes out at the latter but finds he is fighting a shadow; the more fierce his attack, the more elaborate the flattery it arouses.

The thesis declared, Wycherley sets the traditional contestants to argue it. There has been much critical speculation about the relationship between the characters in this play. Are we, with Dobrée,[8] to consider Manly a hero and Freeman an opportunist, or are we to follow the most recent critic of the play, Norman Holland,[9] who considers Manly neurotic and Freeman and Olivia "well-adjusted"? When we recognize the play as formal satire, Freeman's role at once becomes clear; he is the

[8] Bonamy Dobrée, *Restoration Comedy: 1660 to 1720* (Oxford, 1924).

[9] Norman Holland, *The First Modern Comedies* (Cambridge, Mass., 1959).

adversarius. His function is to take a position opposite that of the satirist, Manly, and to provoke the satirist's attack. Freeman's is a type of adversarius very common in Roman satire; he is one of the very number that the satirist hates, who detaches himself from the crowd and draws near to the satirist, where he plays the role of the devil's advocate. Freeman is not on the side of virtue. He does not want to convince Manly that the world is not really full of hypocrites, but rather he champions the position that hypocrisy is the way of the world. He hopes, in effect, to reason the satirist to the side of unreason, to win him to the very vice he stands most firmly against. At the end of the play Freeman's behavior may seem inconsistent with his character (why should he, a hypocrite, tell Manly what he really thinks?). But we must keep in mind that the adversarius need not be consistent to fill his place in the satiric design. All that is required of him is that he maintain a position opposite to that of the satirist.

The relationship of Manly to Freeman is set up in the first act, almost as soon as the play begins. Manly enters upon the scene first and, by the ferocity both of his speech and manner, establishes himself as the fearless satirist, determined to expose and shame hypocrisy wherever he finds it. He begins his mission by cursing Lord Plausible for a "common whore or pickpocket, dangerous to those he embraces" and throws him out of doors. He declares himself a champion of truth and a hater of the world and all its vanities. Once Manly has identified himself as satirist, the adversarius is allowed upon the scene. Freeman, as his name implies, is a typical Restoration *honnête homme;* in an Etheregean play he would be hero. He is a self-declared opportunist who gets along with the world and whose sole motivation is self-interest. He cannot understand the disappointed idealism that makes Manly such a wildly misanthropic champion of truth. But since friendship is easy for him, he offers to be Manly's friend. Manly rejects his offer and this provides the point upon which their basically antagonistic views of life can be revealed, and their roles in the satire clearly laid out.

> *Manly:* . . . you must pardon me, I cannot wish well to pimps, flatterers, detractors, and cowards, stiff nodding knaves, and supple pliant kissing fools. Now all these I have seen you use like the dearest friends in the world.
>
> *Freeman:* Ha! Ha! Ha! What, you observed me, I warrant, in the galleries at Whitehall, doing the business of the place? Pshaw! Court-professions, like court promises, go for nothing, man. But faith, could you think I was a friend to all those I hugged, kissed, flattered, bowed to? Ha! Ha!
>
> *Manly:* You told 'em so and swore it too; I heard you.
>
> *Freeman:* Ay, but when their backs were turned, did I not tell you they were rogues, villains, rascals whom I despised and hated? . . . Why don't you know, good captain, that telling the truth is a quality as prejudicial to a

> man that would thrive in the world, as square play to a cheat, or true love to a whore? (I,i)

That Freeman is a declared opportunist, that he acknowledges his resemblance to cheats and whores, makes him a more complex hypocrite than Lord Plausible, but he is no more virtuous. It is necessary to the satiric design that he openly advocate the vice under consideration, since he and Manly must defend opposing views of good.

In Act I Wycherley closely adheres to the form of verse satire. Having established the necessary antagonism between Freeman and Manly, he must provide a satiric background. His first background (used here in the special sense) is presented, as in verse satire, in the conversation of his adversaries. If we examine one of the key Act I "exchanges" between Manly and Freeman, we find that it is a formal satire in little; that is, it employs all of the devices used in classical verse satire and even forms the pattern of the satiric design in miniature. Freeman provokes the attack with an argument that he knows will draw Manly's fury, that of "everybody does it, so it must be right." Then Manly launches into his counterargument. To illustrate the rationality of his hatred and disgust with the world, he describes a scene—it is the usual crowded, moving "background" of satire. He sketches caricatures of the hypocrites of the world, falling upon every level of society from bishop to fishmonger. Finally, this small satire within a satire is clinched with a recapitulation of the basic disagreement of the two antagonists. Freeman begins with the defense that his behavior grows from a recognition and acceptance of the facts of social life:

> *Freeman:* . . . Observe but any morning what people do when they get together on the Exchange, in Westminster Hall, or in the galleries of Whitehall.
>
> *Manly:* I must confess there they seem to rehearse Bayes's grand dance. Here you will see a bishop bowing low to a gaudy atheist; a judge to a doorkeeper; a great lord to a fishmonger, or a scrivener with a jack-chain about his neck; a lawyer to a sargeant-at-arms; a velvet physician to a threadbare chemist; and a supple gentleman usher to a surly beef-eater; and so tread around in a preposterous huddle of ceremony to each other, whilst they can hardly hold their solemn false countenances.
>
> *Freeman:* Well, they understand the world.
>
> *Manly:* Which I do not, I confess. (I,i)

We might note that while the satirist's attack is upon hypocrisy, he touches tangentially upon one of the traditional complaints of satire, the loss of the old ways when degree was observed and each class respected itself and all other classes. Just as Juvenal is moved to complain again and again about the elevation in society of a freed slave, "whose razor scraped my youthful beard," so Manly is disgusted by the sight of a great lord bowing to a fishmonger. Loss of degree means loss of function. The falsity of social commerce is both the cause and effect of the decay of social function. The participants in Bayes' dance are hollow men, but even the dance itself is a pretense.

Act I, then, establishes Manly and Freeman in their key roles and outlines the basic design that will be repeated throughout the play with increasingly complex modification. The structure of the play does not follow the linear progression of a plot. There is no real plot line, no continuous action that in its unravelling reveals the theme. What plot there is—the deception of an advocate of truth by the only two people whom he had trusted and his subsequent attempts to be revenged upon the woman who had wronged him—merely provides an excuse for the establishment of the real structural relationship upon which the play hinges, that of satirist, adversarius, and background. This basic design is qualified by a satiric substructure and the final undoing of the satirist. But in the first three acts it is maintained, and progressively widened until the satiric field of vision seems universal.

In Act II, besides establishing a satiric substructure that will be discussed later, Wycherley both expands the "background" of his satire and "proves" the spoken satire of Act I in the action that he sets before us. We become aware here of the great advantage that dramatic satire has over verse satire. The verse satirist is restricted in what he can display to his reader by the persona of the satiric spokesman. In the first place, he can show only as much as the satiric persona can see and comment upon and, if he wants to preserve the unity of his structure, he cannot allow his spokesman to range too far. In the second place, the personality of the spokesman acts as a filter through which the scene must pass. The dramatist, on the other hand, can not only present us with the scene at first hand, so that we may observe for ourselves the justice of the satirist's position, but he can also present us with descriptive scenes ("background") in the conversation of characters other than the satiric spokesman. This is the method that Wycherley employs in Act II to expand his satiric background. His satire here is double-edged. He allows free rein to three barb-tongued commentators on high society, Olivia, Novel, and Plausible. In their repartee the satiric vision with which we had been presented in the Act I exchanges is widened and intensified. It is widened because Olivia and company focus their attention upon a different segment of society. We are introduced to the circle of the great, to the "Sir Richard Court-titles" and "Sir John Currents" of the world. It is intensified because we are taken into drawing and conference rooms to see hypocrisy at work. Manly and Freeman, in Act I, had discussed hypocrisy in its mildest and most common form, in men's actions toward one another in public places. Now we see hypocrisy at work. To succeed in the world of high society, we learn, a man must wear many masks, must indeed change his spots several times a day. Olivia describes the activities of one such successful man of mode:

> . . . he endeavors only with the women to pass for a man of courage, with the bullies for a man of wit; with the wits for a man of business, and with the men of business for a favorite at court; and at court for a city-security. (II,i)

At the same time that Olivia, Novel, and Plausible are enlarging the scope of Manly's spoken satire of Act I, however, they are also proving the truth of it in their actions. While they speak, they are revealed to the audience as hypocrites as great as the objects of their barbed wit. For instance, Olivia, who opens Act II with a declaration to Eliza of her hatred of flatterers and her own inability to flatter, turns face completely on the entrance of Novel and Plausible. She had denied knowing Novel, but when he enters and, preparing to begin his catty review of the company he has just left, asks the conventional "d'ye know whence I come now?" Olivia proves to be quite adept at flattery, "From some melancholy place, I warrant, sir, since they lost your good company." Novel and Plausible, thinking themselves rivals for Olivia's affections, alternately flatter and backbite one another. Olivia overtly pours the sweet balm of flattery on both, and roundly libels both in asides. Another dimension is added to the irony of the scene, for each hates in the others the faults of which he himself is most guilty. None of the company can be other than false. All use flattery to enhance themselves in some way, either by gaining the admiration of others, or in the hope that others will prove in some way useful to them. In Act I we are shown that hypocrisy makes fraudulent commerce between the classes of society. In Act II we are shown that, on the personal level, hypocrisy forges masks behind which human beings hide from each other—Olivia, for instance, rebuffs all of Eliza's attempts to drop pretense and speak freely. We are shown the effects of hypocrisy upon love. Olivia uses Novel and Plausible in the cause of her self-aggrandizement, and for gain; she pretends to decide between them, as she had pretended to love Manly, for money. Freeman, the more blithely open opportunist, pursues the Widow Blackacre for her jointure. Every human relationship, as well as every level of society, is shown to be infected with the disease of hypocrisy.

In Act III the satirist and the adversarius are again in the central position (they appear in Act II, but do not stand as the dominant figures throughout, for reasons which will be discussed later). In this act the audience has all three of the components of satire before its eyes, for the satirist and the adversarius operate *within* the satiric background, instead of projecting it from their conversation. There is no plot requirement that demands that Manly appear at Westminster Hall; nothing that he does there furthers the action. It simply provides a crowded, moving scene in which one after another scrambling knave approaches the satirist and provides fuel for his fiery outbursts. The seat of justice, we find, is the scene of the greatest of all hypocrisies. Justice is a mere cover-up for self-seeking; the law, a game in which only the lawyers can be winners.

A dominant figure at Westminster is the Widow Blackacre. While largely a humorous character thrown in for comic effect, she embodies the whole spirit of the scene. The widow's life is an entanglement of the trappings of the law. She is weighed down with briefs, writs, and legal jargon, but she has not the slightest conception of the meaning of justice. The law for the widow, as for the other denizens of Westminster, is a socially acceptable way of deceiving one's fellows for one's own gain. She spends much of her time training her lumpkin son, Jerry, "in the law," that is, in the ways of turning every legal circumstance to profit. She neither values nor understands any good but material good. She will, for instance, deny her integrity on the spot, declaring herself a whore and her son a bastard, to protect her jointure and her life in the courts. Yet even this prodigious lady of the law is no match for the double-dealers of Westminster. Despite all her maneuvering her lawyer will betray her to solicit the favor of a lord. The inhabitants of Westminster cannot be appealed to but by promise of a profit. They recognize neither contract, justice, nor old acquaintance when the opportunity for gain presents itself.

Freeman flourishes in this atmosphere. It is here that he plans to trap the widow, declaring that he is sure that he is "the first man that ever began a love intrigue in Westminster Hall." It is altogether fitting that he should be so comfortably within his element there that he is able to conduct a love intrigue, especially since the object of his love is the widow's money. While Freeman thrives in the country of opportunism, Manly is beside himself with rage. After he has incurred three law suits for boxing the ears of two lawyers and pulling an alderman's nose, he hits upon a method of exposing the hypocrisy of the law sharks and getting rid of them at the same time. To each who approaches him, he offers the opportunity of aiding the cause of justice without hope of gain. To the first, he offers the case of a poor orphan who has lost her inheritance, a case which must be handled *in forma pauperis;* the lawyer hurriedly recalls other pressing business. An alderman who offers to buy Manly a dish of coffee finds himself presented with the prospect of standing city-security for a poor man. He, too, is called away.

It is said that the reason that Wycherley set Act III at Westminster is that he himself had been a student of the law. This external consideration is less important than the internal demand of the play's design. We have observed the enlargement of the basic satiric pattern from Act I to Act II. The scene at Westminster broadens the satiric scope to the widest extent possible in drama. The mild flattery that glosses over the emptiness of social form in Act I, that appears as nipping, snarling backbiting in Act II, becomes in Act III the perversion of justice. Hypocrisy is here a methodized approach to brute-like self-seeking. An almost Platonic progression has been followed that traces the taint of hypocrisy from falsity in personal relationships, to social and class relationships, to the corruption of an abstract principle, justice, upon which rules for the government of nations depend. The satire, therefore, assumes a universal scope, and the final impression is of the whole world engaged in a frantic Bayes' dance of hypocrisy. This, then, is the fullest development of the basic satiric design as it appears in the play. Had Wycherley accomplished no more than the embodiment of this design in the drama, he would yet have gone far in answering the Restoration's demand for the reinstitution of classical form in satire. However, he builds into the structure of the play a satiric substructure that both rounds out the thesis of the satire, by diminishing the character of the satirist himself, and questions the very premises upon which satire rests.

Both the completion of the thesis, or destructive argument of the satire, and the Elizabethan convention of the satyr-satirist, mentioned earlier, demand that Manly be exposed as a practitioner of the vice he rails against. His full disgrace occurs in the last two acts of the play, where the focus of satire is narrowed from the universal field of justice to the soul of one man. However, the deterioration of Manly's character is prepared for as early in the play as the second act. As we have seen, Act I prepares the audience for formal satire (a Restoration audience would not have mistaken that intention). At the end of Act I we are prepared by Manly, whose part we have taken in the first act exchanges, for our introduction to Olivia. She is, we are told, as honest as she is beautiful, possessed of every virtue. The second act opening, then, comes as something of a shock. Instead of the womanly paragon that we had expected, Olivia turns out to be an imitation of Manly, a parody-satirist. Her opening lines, "Ah! cousin, What a world 'tis we live in, I am so weary of it," affect a weary discontent that comes as an echo to Manly's protestations of world-hatred that we have just heard. More surprising still, a new satirist-adversarius relationship is set up between Olivia and her cousin, Eliza, that is an imitation of the Manly-Freeman relationship of Act I. Olivia rails against the world, its vanities and falsity, all the while proclaiming her own plain-dealing, while Eliza subtly baits her, drawing her into contradictions.

Eliza: But what d'ye think of visits—balls?
Olivia: O! I detest 'em!
Eliza: Of plays?
Olivia: I abominate 'em, filthy, obscene, hideous things . . .

Eliza: . . . what d'ye think of the court?
Olivia: How, the court! the court, cousin! . . . my aversion of all aversions!
Eliza: How! the court where———
Olivia: Where sincerity is a quality as much out of fashion and as unprosperous as bashfulness: I could not laugh at a quibble, though it were a fat privy-councellor's; nor praise a lord's ill verses, though I were myself the subject; . . . nor sit to a vain young smile-maker, though he flattered me. In short, I could not glout a man when he comes into a room and laugh at him when he goes out; I cannot rail at the absent to flatter standers-by, I——. (II,i)

In its frankness, its tone, even in its cadences, this speech of Olivia's is an obvious imitation of Manly's "I cannot wish well . . ." speech of Act I. The whole Olivia-Eliza exchange is a parody of the exchanges between Manly and Freeman. But as the verbal encounter between the two women progresses, we realize that an ironic reversal has occurred. The satirist, Olivia, who endlessly protests her virtue, is a hypocrite. The adversarius, Eliza, who makes no claim to being a champion of truth, is a plain-dealer. Step by step, Eliza forces Olivia into contradictions that expose her virtue as mere affectation. Her professed simplicity and disregard for outward show, for instance, are laughed out of court when Eliza reminds her of the six dresses a month that she buys. Her mask of innocence and virtue is pulled aside when Eliza leads her into a discussion of *The Country Wife,* and she proves an expert at detecting *double entendre*. As we have seen, at the entrance of Novel and Plausible, the exposure is completed. Eliza makes the final comment upon Olivia's pose as plain-dealer, "railing is now so common that 'tis no more malice but the fashion." We are led to suspect, then, that attacking hypocrisy can itself be hypocritical.

In the substructure the roles of satirist and adversarius are reversed. On the surface the opening of Act II is a perfect reproduction of the Act I exchanges. Olivia is still, in her speech, manner, tone, the satirist. Eliza, in her function of baiting, drawing comment, opposing, is still the adversarius. Only the inner, moral positions of the adversaries are reversed. What function does this moral reversal serve in the design of the play? Superficially, Olivia's spoken satire reinforces and even widens Manly's spoken satire of Act I. More important, however, Olivia's resemblance to Manly, joined with her inner falsity, renders Manly's role of public defender of truth somewhat suspect. We never appreciate the pomposity and opportunism of Henry IV until we see them parodied in Falstaff. Manly's public protestations, that seem so golden in Act I, tarnish when they are imitated in Act II. In addition, the revelation of Olivia's inner falsity, her private personality of cruelty, exploitation, and the participation in the very faults against which she rails, combined with her public affectation of the virtues of the satirist (plain-dealing, frankness, the defense of truth at any price), prepare us for the full revelation of Manly's character that is to occur in the last two acts. In Olivia we are given a fore-glimpse of Manly *whole*.

But most important, the parody substructure is a commentary upon satire itself. Olivia's resemblance to Manly is the very reason for his love of her: "I knew he loved his own singular moroseness so well as to dote upon any copy of it." Manly thinks Olivia to be honest, above reproach (before his disillusionment) because he thinks she is exactly like him, and he thinks himself above censure. The discovery of this self-esteem in Manly makes us, for an instant, wary of satirists. We realize that the satirist in raging at the vices of others, claims, by implication, to be himself above vice. He thereby leaves himself open to that pride which leads to the inevitable fall. The downfall of Manly is required by the satiric design. But that the satirist should *appear* in the play, and be exposed as a hypocrite serves a second function: to question the very basis of satire itself. The play, then, is not only a well-executed formal satire, but a satirization of satire itself. The mockery that Wycherley directs against his art,

> You rail, and nobody hangs himself; and
> thou hath nothing of satire but in thy face (V,ii)
> . . . for railing is satire, you know, and
> roaring and making a noise, humour. (V,ii)

is built into the very structure of his play.

The final deterioration of Manly is accomplished in Acts IV and V. He becomes a kind of Everyman, a subject of a study in the corrosive effects of hypocrisy upon a single soul. As mentioned early in this paper, the characterization of Manly grows out of the Elizabethan tradition of the satyr-satirist, a figure who, while overtly proclaiming his honest indignation at the vice he observes around him, is in his inner personality subject to the very vices against which he rails. Therefore, he is in his public personality a fearless satirist, and in his private personality a raging satyr, dominated by the traits that the Renaissance particularly associated with satyrs: lust and blind rage. The new Restoration adherence to classical principles forbade the treatment of more than one major vice in a satire. Other vices could be treated only as they arose from, or were related to, the vice under consideration. Hypocrisy being the vice underscored in *The Plain Dealer,* Wycherley could not employ the simple Elizabethan technique of having the satirist rail against lust, and then showing him to be lustful, having him rail against greed, and then showing him to be greedy, etc. He solves the problem by showing the deterioration of Manly's character to be contingent upon his falling prey to the vice he most detests, hypocrisy. Manly's hypocrisy grows out of an attempt to hide the vices of the "satyr" in him; the disintegration of his character is accomplished as the satyr-like qualities of his private personality overwhelm the public personality of the courageous and fearless satirist. As his character degenerates the very qualities that we have admired in him are revealed as vices. For instance, his fearless courage and honesty of Acts I and II become in Acts IV and V brute rage and sadism. When we first encounter Manly he tells us that he is a plain-dealer, in love with the only woman in the world whose honesty matches his own. Once Manly has been disenchanted, his love turns to lust, a lust as ungovernable as his anger, which increases as it is rebuffed. It is in trying to hide his unquenchable lust for Olivia from Freeman, whose scorn he fears, that Manly first plays the hypocrite. At first he finds hypocrisy a difficult game:

> How hard 'tis to be a hypocrite!
> At least to me who am but newly so
> I thought it once a kind of knavery,
> Nay, cowardice to hide one's fault; but now
> The common frailty, love, becomes my shame
> He must not know I love th' unfaithful still. . . . (III,i)

But his desire for Olivia, as it is constantly thwarted, becomes increasingly difficult to bear, and he falls into greater and greater deceit in trying to disguise it. He lies to Freeman, pretending to be above a woman's scorn. Then, he lies to Fidelia, pretending that his various and ever more grotesque attempts to appease his lust (his final plan is to rape Olivia while Fidelia "talks love" to her) are merely the desire for revenge, his object being to punish Olivia, not to satisfy himself. Finally, in telling Vernish, before he knows him to be Olivia's husband, that he has enjoyed her favors, Manly becomes a finished hypocrite, one who lies to gain the good opinion of others. Hypocrisy to hide a deeper emotion becomes hypocrisy for its own sake, and the satirist becomes guilty of the very vice against which he rails. Manly reaches the fullest depth of degradation when, his threat to cut Fidelia's throat if she will not pimp for him proving ineffectual, he bribes her with the promise that if she gets Olivia for him by any means, he will allow Fidelia to stay with him. He knows that Fidelia is loth to go again to Olivia's apartments (she fears rape by Vernish), but he shamelessly exploits her affection for him and those very qualities that he had ridiculed in her at the beginning of the play, her softness and fear of violence. At this, the ultimate depth of his decline, Manly comes full circle and turns into the very creature that he had accused Lord Plausible of being in the opening lines of the play—a hypocrite "like a common whore, dangerous to those he embraces."

This structural reversal of Manly's coming full circle to the opposite pole from his starting position is accompanied by a second ironic reversal.

In Act II Wycherley had Olivia affect Manly's virtues, but showed her to be morally false. As Manly's character declines it grows more and more like Olivia's. As she had consciously imitated his virtues, in the last two acts he unconsciously imitates her vices. For example, in hiding his true feeling from Freeman (end Act III) he imitates Olivia's attempts to hide her feelings from Eliza (Act II, and repeated with exaggerated effect in Act IV). In the scene in Olivia's apartments when Manly, hidden in the dark, watches Olivia's raging lust as she pursues Fidelia, he becomes the mirror image of her. In the first place, his own passion, far from being quenched, is kindled at the sight of Olivia pursuing Fidelia, so that he is like her in bestiality; the similarity of their inner natures is forced upon the attention of the audience. But more important, when he comments upon her depravity ("a goat or monkey were fitter for thee [than a gallant]"), he imitates Olivia's criticism of Novel in Act II; that is, he blames in another a fault that he cannot recognize in himself. The parody substructure, then, makes its final commentary upon the basic satiric design. Olivia's surface resemblance to Manly is reversed to reveal Manly's actual resemblance to Olivia.

With the complete decline of Manly's character the satiric thesis is completed. When Manly's virtue is proven hollow, when he is shown to be of the company of hypocrites, the satiric vision is fulfilled. All the world, every level of society, even the extra-terrestrial realm of abstract ideas is tainted with falsity. The disease is not more wide spread than it is deeply rooted; man is essentially corrupt and beastly. The satiric thesis has become, as it must, an indictment of human nature. Yet the thesis, however elaborate, cannot by itself fill the requirements of the perfect satiric design. The writer of classical satire, Dryden warns, is bound by his form to give some example of virtue.[10] In this play the standard of virtue, the satiric antithesis, is realized through Fidelia. Most critics consider Freeman and Eliza "the comic standard" [11] of *The Plain Dealer*. They are supposed to represent the poet's point of view because they "champion the naughty world." [12] But if we are not to mistake the excessive misanthropy of Manly for the poet's view, neither are we to negate the play's satire by accepting the viciousness that Manly rails against as the standard upon which we are to judge him and the other characters. To accept the "naughty world" (and naughty seems hardly the adjective that lust, deceit, and the perversion of justice should evoke), to take for the poet's viewpoint the satiric thesis itself, is to pervert the whole scheme of the play. Still the critics have argued well that if Manly is too excessive to be a hero, Fidelia is too unreal to be a heroine. If *The Plain Dealer* is viewed as "Restoration Comedy," Fidelia is completely inexplicable. How in the

[10] Dryden, *Essays of John Dryden*, ed. Ker (London, 1900), II, 102.
[11] Kathleen Lynch, *The Social Mode of Restoration Comedy* (New York, 1926), p. 171.
[12] Lynch, p. 171.

Restoration world could there exist a woman who disguises herself as a page to follow her beloved to war, or who woos another woman on his behalf? Fidelia is unreal; she is vestigial. But in her very unreality, her incongruity in the satiric thesis set before us, she fills the demand of the satiric antithesis. She is the virtue that opposes the vice of the thesis; that virtue is weak, is nearly overwhelmed by the evil it stands against, is always an argument for old-fashioned goodness, the return of a simple and golden past.

In the action of the play Fidelia serves as a symbol rather than a character. Her name gives her the flavor of a Morality play figure. She is Faithful to Manly's Everyman. She represents that quiet virtue that follows behind Manly's braggadocio courage, never boasting of its goodness, wishing only to serve. Manly, in the tradition of Everyman, ignores the virtue that is right at hand, and chooses to pursue a reflection of himself, an embodiment of his baser nature. Fidelia, however, remains true to her name, and when she has nearly been murdered, Manly recognizes her and she is given his soul to guide. As a representative of the antithesis, Fidelia is weak, barely noticeable against the glaring vice that surrounds her, and constantly threatened by it (Manly's rage, Vernish's lust). She is also symbolic in that her disguise, materially more real than those of the others, is spiritually less real. Hers, the most overt mask, hides only modesty and virtue.

But more important is that Fidelia recalls the virtues of a former golden age, like that of Juvenal's primitive Rome. In this too, she serves as a symbol. Wycherley has made of Fidelia what I shall call an expanded allusion. It is impossible to miss Fidelia's resemblance to Viola of *Twelfth Night*. Like Viola, she assumes the disguise of a page. Like Viola, she loves a man who loves another woman, and who does not even realize that she herself is a woman. Like Viola, she serves this man, and finally, though it breaks her heart, woos for him the other woman (whose name, significantly, is Olivia). Like Viola, she is wounded in a duel, her true sex is revealed, and she is rewarded for her loyalty with the affection of the man she loves. Wycherley expects us to recognize in Fidelia the allusion to *Twelfth Night,* for it is through her that he brings to our minds the wonderful, green world of romantic comedy against which we are to view the corruption of the world presented in the satiric thesis. Fidelia is too "literary," too romantic to function as a character in that world of knaves and goats. But she comes trailing a vision of the green world of romance, where love and loyalty are "givens," where all obstacles to true love can be overcome, and the height of mischief is to trick Malvolio into yellow garters. The vision forces us to compare Wycherley's Olivia, a libidinous witch, with the gently lovesick Olivia of Shakespeare, to view Manly's attempts at rape against Orsino's sighing, moaning platonism. Or, if such comparisons can occur only in the mind of an attentive reader, and not to a watching audience, still the allusion to *Twelfth Night* is strong enough to recall a golden never-never land of the past. In the best satire this vision of a golden past seems unreclaimable, as it does in *The Plain Dealer.*

Though Fidelia, the satiric antithesis, proves able to survive in the vicious and realistic world of the thesis, she does not conquer it in a glorious "happy ending." It is true that she gets her man, but their union is not accompanied by that restoration of order and the government of love that forms the traditional comic ending. Olivia is exposed, but she and Vernish are neither punished nor banished. The Widow Blackacre proves the triumph of injustice by arriving on the scene in time to assure Olivia that she can sue. Novel and Plausible are rewarded with the recovery of certain jewels that they had given Olivia, and there is nothing in the play to assure us that they will not go on backbiting until the end of time. Most important, Freeman is not cured of his opportunistic outlook by the example of Fidelia. The adversarius's point of view is maintained, for he sees in Manly's "conversion" a mere compromise with good fortune:

> *Manly:* But if I should tell you [Fidelia] . . . that your virtue (since greater than I thought any was in the world) had now reconciled to me to 't, my friend here would say 'tis your estate made me friends with the world.
>
> *Freeman:* I must confess I should; for I think most of our quarrels with the world are just such as we have to a handsome woman; only because we cannot enjoy her as we would do.
>
> *Manly:* Nay, if thou art a plain dealer too, give me thy hand; . . . .
>
> (V,iv)

This, the note upon which the play ends, should give us pause. It should first remind us that Freeman's view, the view of the majority, still exists—is untouched by the virtue and generosity of Fidelia's example. It should also remind us that it is not Freeman's worldliness, but Fidelia's romantic loyalty that has given Manly, the satirist, one ray of hope. But it should also make us question the permanence of Manly's cure. He embraces Freeman here as he had embraced Olivia at the beginning, for being a superficial copy of himself, a seeming plain-dealer. In its ending the play answers the last requirement of the satiric design. It gives us a vision of the vice-ridden world; it gives us an example of virtue, but it remains open-ended. If virtue triumphs, its triumph is equivocal. As in all great satire, the final decision, being whether or not to heed the satirist's harsh demand for reformation of our lives, is left to the audience; the satirist merely presents the alternatives.

This study is part of a larger one on Wycherley's art and is therefore limited by the writer's determination to concentrate in this paper upon a single aspect, satiric structure, in one play. However, if it has achieved its intention, it should have proven that a writer of the Restoration period can yield literary riches if we approach him with minds cleared of the cant about "Restoration Comedy." Wycherley is only chronologically of the Restoration period. From the beginning to the end of his career as a playwright he wrote in traditions that antedate and stretch beyond the forty-year period to which we have confined him—traditions that form the backbone of our literary heritage. The friendship between the old Wycherley and the young Pope, over which biographers have sentimentalized, may be considered as a human relationship symbolic of the continuity of English literary tradition.

Otway Preserved: Theme and Form in *Venice Preserv'd*

by David R. Hauser

Otway's *Venice Preserv'd* has been repeatedly judged one of the finest of Restoration tragedies, yet almost all modern critical discussions have emphasized the play's defects, thereby producing a confusion as to precisely where the excellence of the play resides.[1] Amid the welter of claims and counter-claims the two most comprehensive and influential criticisms levelled at the play are these: that it merely repeats the artificial formula of heroic drama, being "another linguistic machine to magnify the clash of love with honour";[2] and that the "poetic potential" is too low, emotion being presented for its own sake without any relation to the exigencies of the "tragic vision," that the sentiments are "for the most part expressed not through figurative symbols, but by means of explicit and direct description." [3] Without attempting to explain these criticisms away, it will be the purpose of this paper to demonstrate how Otway partially overcomes the obstructions of the heroic conventions to reanimate the dramatic mechanism of his age, and through an examination of the relationship of imagery to plot, to explore means by which the play may be viewed as more organic and more highly wrought artistically than has previously been allowed. As lumbering and bathetic as it may occasionally be, *Venice Preserv'd* is constructed of sound materials which structurally and poetically "prop the fall" of the drama as a whole.

Despite the difficulty in defining any complex literary phenomenon

"Otway Preserved: Theme and Form in *Venice Preserv'd*." From *Studies in Philology,* LV (1958), 481-93. Reprinted by permission of David R. Hauser and the editor of *Studies in Philology,* University of North Carolina Press.

[1] Aline Mackenzie Taylor, *Next to Shakespeare* (Durham, N. C., 1950), pp. 39-72; and "*Venice Preserv'd* Reconsidered," *Tulane Studies in English,* I (1949), 81-118, offer a thorough and interesting defense of the play, together with discussions of its background, form, and language. While I am indebted to her interpretations, I believe that she has not adequately answered the foremost specific objections to the play. I shall have occasion elsewhere in this paper to indicate my dissatisfaction with her arguments.

[2] Wylie Sypher, *Four Stages of Renaissance Style* (Garden City, N. Y., 1955), p. 263.

[3] Bonamy Dobrée, *Restoration Tragedy* (Oxford, 1929), pp. 145-47; Moody E. Prior, *The Language of Tragedy* (New York, 1947), p. 192.

simply and accurately, there has been general critical agreement as to the community of formal and thematic features which constitute the heroic drama. According to Dryden (who was working with previous English and French dramas in mind, as well as the relation of the heroic play to the Vergilian concept of *epos*), the major distinguishing features of the genre are the highly elaborated conflicts of love and honour within the soul of a great man and the epic elevation of style.[4] Furthermore, "painting the passions" had become the foremost business of the tragic poet; in spite of the critics' Aristotelian emphasis on plot, the tendency in most heroic drama was to utilize plot as a vehicle whereby characters could test and display their emotions.[5] The ethic of the Cartesian psychology of the passions furnished the rationale for such display. According to this system, all virtue is the result of proper ordering and control of the passions by a reasoned use of the will, all evil a failure to channel the passions.[6] Thus the strength of an individual soul depends on the strength of the will. A corollary theory, found in Dryden and elsewhere, was that the nobler an individual, the greater the passions.[7] Consequently, a hero in heroic drama gains his exalted position not by great deeds and noble birth alone, but also through great self-control, a necessary premise to heroic action. Man becomes autonomous and is virtually able to guide his fate by the force of his will. An examination of almost any heroic play will bear out the relevance of the passion theories to the heroic world view.[8] The

[4] "An Essay of Heroic Plays," *Essays of John Dryden,* ed. W. P. Ker (Oxford, 1900), I, 150.

[5] See esp. Dryden's "Preface to *Troilus and Cressida,*" *Essays,* I, 220-28. Sypher (pp. 274-81) and Prior (p. 157) discuss the relevance of the passion psychology to heroic drama, as does the unpublished Johns Hopkins University doctoral dissertation of Ernest S. Gohn, "Seventeenth-century Theories of the Passions and the Plays of John Dryden" (Baltimore, 1948). Also pertinent is Brewster Rogerson, "The Art of Painting the Passions," *Journal of the History of Ideas,* XIV (1953), 68-94.

[6] René Descartes, *The Passions of the Soul,* in the *Philosophical Works of Descartes,* trans. and ed. Elizabeth S. Haldane and G. R. T. Ross (Cambridge, 1911), I, esp. 352-54.

[7] See Cleopatra's speech in Dryden's *All for Love,* in the *Dramatic Works,* ed. Montague Summers (London, 1932), IV, 204; cf. the *Spectator,* No. 408 (June 18, 1712): "We may generally observe a pretty nice proportion between the strength of reason and passion; the greatest geniuses have commonly the strongest affections."

[8] In Dryden's *Aureng-Zebe,* for example, a typical heroic play, the characters are tagged by reference to their passions: Aureng-Zebe is "by no strong passion sway'd," whereas the Emperor excuses his lapses from the code of honour by claiming that love "distemper'd" his mind (*Dramatic Works,* IV, 91, 97). The plot moves from one test of self-control to another. The Emperor's passions overcome his reason when he betrays his city and his son Aureng-Zebe so that he may possess Indamora, forgetting his duties as ruler and father. Aureng-Zebe cannot use force to regain Indamora because he would thus be violating his honour as son and subject, but he cannot honorably abandon her, nor does he wish to. Meanwhile, Indamora displays her self-control by resisting the illicit love of the Emperor and later by denying the personal safety to be secured in encouraging the advances of the lawless Morat. When Aureng-Zebe is confronted with his stepmother Nourmahal's love for him, he is placed in the position of either com-

greater part of the heroic code can be explained in terms presented by the passion psychology, and a good deal of the artificiality of the heroic drama derives from the fact that it is based on such an oversimplified view of human behavior.

Otway does not entirely abandon the heroic code; *Venice Preserv'd* is constructed upon a central conflict of love and honour, is deeply saturated in the Platonic conventions of friendship which were characteristic of heroic drama, and above all, depends heavily on the heroic concept of personal honor. Jaffeir intimates in the very first scene that he has lived the life of a heroic man, for he describes his rescue of Belvidera five years prior in epic terminology.[9] When Pierre solicits his aid in the conspiracy, he states that "I am fit for Honour's toughest task" (II, 148). His final act, the "mercy killing" of Pierre on the scaffold, is his daring attempt to regain the attributes of heroism which his betrayal of the conspiracy had lost him. Pierre, whose impetuosity and bravado have been taken for heroism by most readers, constantly proclaims his adherence to the heroic code, especially when he appears before the Senate in Chains:

> When you, great Duke, shrunk, trembling in your Palace, . . .
> Stept not I forth, and taught your loose Venetians
> The task of honour and the way to greatness? (IV, 236-40)

The conspirators believe themselves to be undertaking a vastly noble cause, and when a minor quarrel develops among them, they are thus silenced by Bedamar:

> Thieves and Rogues
> Fall out and brawl: Should Men of your high calling,
> Men separated by the Choice of Providence,
> From the gross heap of Mankind . . .
> T'adorn the bravest purpose it e'er smil'd on;
> Should you like Boys wrangle for trifles? (II, 222-28)

Even Belvidera feels the tug of the heroic code. When confronted with the plans for the conspiracy, she immediately apprehends the conflict between her love for Jaffeir and her duty to her father, and it is the latter she obeys as she persuades Jaffeir to expose the plot.

---

promising his honour by participating in the immoral relationship or, it seems at the time, ignominiously dying. Only by restraining the passions throughout many temptations is Aureng-Zebe eventually able to triumph, becoming reunited with Indamora and either killing or converting his antagonists. Thus the play not only develops through a series of conflicts between love and honour (as Sypher, pp. 262-63, and Prior, pp. 158-61, have illustrated), but these conflicts are resolved only within the ethic of the passion psychology.

[9] *The Works of Thomas Otway*, ed. J. C. Ghosh (Oxford, 1932), II, 205, ll. 36-48. All further references will be to the line numbering in this edition.

But whereas honour is the ideal, it is rarely sustained in the action of the play itself. The focal point of the tragedy is Jaffeir's failure to uphold his oath to the conspirators, thereby condemning his friends and preserving his enemies. The number of broken oaths elsewhere in the play is astounding. In Act I (298), for example, Jaffeir swears that he will avenge Belvidera's grief at being evicted from their home, yet in actuality he eventually gives her much greater cause for grief. Jaffeir hands Belvidera over to the conspirators as a pledge of his good faith, for if he proves unworthy of their trust they are to execute her, but in spite of his betrayal the execution does not occur. Belvidera assures Jaffeir that she will keep whatever secret is preying upon his mind, yet when she learns of the conspiracy she desires to reveal it at once. Although the Senate swears to pardon the plotters in exchange for Jaffeir's information, it breaks its word and has them hanged. Pierre vows never again to hold "communion, Friendship or interest" with Jaffeir (IV, 365), but in the next act the two become reconciled. Even the grotesquely comic Antonio "resolves" not to leave Aquilina's house, yet he is beaten out immediately after his vow (III, i, 128). While the forswearing of oaths is unthinkable in heroic drama, in *Venice Preserv'd* the will is not in absolute control of events; emotions war against the will and often counteract it.[10]

Otway's more realistic view of human behavior springs from his conception of man's ambivalent nature. At several points in the play he establishes the bases upon which his characters operate. In Act III Jaffeir begins to doubt the good will of the conspirators after he learns that Renault, the leader of the venture, has attempted to rape Belvidera. He says in soliloquy:

> Heav'n! where am I? beset with cursed Fiends,
> That wait to Damn me: *What a Devil's man,*
> *When he forgets his nature.* (ii, 302-04. Italics added)

Man contains great capacity for evil as well as good, as is emphasized by Priuli's utterance, "The vilest Beasts are happy in their off-springs,/While onely man gets traitours, whores and villains" (V, 15-16). In Act IV, following Belvidera's success at persuading Jaffeir to reveal the plot to the Senate, Jaffeir exclaims while contemplating his love for his wife, "Why was such happiness not given me pure?" (85). Man, then, may be good or heroic at a given moment, but his nature is such that he cannot sustain his goodness or heroism. Renault's comment, "Clocks will go as they are set: But Man,/Irregular Man's ne're constant, never certain" (II, 206-07) serves as an epigraph to describe the world in which *Venice Preserv'd* takes place.

[10] Aureng-Zebe's first words are "My Vows have been successful as my Sword" (*Dramatic Works,* IV, 96), and this attitude prevails throughout the play.

Consequently, Otway's heroes are not invariably courageous and his villains contain some seeds of virtue. Priuli appears in the first act as a merciless persecutor of his daughter and her husband, but by the final act he relents, Lear-like, pledging "I'll henceforth be indeed a father" (116). The Senate, although corrupted by degenerates like Antonio and apparently inured to treacherous practices such as the breach of faith with Jaffeir, can react nobly on occasion; when the conspiracy becomes known, Priuli speaking for the Senate states bravely:

> Let's not be tamely butcher'd, but doe something
> That may inform the world in after Ages,
> Our Virtue was not ruin'd though we were. (IV, 126-28)

Renault, the sinister caricature of Shaftesbury who lies about his custody of Belvidera when confronted by Jaffeir, has doubts about the moral validity of the conspiracy; in his first speech he ruminates on the dangerous folly involved in satisfying his ambitious urge for power (II, 196-202). Indeed, the nature of the conspirators as a whole is ambiguously presented. From one point of view they sincerely desire to dispose of a tyrannic, corrupt government, they are ideally pursuing the "Common Good." And when they are executed they all die bravely. Yet Jaffeir comes to realize that a good deal of the motive force behind the plot is the personal discontent of base men. In their first conversation the conspirators reveal their misguided nature by the allusions they make. Pierre refers to Brutus as a "Gallant Man" (a debatable view in a commonwealth threatened with rebellion), and Renault picks up this strand of thought, almost parodying the entire conspiracy:

> Yes, and *Cateline* too:
> Tho story wrong his Fame: for he conspir'd
> To prop the reeling Glory of his Country:
> His Cause was good.

Bedamar carries out the implicit comparison:

> And ours as much above it,
> As *Renault* thou art Superior to *Cethegus,*
> Or *Pierre* to *Cassius.* (II, 247-55)

Even if Brutus' gallantry might be defended, the other figures mentioned are far from admirable—Cateline, who was reported to have "deflowered his virgin daughter," Cethegus, a dissolute soldier of fortune, and Cassius, who undertook to shake the state because of personal slights.[11] Thus the

[11] For "characters" of these men see Plutarch's lives of Brutus and Cicero, Sallust's *History of Cateline's Conspiracy,* esp. sect. 5, and Dio Cassus' *Roman History,* books xxxvi, xxxvii, xliv. See as well R. G. Ham, *Otway and Lee: Biography from a Baroque Age* (New Haven, 1931), pp. 195-98, for a discussion of the influence of Lee's *Lucius*

plotters condemn themselves in the very act of reaffirming their own proper motives.

Pierre also partakes of the general self-deception. Possessed of great élan and courage, he seems a totally admirable character, eminently clear-sighted as to the evils and injustices of life. In his first appearance he introduces Jaffeir to a realm of ideas completely new, the universal hypocrisy and innate greed of mankind. He is seemingly dedicated to the cause of humanitarian amelioration. Yet his vision is blurred with respect to the conspirators in that he believes them also wholly dedicated to the "Cause." Even after he learns of Renault's attack on Belvidera he is so caught up in the impending action that he refuses to look at the evil inherent in the conspiracy. Furthermore, he fails to see that he has entered the plot for purely personal motives—Antonio has purchased his mistress and has lodged a complaint against him in the Senate, which has publicly censured him for violating senatorial "privilege." Just prior to his execution he refuses the aid of a priest, who, he claims, wishes "to lead my Reason blindfold" (V, 384-85); he feels that he has lived a good life because he has never broken peace with a heaven he does not believe in "by cruel murthers, Rapine, or perjury, or vile deceiving" (376-77). What he fails to recognize is that if the plot had succeeded he would have been responsible for the very crimes he eschews.[12]

Even the "beauteous Belvidera" is not an unmixed blessing. Her love for Jaffeir remains unhesitatingly constant, and she alone among all the characters consistently sees through the sham idealism of the conspiracy. Yet she is peculiarly blind to the masculine concept of personal honour. In her reference to Lucretia (III, ii, 8-10) she too quickly infers that Jaffeir has deserted her; she boasts of her "Roman constancy" and compares

---

Junius Brutus on *Venice Preserv'd*. Ham notes Otway's borrowings for the Belvidera-Jaffeir relationship and for the play's dénouement, but Otway may well have developed his conspirators with Lee's play in mind. *Brutus* was almost immediately banned, because the censor found in it "Scandalous Expressions & Reflections" upon the government and because its hero, a rebel, was portrayed too sympathetically. Otway was to make no such mistake.

[12] Mrs. Taylor (*Next to Shakespeare,* p. 51) claims that Pierre and Jaffeir plot against the state "under the provocation of personal injury, but the state to them means Antonio and Priuli, and the satisfaction they seek is only that which is sanctioned by the gentleman's code." I find this explanation of dramatic characters by reference to Cavalier mores unconvincing, especially when Otway has given us all we need within the play itself to understand the actions of his characters. Furthermore, following her premises, Mrs. Taylor is forced to conclude that Otway is unsuccessful in his depiction of Pierre, for "there still lingers more than a suggestion of political idealism." But if we view Pierre as a man who confuses personal injury with universal injustice, it is not necessary to criticize Otway for what many readers have found to be his most successful character. While a drama is necessarily of its own time, it must transcend time if it is to be valid tragedy, and if my reading of the play is at all correct, *Venice Preserv'd* exists both within and without the 1680s.

herself to Brutus' wife, Portia, yet she cannot understand any possible reason for Jaffeir's participation in the conspiracy; she even believes that Jaffeir is capable of murdering her.[13] In the final act she is guilty of falsehood when she goes before her father to plead for Pierre's pardon. She does not intimate that the reason she wishes Pierre spared is to preserve her own and Jaffeir's "future Quiet," but instead plays upon her father's emotions, saying that Jaffeir will kill her unless she performs his will (80-111). Furthermore, she so completely misunderstands Jaffeir that she believes they can return to their former way of life after his betrayal (V, 275-78). Even though she may be skilled in persuasive rhetoric, Belvidera lacks sensitivity to the emotions of others.

Venice Preserv'd, then, takes place in a world of ambivalence where good and evil are inextricably mingled and where the human mind is not always capable of distinguishing between them. In this respect Otway has radically departed from the heroic world view in which the strong will can control its destiny by ordering the passions. Dryden's Indamora can rely on her inner order to meet all emergencies:

> Unsetled Virtue stormy may appear:
> Honour, like mine, serenly is severe.[14]

But Belvidera, no less "honourable," is driven mad by circumstances beyond her control. Yet a complex cosmology does not assure complex art; the other objection to the play, that it lacks sufficient poetic strength and that the language is ordered in the interests of passion rather than drama, is the more formidable. While no amount of discussion can alter the diffuseness of much of the verse, it is possible to view Otway's poetic organization as perhaps more profound than has heretofore been allowed, to see an integration of theme and form.

Venice Preserv'd abounds in cosmic references: Heaven and Hell, devils and angels, Creation, the planets. While these images had also appeared in heroic drama, Otway fuses them into a coherent pattern through which a good share of the meaning of the play emerges. At the opening of the play Priuli expresses his hate for Jaffeir, informs him that he is financially

[13] The use of the Portia allusion is an interesting example of the neo-classical technique of imitation; that is, the addition of a dramatic value to a given context by juxtaposing a well-known situation from classical literature (or any other literature) with the present one, and allowing the parallels and contrasts to modify the surface statement. Here Belvidera is revealed as less heroic than Portia, who demonstrated her ability to receive confidences by wounding herself in the thigh before approaching her husband Brutus. Belvidera's "Roman constancy" is simply rhetorical; she claims fidelity but when put to the test cannot stand by her husband at the expense of her father. Later in the play she will exclaim, "Where's now the Roman Constancy I boasted?" (IV, 391). Thus once again Otway expresses the frailty of the human will, this time indirectly.

[14] Dryden, *Dramatic Works,* IV, 127.

ruined, and curses him with, among other things, everlasting poverty: "Get Brats, and Starve" (110). Jaffeir is perfectly willing at this point to continue life on the humble, non-heroic plane so long as he has his beloved Belvidera to share it with him. But he then meets Pierre, who forcibly impresses on him the weight of evil and injustice operative not only in his personal misfortune but in society as a whole, and Pierre thus reanimates the heroic code within Jaffeir. Jaffeir ponders the meaning of what he has learned in a soliloquy which takes the form of a prayer; he asks Heaven why "Thou mad'st me what I am, with all the Spirit,/Aspiring thoughts and Elegant desires/That fill the happiest Man?" (I, 308-15). Yet at the end of the first act he is again reconciled to the humble life by Belvidera.

But Jaffeir has promised to meet Pierre at midnight, and as he goes to the meeting he is filled with the foreboding that he is about to sell his soul to the Devil (II, 66-76). When Pierre gives him a bag of money, "something to buy Pins," he feels that the Devil is before him (99-100). Pierre praises the "Cause," claiming "There's no Religion, no Hypocrisie in't," thereby indicating that Jaffeir is being further drawn away from the Heaven to which he had earlier prayed. Jaffeir swears his allegiance with a mighty oath which irrevocably alienates him from the humble life:

> I do, by all those glittering Stars,
> And yond great Ruling Planet of the Night!
> By all good Pow'rs above, and ill below! (177-79)

Now Jaffeir, says Pierre, has become "fit to disturb the Peace of all the World,/And rule it when it's wildest" (186-87). Jaffeir becomes one of the conspirators who ironically adumbrate their own alliance with evil by the remark, "Hell seize that Soul amongst us, it can frighten" (II, 212), although later they are all frightened by Pierre's vehement defense of Jaffeir. When Jaffeir surrenders Belvidera as a pledge of his good faith he indicates that the nonheroic life is far behind him:

> Oh *Belvidera!* we must change the Scene
> In which the past Delights of Life were tasted:
> . . . we must learn to watch
> Our labours late and early every Morning . . .
> Rise to our toils, and drudge away the day. (II, 367-72)

By joining the conspiracy Jaffeir has ended his Adam-like innocence and has embarked upon what is figuratively established as the work of the Devil. Belvidera understands this: to her the plotters "look as Hell had drawn 'em into League" (III, ii, 100), but Jaffeir realizes how far he has been corrupted only after Belvidera exposes Renault's attempted rape. Then Jaffeir fervently desires release from his "pact":

> What, be a Devil! take a Damning Oath
> For shedding native blood! Can there be a sin
> In merciful repentance? (III, ii, 270-72)

Yet Jaffeir cannot extricate himself from his pact merely by repudiating his aid in the conspiracy, for he has impetuously sworn an oath to his friend and has given up his wife as a hostage. He would "rather see the face of Hell,/Than meet the man I love" as he goes to the Senate to expose the plot (IV, 97-98). But he does meet Pierre, who refuses to let him tell of his attempt to gain full pardon for the conspirators, and who strikes him, exclaiming, "What whining Monk art thou? What holy cheat" (287), referring to a previous conversation and classing Jaffeir with the generality of mankind, who are hypocrites. At this point Jaffeir is roused from his lethargic acceptance of sin to self-defense, not on the grounds that he has acted rightly, but that he still loves and sympathetically suffers for Pierre. The innate charity of Jaffeir's character had appeared earlier; when Pierre had mentioned the "Cause," Jaffeir had replied, "Curst be the Cause, though I thy friend be part on't:/Let me partake the troubles of thy bosom" (I, 222-23). As Pierre spurns Jaffeir's sympathy, Jaffeir offers himself as a martyr, exclaiming that Pierre may "heap wrongs on my poor head," yet he will bear them until "wounded by my sufferings, thou relent,/And raise me to thy arms with dear forgiveness" (IV, 339-44). But Pierre, bound to the heroic code, refuses to accept sympathy and "excommunicates" Jaffeir from his friendship.

Jaffeir mistakenly attempts atonement by carrying out his pledge to sacrifice Belvidera, but again his charitable nature prevents him from accomplishing the deed, and he reaches the depths of self-abasement:

> I am, I am a Coward; witness't Heaven,
> Witness it, Earth, and every being Witness. (IV, 520-21)

By the time of the final meeting with Belvidera he has resolved to commit suicide, and he no longer desires revenge; he admits that he still loves her and under the influence of his reawakened love he forgives her for her part in his degradation. He "blesses her unaware" so that they part reconciled, even though the scene is so painful to Belvidera that she is driven mad (V, 291-317). The reconciliation with Belvidera symbolizes Jaffeir's final acceptance of the hard terms life offers, and thus when Jaffeir provides an honorable death for Pierre by saving him from the rack, he has found the means to complete the redemptive process already well under way. He is able to expiate his sins by satisfying the demands of Pierre's code, thereby sacrificing his life for the needs of another. It is at this point that the heroic and the humble ways of life (to both of which Jaffeir owes allegiance) become reconciled.[15]

The roles of Belvidera and Pierre support this symbolic identification of Jaffeir with the sin and redemption motif. Throughout the play Belvidera is associated with angels, goodness, and faith. She first appears on the arms of two "virgins," a pose reminiscent of innumerable Renaissance paintings of the wounded Christ supported by women or angels. Jaffeir states that "Angels are painted fair, to look like you" (I, 339), and he feels that poverty would be a veritable Eden with her (I, 382-95). She intuitively sees the conspiracy as a "hellish Trust" (III, ii, 107), and she has the power to frighten off evil in the form of Renault. At one point Jaffeir envisions her as a priestess leading him to holy sacrifice (IV, 87-94). More significantly, she serves to redeem Jaffeir temporarily each time she encounters him; especially vital is her role in convincing him to betray the plot, for she appeals to his "piety" as well as his love. She acts as the agent for Jaffeir's redemption by presenting the example of willing martyrdom which Jaffeir will follow on the scaffold. Jaffeir states:

> The Seal of providence is sure upon thee.
> And thou wert born for yet unheard of wonders:
> Oh thou wert either born to save or damn me! (IV, 524-26)

Ultimately Belvidera is destroyed because she takes upon herself the sins of her husband (V, 307-14), but she teaches Jaffeir how he, in turn, can assume the burdens of Pierre, and thereby complete his salvation.

Pierre fits coherently into this essentially religious pattern. Deluded himself as to the true reason for his actions, he is able to blind Jaffeir by the power of friendship. Early in the play Pierre intimates the unacknowledged truth, that his personal motives are stronger than his patriotism:

> A Souldier's Mistress *Jaffeir's* his Religion,
> When that's prophan'd, all other Tyes are broken. (I, 199-200)

In the oath-taking scene Jaffeir, apprehensive of evil, says upon the entry of Pierre, "I but half wisht/To see the Devil, and he's here already" (II, 99-100). Indeed, Pierre's high-sounding phrases on the necessity of liberty

[15] Mrs. Taylor states that in Otway's play the "heroic is disintegrating under the weight of the pathetic but the heroic convention is nonetheless a powerful influence; between it and the pathetic, though there may be a truce, there cannot be a peace" (*Next to Shakespeare*, p. 70). While there is much truth in this observation, I believe that Otway effects a reconciliation to this extent: Jaffeir fulfills the demands of the pathetic (or humble, as I have chosen to call it) by sacrificing his life for the needs of another, regardless of his valuation of those needs, yet he also makes partial restitution for his breach of heroic action in forswearing his oath to Pierre and the conspirators. Jaffeir thus becomes the point at which the pathetic and heroic merge, and although this resolution cannot avert the tragedy, it can place the action in a new perspective.

closely echo the Miltonic Satan, just as the plotters discuss their rebellion in terms strongly reminiscent of Milton's counsel in Hell. There dwells a "God-like" nature in Pierre, but it is perverted in the interests of pride and personal heroism. At the execution, Pierre refuses the consolation of the priest, saying that he has lived a just, if godless, life, and that he holds no respect for "signs of Faith" (V, 388). But Pierre relents towards Jaffeir and forgives him, so that the final sacrificial act by Jaffeir consummates both their reunion in profound friendship and Jaffeir's restitution of honor. The priest at this point, thinking only in abstract theological terms, cries "Damnable Deed!" but Pierre says "Now thou hast indeed been faithful" (V, 467). Thus Jaffeir, who had earlier hoped for peace with Belvidera (III, ii, 24-25) and who had expressed his inner chaos by macrocosmic imagery (V, 219-27), is now able to say as his final utterance, "I'm quiet" (478).

But no simple triumph is possible on the human level in Otway's view of human nature. With Jaffeir's redemption comes the pitiable insanity and death of Belvidera, who had made Jaffeir's recovery possible. She is too weak, as any mortal would be, to bear both the burden of her husband's sins and her own emotional pressures. Thus the series of personal relationships between Jaffeir, Belvidera, and Pierre ends in grim irony: the Satanic Pierre is the means whereby Jaffeir's salvation is effected; the angelic Belvidera is crushed, not by evil, but by her own goodness; the vacillating Jaffeir eventually redeems himself and aids Pierre, but causes the death of the person he loves most, the one who released him from his "pact" with evil. *Venice Preserv'd* avoids the artificial resolution of heroic drama, and in so doing manifests profound tragedy.

Thus when a critic claims that Pierre's speeches about "my Proselyte" and the "mechanic" nature of prayer do not "fuse into any sort of coordinate relation with the play as a whole," [16] he neglects to examine the imagistic texture of the complete play. Whereas Otway's primary interest was undoubtedly "painting the passions," he has accomplished this on a carefully laid symbolic foundation which serves to unify the more superficial plot structure. If the language of the play is ordered in the interests of emotion, that emotion is also ordered so that it expresses a realistic and complex view of human problems and behavior. *Venice Preserv'd* may not poetically be "next to Shakespeare," but it is nevertheless sound tragedy.

[16] Prior, p. 188.

Love for Love

by Norman N. Holland

Congreve's third comedy, *Love for Love,* surely his most neatly conceived and executed, was a *succès fou* when it was first produced on April 30, 1695, at the new theater Lincoln's Inn Fields, and it has been a favorite of critics and audiences ever since. Almost as though Congreve were testing his own innovations, he wrote his third play about three different kinds of knowledge, three different ways of life—we might call them presocial, social, suprasocial.

The high or "suprasocial" plot deals with Valentine Legend's courtship of the lovely Angelica. Already at the opening of the play, he has run heavily into debt in his efforts to win her, while she, in a manner not entirely becoming, has kept up an appearance of complete indifference. Even when Valentine gets into more and more trouble, she ignores his declarations of love. Sir Sampson Legend, Valentine's father, tries to disinherit him in favor of his younger brother, the sailor Ben, and even tries to marry Angelica himself. Tattle, an indiscreet beau, also tries to marry Angelica, and Mrs. Frail, a none too virtuous lady, tries to marry Valentine, who is at this point reduced to feigning madness. Mad or not, he and his servant Jeremy dupe Mrs. Frail and Tattle into marrying each other; but still none of his schemes to win Angelica, even his feigned madness, succeeds until he finally agrees to renounce his estate and consent to his father's marrying her. Then, she says his love is true and accepts him.

Valentine in this high plot progresses from lover to poet to madman to martyr, almost as though Congreve were remembering:

> The Lunaticke, the Louer, and the Poet
> Are of imagination all compact. . . .
> And all their minds transfigur'd so together,
> More witnesseth than fancies images,
> And growes to something of great constancie,
> But howsoever, strange, and admirable.[1]

[1] *A Midsummer-Night's Dream,* V.i.7ff.

His progress is through three confinements. In Act I, he is forced to remain in his house to elude his creditors, having run heavily into arrears in his pursuit of Angelica. At this stage, he contemplates becoming a poet to support himself. In the second confinement (Act IV), he agrees to relinquish his estate to get his father to pay his creditors, and, to avoid signing the final papers and to get Angelica's sympathy, he feigns madness, confining himself to his house again. In his third confinement (Act V)—this one metaphorical—he actually relinquishes his estate and Angelica, but she rescues him and accepts him. "I yield my Body as your Prisoner," he says (330).[2] His progress involves the familiar neoclassic coupling of religion, love, and the *furor poeticus,* as aspects of the irrational. "The divine Part of me, my Mind," he says to Angelica, "has worn this Masque of Madness, and this motly Livery, only as the Slave of Love and menial Creature of your Beauty" (308). Thus Valentine's friend, Scandal, can comment drily on his wish to write satire: "Who would die a Martyr to Sense in a Country where the Religion is Folly?" (223). In the context, it is completely appropriate that Valentine's final effort to win Angelica is to feign lunacy, for "He that was so near turning Poet yesterday Morning, can't be much to seek in playing the Madman to Day" (286).

Valentine's progress through confinements relates to knowledge as well as to madness. When Scandal suggests to Angelica that her indifference to Valentine is an affectation of ill nature, Valentine ruefully makes a remark which is a key not only to this play but to all of Restoration comedy: "I know no effectual Difference between continued Affectation and Reality" (262). His failure to realize that outside society there is a difference and his related failure to seek Angelica through something other than a show or "affectation" are what keep him from winning her. *Love for Love,* like most of the comedies we have considered, is based on the idea of an education or therapy, and this is the point at which Valentine needs education: that there is a reality which is higher and larger than "continued Affectation."

In all his schemes to win Angelica, Valentine neglects the one method that finally succeeds—directness. He pretends to poetry, to madness, and to devotion; not until the finale does he resort to a simple direct proposal

[2] The edition to which I refer is: *Comedies by William Congreve,* ed. Bonamy Dobrée, The World's Classics (London: Oxford University Press, 1925), pp. 213-332. The numbers in the text refer to pages in this edition, but they may be related to other editions by the following table:

Act I: 219-240.
Act II: 240-261.
Act III: 261-286.
Act IV: 286-311.
Act V: 312-331.

with obvious evidence of his sincerity. When he plans to turn poet, he tells his servant Jeremy:

> Now I am poor, I have an Opportunity to be reveng'd on 'em all; I'll pursue *Angelica* with more Love than ever, and appear more notoriously her Admirer in this Restraint, than when I openly rival'd the rich Fops, that made Court to her; so shall my Poverty be a Mortification to her Pride, and perhaps make her compassionate the Love, which has principally reduc'd me to this Lowness of Fortune. (220)

Despite his protestations, though, he is keeping a barrier between himself and Angelica, trying to create a "Mortification to her Pride," rather than a direct bond between them. His feigning madness is another ruse. Angelica quickly realizes it is and resolves to "play Trick for Trick" (288). She refuses to recognize that he is feigning, even when he says:

> You see what Disguises Love makes us put on; Gods have been in counterfeited Shapes for the same Reason; . . . Nay Faith, now let us understand one another, Hypocrisie apart,—The Comedy draws toward an end, and let us think of leaving acting, and be our selves; and since you have lov'd me, you must own, I have at length deserv'd you shou'd confess it. (308)

In effect, Valentine still keeps a distance between them, revealed by his speaking of "acting." He has soiled his relationship with Angelica as she promptly makes him confess:

> *Valentine:* My seeming Madness has deceiv'd my Father, and procur'd me time to think of Means to reconcile me to him; and preserve the right of my Inheritance to his Estate; which otherwise by Articles, I must this Morning have resign'd: And this I had inform'd you of to Day, but you were gone, before I knew you had been here.
>
> *Angelica:* How! I thought your Love of me had caus'd this Transport in your Soul; which it seems you only counterfeited; for mercenary Ends, and sordid Interest. (308-309)

She meets his social show with an answer in social terms and demands instead that he show real madness: "I'll tell you two things before I leave you; I am not the Fool you take me for; and you are mad, and don't know it" (311). Thus, too, Angelica replies to Tattle's proposal: "O fie for shame, hold your Tongue, A passionate Lover, and five Senses in perfection! when you are as mad as *Valentine,* I'll believe you love me, and the maddest shall take me" (304).

In this "mad" scene with its echoes of *Hamlet* and *The Plain-Dealer,* Valentine takes on some of the character of the playwright. Valentine's statement about his "Comedy" certainly supports this view, as do the frequent references to art and artifice. But, as in *The Way of the World,* drama is tested and found wanting. Valentine has in no sense achieved completeness by becoming inspired and literary. On the contrary, Valentine has yet to learn what Angelica's trial of his constancy has to teach him—"real" madness.

He must prove to her that the underlying reality, "the naked Hook" that one gets when the bait (appearances and disguises) is thrown off (268), is worth the loss of liberty and the chase. He must, in other words, prove that Vainlove in *The Old Batchelor* is wrong, that indeed Angelica herself is wrong when she says: "Uncertainty and Expectation are the Joys of Life. Security is an insipid thing, and the overtaking and possessing of a Wish, discovers the Folly of the Chase. Never let us know one another better; for the Pleasure of a Masquerade is done, when we come to shew our Faces" (310-311). To prove her statement wrong, when the other characters show it is clearly right for the ordinary social world, Valentine must show a "real" madness, that lifts him above ordinary social realities. That "real" madness comes when Valentine consents to ruin himself simply, as he believes, to please her. He has come, in effect, to the knowledge that the final reality is not affectation, but expectation: "He that loses Hope may part with any thing" (328).

When he resigns both his love and his money, Angelica accepts him. He sees her then as a kind of religious fulfillment. The idea is implicit, of course, in her name. Valentine had commented on it in the mad scene: "You're a Woman,—One to whom Heav'n gave Beauty, when it grafted Roses on a Briar. You are the Reflection of Heav'n in a Pond, and he that leaps at you is sunk" (306). The religious or neoplatonic imagery gets particularly strong in the finale. *"Tattle,"* says Valentine to the foppish rival whom he has tricked into marrying Mrs. Frail, "You would have interposed between me and Heav'n; but Providence laid Purgatory [i.e., Mrs. Frail] in your way—You have but Justice" (330). Even the cynical Scandal is converted; he says to Angelica:

> *Scandal:* There is a third good Work, which I, in particular, must thank you for; I was an Infidel to your Sex, and you have converted me. . . .
> *Angelica:* . . . Men are generally Hypocrites and Infidels, they pretend to Worship, but have neither Zeal nor Faith: How few, like *Valentine,* would persevere even to Martyrdom, and sacrifice their Interest to their Constancy! In admiring me, you misplace the Novelty.
>
> The Miracle to Day is, that we find
> A Lover true: Not that a Woman's kind. (331)

In other words, the end of Valentine's education is to bring him to a higher kind of reality, a Providence or God's justice, that transcends the chance and show of ordinary social reality. Valentine here shows, like Manly, overtones of the Kierkegaardian hero: he makes the final act of resignation in giving up all he hopes for, his love and his estate, and then achieves what he had given up.

In spite of the neoplatonic religious imagery, much of the material of *Love for Love* is concerned with Locke's conception of man, published five years before the play. Thus, Valentine demands of his father: "If you don't mean to provide for me, I desire you would leave me as you found me."

> Sir *Sampson:* With all my Heart: Come, uncase, strip, and go naked out of the World, as you came into't.
>
> *Valentine.* My Cloaths are soon put off:—But you must also deprive me of Reason, Thought, Passions, Inclinations, Affections, Appetites, Senses, and the huge Train of Attendants that you begot along with me. . . . I am of myself a plain easie simple Creature; and to be kept at small Expence; but the Retinue that you gave me are craving and invincible. (251)

Part of Valentine's education in the play is to realize that his social desires are not part of his intrinsic nature. When he came naked into the world, he was a *tabula rasa.* Indeed, he says to Angelica, "You are all white, a Sheet of lovely spotless Paper, when you first are born; but you are to be scrawl'd and blotted by every Goose's Quill" (306)—a quite accurate statement of Locke's idea that we come into the world as clean slates, and our minds are made up of the accumulated scribblings on the slates by all our experiences. The play is so Lockean that there are two actual *tabulae rasae,* the presocial "naturals," Ben and Prue.

Ben is Valentine's younger brother, a boorish but likable sailor. He has come home to see his father, Sir Sampson Legend, who is trying to force Valentine to sign over his estate to his younger brother. Prue is the boorish, countrified daughter of the silly astrologer Foresight. Foresight and Sir Sampson plan a match between the "Sea-Beast" and the "land-Monster," but their plans fail when the couple fall out and when Valentine manages to avoid signing the document dispossessing him.

Whereas Valentine and Angelica in the course of the play come *through* the obstacles of society to their neoplatonic, suprasocial status at the end of the play, Ben and Prue are *pre*social, barely beyond the *tabula rasa* stage. Shortly after *Love for Love* appeared, Congreve wrote to Dennis, describing among other things this type of character:

> Under this Head may be ranged all Country-Clowns, Sailors, Tradesmen, Jockeys, Gamesters and such like, who make use of *Cants,* or peculiar *Dialects* in their several Arts and Vocations. One may almost give a Receipt for the Composition of such a Character: For the Poet has nothing to do, but to collect a few proper Phrases and terms of Art, and to make the Person apply them by ridiculous Metaphors in his Conversation, with Characters of different Natures. Some late Characters of this kind have been very successful; but in my mind they may be Painted without much Art or Labour;

since they require little more, than a good Memory and Superficial Observation.[3]

Dr. Johnson said of Ben, with admirable simplicity, "The Sailor is not accounted very natural, but he is very pleasant,"[4] and Coleridge remarked of Congreve's characters generally, "There is no growth from within."[5] In the case of Ben, at least, this character structure is exactly what is called for. Ben is unnatural because Congreve was drawing a "natural man," an intellectual construct. By making Ben less lifelike, Congreve makes us more aware of the character as symbol.

Ben's sea-jargon sets him off from the other people in the play, and his seaworthiness suggests his association with nature and sincerity: "Flesh, you don't think I'm false-hearted, like a Land-Man. A Sailor will be honest, tho'f may-hap he has never a Penny of Mony in his Pocket—May-hap I may not have so fair a Face, as a Citizen or a Courtier; but for all that, I've as good Blood in my Veins, and a Heart as sound as a Bisket" (283). When Sir Sampson tries to coerce Ben into marriage, he is fighting nature itself: "If so be, that I ben't minded to be steer'd by him; 'tis as tho'f he should strive against Wind and Tide" (283).

Ben and Prue, being presocial, have "natural" sexual desires that they do not conceal, as when Prue, in a manner reminiscent of Hippolita, says: "Now my Mind is set upon a Man, I will have a Man some way or other. Oh! methinks I'm sick when I think of a Man; and if I can't have one, I wou'd go to sleep all my Life: For when I'm awake, it makes me wish and long, and I don't know for what—And I'd rather be always asleep, than sick with thinking" (321).

While Ben is of the sea, Prue is of the land and hence more naturally inclined toward the social pretenses to which the foppish beau Tattle introduces her: "All well-bred Persons Lie—Besides, you are a Woman, you must never speak what you think: Your Words must contradict your Thoughts; but your Actions may contradict your Words." "O Lord," cries Prue delightedly, "I swear this is pure,—I like it better then our old fashion'd Country way of speaking one's Mind" (259-260). Ben, however, finds social pretense unnatural; he tells her, "It's but a Folly to lie: For to speak one thing, and to think just the contrary Way; is as it were, to look one way, and to row another" (272). Neither Ben nor Prue has the proper social habit of concealing what one thinks, and as a result they can quickly see their natural mismatch and quarrel over it (272-273).

There is a curious kinship between Ben and Prue, the presocial people,

[3] "*Mr.* Congreve, to *Mr.* Dennis *Concerning Humour in Comedy*," *ibid.*, p. 7.

[4] Samuel Johnson, *Lives of the English Poets*, ed. George Birkbeck Hill (3 vols.; Oxford: Clarendon Press, 1905), II, 218.

[5] Coleridge, "On Wit and Humour," *Coleridge's Miscellaneous Criticism*, ed. Thomas M. Raysor (Cambridge: Harvard University Press, 1936), p. 443.

and Valentine and Angelica, the suprasocial people. Throughout the play, both Ben and Angelica are free of the pretenses of society; Valentine becomes free at the end, and Prue is free at the beginning (though she learns pretense from Tattle). It is as though Congreve were saying the highest social wisdom is the naturalness of those who never saw society. Thus, Angelica establishes a naturalness like Ben's when she says: "Passions are unreasonable and involuntary; if he loves, he can't help it; and if I don't love, I can't help it; no more than he can help his being a Man, or I my being a Woman" (289). Prue uses a neoplatonic image such as we would expect from Valentine or Angelica, when she asks about making love, "Is it like the Catechism?" (259). (The connection between presocial and suprasocial is made even stronger by the fact that one of the first things Prue learns is that love in society is *not* like the catechism: one must say the opposite of what one believes.) Valentine calls himself and his brother "Twin-Stars, and cannot shine in one Sphere; when he rises I must Set" (267), like opposed "suns."

The presocial and suprasocial characters share as one form of naturalness the fondness for perpetually seeking that was Vainlove's humor in *The Old Batchelor*. Angelica shows it in her speech, "Uncertainty and Expectation are the Joys of Life" (310-311). Ben shows it when he says, "I love to roam about from Port to Port, and from Land to Land: I could never abide to be Port-bound, as we call it: Now a Man that is marry'd, has as it were, d'ye see, his Feet in the Bilboes, and may-hap mayn't get 'em out again when he wou'd" (270). Valentine, however, differs from Ben precisely at this point when in the closing scene he yields himself to Angelica as her "Prisoner" (330). Prue also differs from Ben in the matter of perpetual seeking: Ben seeks freedom; Prue just wants to get into the social swim.

Thus, society lies between the "naturalness" of the presocial people on the one hand and on the other the "naturalness" of the suprasocial people. The social group is composed of a younger generation (Tattle, Scandal, Mrs. Frail, and Mrs. Foresight) and an older generation (Sir Sampson and Foresight). Tattle, after a flirtation with Prue, tries to dupe Angelica into marrying him. Mrs. Frail, after a flirtation with Ben, tries to dupe the supposedly mad Valentine into marrying her. Tattle disguises himself as a friar for the purpose, Mrs. Frail as a nun, and suddenly by the deft doings of Valentine's servant Jeremy, they find themselves married to each other. Tattle mangles reputations by pretending to mend them; his friend Scandal mangles reputations by direct attack. Even Scandal is impressed, though, by Mrs. Foresight's *sang-froid*—he seduces her, and she pretends not even to know him the next day. Congreve may have had a real person in mind when he drew Mrs. Foresight, for one of his poems, "To Doris," says:

But who o'er-night obtain'd her Grace,
She can next Day disown,
And stare upon the Strange-Man's Face,
As one she ne'er had known.
So well she can the Truth disguise,
Such artful Wonder frame,
The Lover or distrusts his Eyes,
Or thinks 'twas all a Dream.[6]

Finally, there is some comedy of humors associated with the old astrologer Foresight and Sir Sampson, Valentine's tyrannical father, who is trying to marry Angelica himself. Together, these two represent the older generation in society.

The essence of society in this as in other Restoration plays is the separation of appearances from nature. Most of the material in the somewhat slow first act serves to set the tone of the social world; for example, the amusing episode—otherwise irrelevant—of Trapland. He comes to collect £1500 from Valentine, who in turn tries to divert him from his purpose by plying him with several glasses of sherry and talk of a widow Trapland admires. Unfortunately, however, the moneylender returns to business and Scandal says, "I'll rip up his Stomach, and go the shortest way to his Conscience" (228). "He begs Pardon like a Hangman at an Execution" (229). The impression we get is of a dog-eat-dog world. Everyone in it, debtor or creditor, is equal in appetite, whether for drink, sex, or money. Everyone masks his motives of self-interest as Valentine does in fawning on Trapland or as the moneylender himself does: "Sincerely, I am loth to be thus pressing, but my Necessity—" (229). We get the impression, too, of the whirligig of improvisation and intrigue that goes into living in such a world when one of Trapland's tipstaffs says, "We have half a dozen Gentlemen to arrest in *Pall-mall* and *Covent-Garden;* and if we don't make haste the Chairmen will be abroad, and block up the Chocolate-Houses, and then our Labour's lost" (228). This is a world in which critics are dogs and poets hunters, and "If you can't be fairly run down by the Hounds, you will be treacherously shot by the Huntsmen" (223). This is the world of which Valentine says, "I know no effectual Difference between continued Affectation and Reality" (262).

Living in this social world calls for the ability to see through appearances, which means knowledge—and several different kinds and levels of knowledge occur among the social people. Foresight, the old astrologer, holds what had become in Congreve's day an outmoded Renaissance and medieval belief in direct supernatural influence on the physical world. He believes that certain appearances—stars, moles on the face, and the

[6] *The Mourning Bride, Poems & Miscellanies,* ed. Bonamy Dobrée, The World's Classics (London: Oxford University Press, 1928), p. 286.

like—show the hidden aspects of the present and future. His belief is based on the facile assumption that all these events are controlled equally by supernatural influence. I "Can judge of Motions Direct and Retrograde," he says, "of *Sextiles, Quadrates, Trines* and *Oppositions,* Fiery *Trigons* and Aquatical *Trigons.* Know whether Life shall be long or short, Happy or Unhappy, whether Diseases are Curable or Incurable. If Journeys shall be prosperous, Undertakings successful; or Goods stoll'n recover'd" (247). Foresight judges people by physiognomies and events by his crackbrained astrological predictions. His knowledge of both persons and events is utterly false, and as if to prove the point he is cuckolded.

Sir Sampson uses another kind of outmoded knowledge. He believes in a kind of Elizabethan "nature" in which a father's authority is like a king's—absolute, divinely ordained: "I warrant my Son thought nothing belong'd to a Father, but Forgiveness and Affection; no Authority, no Correction, no Arbitrary Power; nothing to be done, but for him to offend, and me to pardon" (246). For him, therefore, personal experience—particularly travel and family relations—is the core of reality: "I . . . know the World, and Men and Manners," he says (295):

> There's no time but the time present, there's no more to be said of what's past, and all that is to come will happen. If the Sun shine by Day, and the Stars by Night, why, we shall know one another's Faces without the help of a Candle, and that's all the Stars are good for. . . . I know the length of the Emperor of *China's* Foot; have kissed the *Great Mogul's* Slipper, and rid a Hunting upon an Elephant with the Cham of *Tartary,*—Body o' me, I have made a Cuckold of a King, and the present Majesty of *Bantam* is the Issue of these Loyns. (246-247)

His fatherhood, he believes, gives him absolute rights over Valentine (250) and anything other than complete submission on his son's part is "unnatural." Yet, as if to give him the lie, his son Ben, the "Hopes of my Family" (267), shows a lamentable lack of such "nature":

> *Ben:* Well Father, and how do all at home? How does Brother *Dick,* and Brother *Val?*
> Sir *Sampson: Dick,* body o' me, *Dick* has been dead these two Years; I writ you word, when you were at *Legorne.*
> *Ben:* Mess, that's true; Marry I had forgot. *Dick's* dead as you say—Well. (269-270)

Later, Ben says, "It seems Brother *Val.* is gone mad, . . . but . . . what's that to me?" (298). Furthermore, despite his protestations in favor of the "natural," Sir Sampson's words and actions are most remarkably unnatural. His only actions in the play are to try and reverse the natural positions of older and younger brother and to attempt to marry a woman thirty-odd years younger than himself. Over and over, he makes exclamations like, "Body o' me, why was not I a Bear? that my Cubs might have liv'd upon sucking their Paws." "What, wouldst thou have me turn Pelican, and feed thee out my my own Vitals?" (252-253). Valentine turns the tables on this walking *Pseudodoxia Epidemica* by counterfeiting a disorder in nature, madness: "Indeed, I thought, Sir, when the Father endeavoured to undo the Son, it was a reasonable return of Nature" (328). It is fitting that the lesson Sir Sampson learns in the play is, "Learn to be a good Father, or you'll never get a second Wife" (329).

Valentine's servant Jeremy and Scandal use another kind of knowledge, a skeptical naturalism representative of the younger people in the social group. They reject philosophy, poetry, love, and other intangibles in favor of belly-knowledge (I, i and ii), and they are the most successful characters within the ostensibly rational social framework. This fact, typical in Restoration comedy, hints that for the social people this is the best answer. Thus, Jeremy says of his master's reading philosophy: "Does your *Epictetus,* or your *Seneca* here, or any of these poor, rich Rogues, teach you how to pay your Debts without Mony? Will they shut up the Mouths of your Creditors? Will *Plato* be Bail for you? Or *Diogenes,* because he understands Confinement, and liv'd in a Tub, go to Prison for you?" (220). Wits, to him, are only a poor substitute for money (287).

To Mrs. Foresight, family relations are not real at all. "By my Soul," she cries, when Prue speaks to her, "I shall fancy my self old indeed, to have this great Girl call me Mother" (256). If parenthood can be concealed, it ceases to exist. For her, as for Mrs. Frail and Tattle, reputation is reality. "How can any Body be happy, while they're in perpetual Fear of being seen and censur'd" (254). Thus, Scandal, meeting Mrs. Foresight the morning after he has slept with her, is finally reduced by her denials to commenting, "This I have heard of before, but never believ'd. I have been told, she had that admirable Quality of forgetting to a Man's Face in the morning, that she had lain with him all Night, and denying that she had done Favours with more Impudence, than she cou'd grant 'em" (297). In effect, the previous night becomes unreal. So too, for Mrs. Frail and Tattle, only the realization that their marriage will be published makes it real to them (326).

Among the social people, Tattle and Scandal are contrasted throughout the play. Though both base most of their actions on reputation, Tattle pretends secrecy and openly undercuts his pretense. Scandal cries down the vices of the age and secretly undercuts his railing. "The Liberty I take in talking, is purely affected for the Service of your Sex," he tells Mrs. Foresight, "He that first cries out stop Thief, is often he that has stol'n the Treasure" (282). Low in social acumen, Tattle is finally duped, because he thinks the "real" thing is not what people say, but what they do, as he explains to Prue (259). Scandal is more acute. He realizes as Valentine does that in society there is "no effectual difference between continued Affectation and Reality" (262). He realizes what a playwright like Etherege was laughing at; namely, the confusion of the pretended self with "real" self that results from continued pretense. Scandal cannot go beyond this knowledge and remain in the social framework. For a reality that is not "continued Affectation," he must be converted to the religion of love in the final scene. He is, at the end of the play, almost ready to cross the boundary between the social and suprasocial people.

Thus, plot, character, humors, language, in short, all the elements of the play are tailored to bring out in terms of different kinds of knowledge the distinctions among the presocial, social, and suprasocial people. The accompanying diagram shows the relations among the three groups.

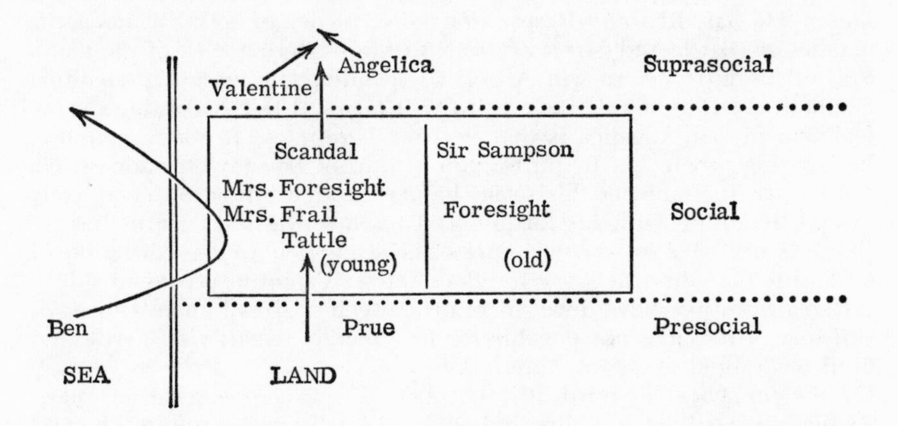

The knowledge necessary for living in the social whirl separates Ben and Prue, who do not have it yet, from the social people who do and from Valentine and Angelica who are rising above it. Ben, Valentine, and Angelica are all seeking something outside the ordinary social framework. Ben, separated from the others by being a "Sea-Beast," is beyond social distinctions. He refuses to come to rest, but Valentine and Angelica, by the end of the play, have gone beyond society as they wanted to. One critic notes that Ben "seems out of place";[7] that is Congreve's point—Ben is a "natural" man in this highly unnatural society. Prue, on the other hand, seeks only social status. Scandal, who has it, is converted at the end to seeking what Valentine and Angelica have found, while the rest of the purely social people are confined to a box of their own making. As if to make the point, Congreve contrasts the tricked

[7] Allardyce Nicoll, *A History of Restoration Drama, 1660-1700* (Cambridge: Cambridge University Press, 1928), p. 231.

marriage of Tattle and Mrs. Frail with the real betrothal of Valentine and Angelica: the hero and heroine speak of their marriage as heavenly, a kind of true religion; Tattle and Mrs. Frail were disguised as a friar and a nun to wed.

The diagram looks as though Congreve had taken one of Etherege's plots and framed around it the actions of Ben, Valentine, and Angelica, thus giving his play a theme that rises above the purely social world. Within that world, people confine themselves to purely social aims, trying to see through the shell of appearances, pretenses, affectations, and dissimulations to real nature. In a sense that is just what the author has done: the action of the play is to make Valentine bring his real nature out from under the shell of pretenses he has drawn round himself. In so doing, Valentine grows out of the limited social world into something larger. He has, like any Restoration hero, plenty of social acumen; he marries off Tattle and Mrs. Frail as if with a dexterous flick of the hand. Yet all his intrigues to win Angelica—spending his money, pretending madness, even his simple attempt to visit her—all fail. Valentine's problem in winning Angelica is that he is still too close to social pretense; he is trying to win her by putting on a show of poverty or madness. He must learn to transcend his social habits through an action completely asocial, resigning both his fortune and his love; he must learn that intrigue is not effective on the suprasocial level. It is to the education of Valentine that the title *Love for Love* refers: Valentine learns to substitute real love for showy love. In return Angelica gives him real love for real love, a response not possible for love merely social; viz., Tattle and Frail or Scandal and Mrs. Foresight.

Love for Love, linguistically, is much like Congreve's earlier plays. The imagery still has the three-dimensional quality we found in *The Old Batchelor*. Ben's voyaging is keyed into the passage of time, and both suggest a forward movement. There is the conversion upward in the somewhat hackneyed neoplatonism of Valentine and Angelica and the conversions downward in the speeches of the social people. The confusion of appearance and nature and social and sexual intercourse among the social people generally suggest the same transverse motion as the consuming-consumed metaphors of *The Old Batchelor*. Increasingly, however, Congreve gives the usual tropes of Restoration comedy only to the people confined in the social whirligig. Thus, Scandal dismisses dreaming in favor of "willing, waking Love" (286), a conversion downward. He attacks honour and conscience: "Honour is a publick Enemy, and Conscience a Domestick Thief; and he that wou'd secure his Pleasure, must pay a Tribute to one, and go halves with t'other" (281). In the same way Tattle converts Valentine and Angelica's love to weight: "You will pardon me, if from a just weight of his Merit, with your Ladiship's good Judgment, I form'd the Ballance of a reciprocal Affection" (263).

The right-way-wrong-way simile is a resource of description only for the social people. Tattle decides that the universities are all right for servants, "But the Education is a little too pedantick for a Gentleman" (317), a remark that tells us more about Tattle's idea of a gentleman than about the nature of a seventeenth-century university education. Mrs. Foresight says, as she is offering Prue up to Tattle, "They're all so, Sister, these Men—they love to have the spoiling of a young thing, they are as fond of it, as of being first in the Fashion, or of seeing a new Play the first Day" (257). Mrs. Frail, when she is trying to trick Ben into marrying her, says: "You know, marrying without an Estate, is like Sailing in a Ship without Ballast. . . . And tho' I have a good Portion; you know one wou'd not venture all in one Bottom" (283). The contrast is between right and wrong ways of comparing marriage to a vessel: marriage being like a vessel because it requires steadiness represented by ballast (a conversion downward of emotional solidity) and marriage being like a vessel because it is a commercial venture. By contrast, the suprasocial people, Valentine and Angelica, speak a language fraught with cosmological implications—almost in the Elizabethan manner.

The imagery, as well as the figures of speech, is no longer as loose as in *The Old Batchelor*. There is less reliance on isolated image clusters than in Congreve's earlier plays. Imagery is largely controlled by character: astrological images for Foresight, for example, or nautical images for Ben. Each character has a specific area of experience to which he belongs. He is, in effect, placed at a point along one of the three axes [in a previous diagram] rather than at their intersection.[8] His choices, represented by his similes, are more limited. Ben is confined to the continual forward movement of perpetual seeking. The social people are limited to their transverse relations. Valentine, though the most free, moves only upward. Language does not pull apart from action; rather, it constantly tests knowledge, establishing the character's position and the choices open to him. This parallel motion of language and action is what makes us think this the most "stageable" of Congreve's plays. The inside-out quality we saw in the relation of language and action in *The Old Batchelor* is retained in the form of a central paradox: Valentine and Angelica escape the social world by finding a liberating confinement within it.

In another sense, *Love for Love* marks a distinctly new stage in Congreve's development as a comic dramatist. In this epistemological comedy, he contrasts two worlds and two kinds of knowledge: the realistic social world, apparently rational, and the intuitional and unrealistic su-

[8] The diagram referred to places man between coördinates of reason and passion, between consuming and being consumed, and between time and relation to others. In addition, it pictures man not only in a coördinate system but also capable of being a spectator of reality and of "conversion" up or down. [ED.]

prasocial world of aims and seeking. The heart of the irony—it is, of course, the same as that of *The Plain-Dealer*—is that the realities of society are deceptive and social aims limited. The relation among Valentine, Scandal, and Tattle is still faintly like that among Manly, Freeman, and Vernish; the thematic contrast is still between the two worlds of Manly-Valentine and Freeman-Scandal. "Real" reality and success, the fusion of "real" natures, are lodged in the intuitional. Intrigue, with its specious logic of plots and pretenses, is left a role subordinate to naturalness, "generous," irrational, and ingenuous action.

There is a corresponding change in the position of the isolated individual. I come increasingly to the conclusion that *The Plain-Dealer* is the single most important influence on Congreve, and if we consider that play as a kind of first stage in his development, we see a slow growth. At first the deviant individual is a central figure—Manly. As Congreve develops from Heartwell to Ben to Sir Wilfull Witwoud in *The Way of the World,* the solitary one moves further and further out toward the periphery of the action, though still retaining his original function of casting a comic perspective on it. In the last two plays, this figure becomes alien, one coming from elsewhere and going elsewhere, one "passing through" the social whirl. Ben goes through society in a spatial voyage in much the way that Valentine "passes through" in a psychological voyage. Valentine grows up to be able to make his way in society and then rises above it. Although Ben's voyage is analogous to Valentine's voyage of life, they travel at right angles to each other; they are "Twin-Stars and cannot shine in one Sphere."

By juxtaposing the two brothers, one foolish but essentially good, and the other both clever and good, Congreve continues the shift in the comic axis we noted in *The Double-Dealer.* Goodness and cleverness are no longer to be equated; the ethic of Etherege is gone. Knowledge to Congreve serves a different function. No longer does it simply enable the hero to succeed in a corrupt and foolish society. In this play it becomes a means to a larger freedom, and that freedom is not necessarily denied to the ignorant man—Ben. But while Ben's freedom means a physical escape from society, Valentine's freedom is a greater thing, a spiritual freedom. The action of *Love for Love* perfectly exemplifies the last phase of Restoration comedy. The hero retreats from the social world of deception and illusion to a personal haven of psychological truth and emotional sincerity. He discovers the heart behind the mask.

Congreve's Last Play

by Thomas H. Fujimura

Congreve's last play, *The Way of the World* (1700), had far less success than the earlier comedies; and he perhaps foresaw this, for he declared in the dedication that the play was not prepared for the general taste then prevalent, which was for farce and show. He explained that instead of the gross fools currently represented on the stage, he would present some characters who should appear ridiculous because of their false wit. The result is a comedy of wit, embodying the familiar ingredients of Witwouds who are exposed for their defective wit, Truewits who outwit others and engage in wit combats, and rivals who are outwitted. Yet this did not produce a warm response in the audience.

The ill-success of the play cannot be attributed to a radical change in popular taste since the performance of his last comedy. Congreve himself complained that the critics were not perceptive, and that they missed the distinction between the character of Truewit and Witwoud, which, rather than "manners," is the theme of the play. Some modern critics explain the ill-success by stating that the plot is not strong and that the chief excellence of the play is stylistic.[1] But it is not certain that they have put their finger on the chief weaknesses of the play. The plot of *The Way of the World* is actually superior to that of *Love in a Wood* or *The Old Batchelor,* which both met with greater success. In fact, the situation in the play is the familiar one of Truewits outwitting rivals and guardians, exposing Witwouds, and at the same time conducting a wit combat between themselves.

More probably the play did not appeal to popular taste because it lacks the strong naturalism and the easily apprehended comic wit of *Love for Love,* and because it shows deficiencies as a comedy of wit. Mrs. Millamant hit the weak point of Mirabell, and also of the play, I think, when

[1] Cf. Palmer, *The Comedy of Manners* (London, 1913), p. 189. [The edition of Congreve quoted in this chapter is *Comedies by William Congreve,* ed. Bonamy Dobrée (London, 1944). ED.]

she cried, "Sententious Mirabell!" For, indeed, the play is too full of serious reflections and learned allusions, unrelieved by naturalistic touches and by sceptical and sexual wit. Mirabell, for example, caps a couplet of Suckling's that Mrs. Millamant has just spoken; Lady Wishfort, who has Quarles, Prynne, Bunyan, and Collier in her closet, speaks familiarly of a character in *Don Quixote*; and even the boorish Sir Wilfull lards his speech with a reference to Pylades and Orestes. Finally, there is the intrusion of sense and sensibility to such a degree that it mars the play as wit comedy.

The Way of the World has always been a problem for the "manners" critics: it is considered the best comedy of manners—and yet it is admittedly not very successful on the stage (though the perfect comedy of manners will always be unsuccessful theatrically because its chief merits must be stylistic). The relative ineffectiveness of the play can be explained more plausibly, I think, on the grounds given above: it is not as good a comedy of wit as *The Man of Mode* or *Love for Love*. Despite a pair of elegant Truewits and a fine Witwoud, it lacks not only a strong naturalistic substratum but sceptical and sexual wit, comic wit that is easily grasped, and a consistent attitude toward life.

The character of Mirabell is perhaps the best illustration of this deficiency: he is the Restoration rake in the process of being transformed into a Wit of the age of sense and sensibility. His predominant characteristic as a Truewit is his judgment rather than fancy, and he is more addicted to *sententiae* than to similitudes. When Mirabell is metaphorical, his observation is just but not striking, as in his remark on Lady Wishfort: "An old Woman's Appetite is deprav'd like that of a Girl—'Tis the Green-Sickness of a second Child; and like the faint Offer of a latter Spring, serves but to usher in the Fall; and withers in an affected Bloom" (II, iii). He is capable of finely balanced phrases, but his remarks are characterized by subtlety of thought and elegance of expression rather than by striking figures of speech. The repartee of Mirabell and Fainall, in which the latter tries to sound out Mirabell's feelings toward Marwood, is characteristic of his elegant speech:

> *Fainall:* You are a gallant Man, *Mirabell*; and tho' you may have Cruelty enough, not to satisfie a Lady's longing; you have too much Generosity, not to be tender of her Honour. Yet you speak with an Indifference which seems to be affected; and confesses you are conscious of a Negligence.
>
> *Mirabell:* You pursue the Argument with a Distrust that seems to be unaffected, and confesses you are conscious of a Concern for which the Lady is more indebted to you, than is your Wife. (I, i)

The reply is a beautiful "turn," and shows great judgment, but it lacks the force and concreteness that similitudes alone can give. How different this is from the blunt retort of Horner to Pinchwife, or Dorimant's rough raillery. Mirabell is no longer the plain-dealing Truewit; instead he is ironical, and launches insinuations on the sea of conversation. He has become introspective and detached, and he is too elegant to engage in too direct repartee.

As a man of sound sense, Mirabell also displays a modesty of behavior that one does not find in Truewits like Bellmour or Dorimant. He believes that good nature and true wit go together, and he rebukes Petulant for his senseless ribaldry in the presence of women:

> *Mirabell:* But has not thou then Sense enough to know that thou ought'st to be most asham'd thy self, when thou has put another out of Countenance.
>
> *Petulant:* Not I, by this Hand—I always take Blushing either for a Sign of Guilt, or ill Breeding.
>
> *Mirabell:* I confess you ought to think so. You are in the right, that you may plead the Error of your Judgment in defence of your Practice.
>
> Where Modesty's ill Manners, 'tis but fit
> That Impudence and Malice pass for Wit. (I, ix)

This is a reflection of Congreve's own sensible and affectionate nature, and it shows how far the Truewit has been transformed from the malicious and naturalistic Dorimant and Horner. Mirabell also knows his own weaknesses too well to be carefree and gay. Like Valentine, he exclaims, "A Fellow that lives in a Windmill, has not a more whimsical Dwelling than the Heart of a Man that is lodg'd in a Woman." But where Valentine dismisses the thought with a witticism, Mirabell, more sadly and sententiously, observes, "To know this, and yet continue to be in Love, is to be made wise from the Dictates of Reason, and yet persevere to play the Fool by the force of Instinct" (II, vi).

Mirabell is also a Truewit with some principles. He is libertine enough to lie with more than one woman, but he is sensible enough to be discriminating. Despite the advantages to be gained, he refuses to satisfy Marwood's passion—perhaps because he loves Mrs. Millamant; and though he made love once to Lady Wishfort in an effort to win Mrs. Millamant, he would not stoop to debauch the old lady. Mrs. Fainall, we gather, was an attachment of the past, before he fell in love; and since she was a widow at the time, and hence, according to the naturalistic conception of widows, very inflammable, he could hardly be blamed for satisfying her sexual appetite as well as his own. When the play opens, Mirabell has apparently broken off all relations with her, and he is pursuing matrimony with a serious purpose. In the "proviso" scene he stipulates that his son must not suffer from any fanatical wish on his wife's part to be fashionable. "I denounce against all strait Lacing," he tells Mrs. Millamant, "squeezing for a Shape, 'till you mould my Boy's Head like a Sugar-loaf; and instead of a Man-Child, make me Father to a

Crooked-billet" (IV, v). Mirabell is probably the first Truewit so sensible as to begin worrying about his offspring at the time he proposes to his mistress. He is prudent enough, too, to make some concessions to reputation II, iii), and he is the one who expresses the ostensible moral of the play, "That Marriage Frauds too oft are paid in kind" (V, xiv). "Sententious Mirabell," as Mrs. Millamant so aptly calls him, is not so attractive a figure as Valentine, for the playful attitude of the Truewit is sobering into a concern with the sound conduct of life. If there is a flaw in Mirabell, it is not his supposed cynicism, but his sobriety.

Mrs. Millamant, like Mirabell, shows the influence of the coming age in her increased sensibility. It is quite false to her nature to characterize her as "the most witty and fearless of Dianas" whose courtship is unmarked "by one moment of real hesitation or by the disclosure of one palpitation of the heart." [2] If there is a serious criticism of her as a Truewit, it is that she has too many palpitations of the heart. She has something of the seriousness and sensibility of Araminta, plus a little of the charming affectation of Belinda. But she is much more fanciful and whimsical in her wit, with a lightness of touch uniquely hers, and a sensibility extremely refined.

It is her whimsical wit that makes her seem so airy, and one suspects that this is the becoming affectation of which Mirabell is enamoured. She declares that she is pestered with letters—"O ay, Letters—I had Letters—I am persecuted with Letters—I hate Letters—No Body knows how to write Letters; and yet one has 'em, one does not know why—They serve one to pin up one's Hair" (II, iv). Then she plays with the conceit that only letters in verse are good—for mere prose will not curl her hair. How charming is this mixture of whimsical petulance and feminine il logic, of fancy flitting playfully from inconsequential thought to inconsequential thought.

But this is mere affectation on her part, intended for public consumption, to conceal her deep affection for Mirabell. She adopts the same whimsical tone toward him because she does not want to make a public confession of her love, and she is a little pained that he is not perspicacious enough to penetrate her playful disguise:

> *Mrs. Millamant: Mirabell,* Did you take Exceptions last Night? O ay, and went away—Now I think on't I'm angry—No, now I think on't I'm pleas'd—For I believe I gave you some Pain.
>
> *Mirabell:* Does that please you?
>
> *Mrs. Millamant:* Infinitely; I love to give Pain.
>
> *Mirabell:* You wou'd affect a Cruelty which is not in your Nature; your true Vanity is in the Power of pleasing.
>
> *Mrs. Millament:* O I ask your Pardon for that—Ones Cruelty is ones Power,

[2] Ashley H. Thorndike, *English Comedy* (New York, 1929), p. 324.

> and when one parts with ones Cruelty, one parts with ones Power; and when one has parted with that, I fancy one's old and ugly. (II, iv)

Mrs. Millamant has a great deal of judgment, though she prefers not to display it as Mirabell does, and she even tolerates Petulant and Witwoud, as Marwood suspects, so that she may disguise her affair with Mirabell (III, x). When he blindly accuses her of lacking judgment in conversing with such fools, she answers with the mixture of sense and whimsicality that is characteristic of her wit:

> *Mrs. Millamant:* I please my self—Besides, sometimes to converse with Fools is for my Health.
>
> *Mirabell:* Your Health! Is there a worse Disease than the Conversations of Fools?
>
> *Mrs. Millamant:* Yes, the Vapours; Fools are Physick for it, next to *Assafoetida.* (II, v)

Her whimsical wit is a shield which she holds up against the world, against Marwood and Lady Wishfort, and even against Mirabell.

Mrs. Millamant is a highly cultivated woman, so sensitive and fastidious that she wishes to avoid the grossness of wrangling and raillery. She has an aversion to illiterate men; and at times there is almost a touch of pedantry in her speech, as when she says: "There is not so impudent a Thing in Nature, as the sawcy Look of an assured Man, confident of Success. The Pedantick Arrogance of a very Husband, has not so Pragmatical an Air" (IV, v). One of the most amusing scenes in the play is her encounter with the boorish Sir Wilfull when she is reciting to herself some verses of Suckling, of whom she is very fond:

> *Mrs. Millamant:* Natural, easie *Suckling!*
>
> *Sir Wilfull:* Anan? *Suckling?* No such Suckling neither, Cousin, nor Stripling: I thank Heav'n I'm no Minor.
>
> *Mrs. Millamant:* Ah Rustick, ruder than *Gothick.* (IV, iv)

The airy disdain of her retort brushes lightly against him like the wings of a butterfly against an ass: she is too refined and subtle for a grosser stroke in a situation so absurd.

Mrs. Millamant is not without malice, however, though this side of her nature is usually well concealed beneath her affected whimsicality. She is not above teasing Mirabell when he is too serious, and there is some malice in her remark to Mrs. Fainall: "Dear *Fainall,* entertain Sir *Wilfull*—Thou hast Philosophy to undergo a Fool, thou are marry'd and hast Patience" (IV, ii). When charged by the madly jealous Marwood with having Mirabell as a lover, Mrs. Millamant does not spare her rival. She exclaims at the constancy of Mirabell, and swears that if she thought she had power over him, she would command him to show more gallantry: " 'Tis hardly well bred to be so particular on one Hand, and so insensible on the other. But I despair to prevail, and so let him follow his own Way. Ha, ha, ha. Pardon me, dear Creature, I must laugh, ha, ha, ha; tho' I grant you 'tis a little barbarous, ha, ha, ha" (III, xi). When Marwood becomes violent in her language, Mrs. Millamant does not retort directly, but carries out her revenge in a manner more becoming a Truewit by having a malicious song sung before Marwood:

> 'Tis not to wound a wanton Boy
> Or am'rous Youth, that gives the Joy;
> But 'tis the Glory to have pierc'd a Swain,
> For whom inferior Beauties sigh'd in vain. (III, xii)

To such subtle raillery there is no reply, and Mrs. Millamant has the advantage over Marwood because of her superior wit.

Mrs. Millamant is better, however, when her real feelings come to the surface, and reveal her in her true nature, as a woman of sincerity and deep feeling but, at the same time, a Truewit with judgment and an awareness of decorum. This side of her is best demonstrated in the famous "proviso" scene in which she capitulates to Mirabell. In this courtship scene, she tells Mirabell that she will not have any of "that nauseous Cant" of affection, such as "Wife, Spouse, my Dear, Joy, Jewel, Love, Sweet-heart, and the rest," which passes for legal currency between husbands and wives in public; she would rather be distant before others, and love each other sincerely in private (IV, v). As a Truewit, she loves good taste, restraint, and sincerity above false show and cant. She is also independent enough to demand freedom to live a life of her own, instead of having her whole nature circumscribed in the title of a wife.

Till the very end she retains mastery of herself and her emotion; and because she is afraid of losing her self-control she hides under a cloak of whimsicality:

> *Mrs. Millamant:* Well then—I'll take my Death I'm in a horrid Fright— . . . I shall never say it—Well—I think—I'll endure you.
> *Mrs. Fainall:* Fy, fy, have him, have him, and tell him so in plain Terms: For I am sure you have a Mind to him.
> *Mrs. Millamant:* Are you? I think I have—and the horrid Man looks as if he thought so too—Well, you ridiculous thing you, I'll have you—I won't be kiss'd, nor I won't be thank'd—Here kiss my Hand tho'—So, hold your Tongue now, don't say a Word. (IV, v)

She is a Truewit till the last, but when Mirabell departs, she breaks down and confesses to her friend:

> *Mrs. Millamant:* Well, if *Mirabell* should not make a good Husband, I am a lost thing;—for I find I love him violently.
> *Mrs. Fainall:* So it seems; for you mind not what's said to you. (IV, vii)

In addition to her judgment and sense, Mrs. Millamant has a real capacity for deep feeling, and her love for Mirabell is all the more impressive because she has such mastery over it. She remains a Truewit throughout the play, but the warring elements of deep feeling and of an unusually clear and perspicacious mind threaten at times to destroy her equanimity. She is a more subtle and profounder creation than any other female Truewit in wit comedy, but her capacity for deep feeling and her sensitive nature come close to transforming her into a woman of sensibility.

In contrast to the two Truewits, Fainall and Marwood are distinctly unattractive figures, with some resemblance to Maskwell and Lady Touchwood. Fainall has the marks of a Wit: he is a true libertine; he has perspicacity, considerable judgment, and a ready tongue; and in the naturalistic atmosphere of *The Man of Mode,* he would have been quite at home beside Dorimant. But in the increasingly moral atmosphere of Congreve's play, he is condemned as a complete egoist intent only on his own pleasures. Mirabell describes him thus: "I knew *Fainall* to be a Man lavish of his Morals, an interested and professing Friend, a false and a designing Lover; yet one whose Wit and outward fair Behavior, have gain'd a Reputation with the Town, enough to make that Woman stand excus'd, who has suffer'd her self to be won by his Addresses" (II, iii). Fainall possesses the graces of the Truewit, but he is condemned by Mirabell because he is naturalistic in his principles. It is important to note, too, that it is Fainall, and not Mirabell, who exemplifies the title of the play; for it is he, and not Mirabell, who accepts infidelity in matrimony and friendship as "all in the Way of the *World*" (III, xviii). He is sometimes entertaining in his wit, as in the fanciful sophistry of his exchange with Marwood: "Marriage is honourable, as you say; and if so, wherefore should Cuckoldom be a Discredit, being deriv'd from so honourable a Root?" (III, xviii). He has the marks of a Truewit, especially in his distinction of speech; but he is outwitted by his cleverer adversaries, as is Marwood, who plays the scorned woman with some violence.

The play has a fine gallery of Witwouds and Witlesses, for Congreve's main purpose in writing was to bring out the contrast between these creatures and the Truewits. Among the coxcombs, Witwoud is easily the most amusing, though he is the cause for the familiar charge that Congreve made his coxcombs too witty. But, as Congreve observed to Dennis, witty remarks are expected from a witty man, "and even a *Fool* may be permitted to stumble on 'em by chance." [3] The best criticism of Witwoud is to be found in the comments of Mirabell:

> *Fainall:* he has something of good Nature, and does not always want Wit.
> *Mirabell:* Not always; but as often as his Memory fails him, and his com-

[3] Congreve, *The Mourning Bride, Poems & Miscellanies,* ed. Bonamy Dobrée (London, 1928), p. 2.

mon Place of Comparisons. He is a Fool with a good Memory, and some few Scraps of other Folks Wit. He is one whose Conversation can never be approv'd, yet it is now and then to be endur'd. (I, v)

No doubt Witwoud sometimes says amusing things, but they are forced pell-mell on whatever company may be present. His lack of decorum (true wit) is quite evident on his first appearance:

Mrs. Millamant: Dear Mr. *Witwoud,* Truce with your Similitudes: For I am as Sick of 'em—
Witwoud: As a Physician of a good Air—I cannot help it, Madam, tho' 'tis against my self.
Mrs. Millamant: Yet again! *Mincing,* stand between me and his Wit.
Witwoud: Do, Mrs. *Mincing,* like a Skreen before a great Fire. I confess I do blaze to Day, I am too bright. (II, iv)

He is at best a buffoon who will raise a laugh at any price, even at his own expense, because he is deficient in judgment; and in this role he is simply a refinement on similar characters by Etherege and Wycherley.

Sir Wilfull as the boorish Witless is again not new; but unlike most fools, he has a redeeming feature in his good nature. Petulant is also an old character, patterned in part after Captain Bluffe: he is irascible, affects brevity, and breathes fire. "If Throats are to be cut," he mutters, "let Swords clash; snug's the Word, I shrug and am silent" (I, ix). He is rebuked, too, by Mirabell for uttering senseless ribaldry before ladies, like the boor that he is. The crude, witless raillery of Sir Wilfull and Petulant is exposed amusingly in an encounter between the two:

Petulant: Sir, I presume upon the Information of your Boots.
Sir Wilfull: Why, 'tis like you may, Sir: If you are not satisfy'd with the Information of my Boots, Sir, if you will step to the Stable, you may enquire further of my Horse, Sir.
Petulant: Your Horse, Sir! Your Horse is an Ass, Sir! (III, xv)

Among these ridiculous figures, the most striking creation is Lady Wishfort, and she has been highly praised by some modern critics. But I imagine that Congreve himself did not regard her too highly, because she is not sufficiently natural, and the ingredients of her character are too apparent. Like Sir Sampson, she is addicted to extreme forms of metonymy and exaggerated similitudes. To Peg, she cries, "Paint, Paint, Paint, dost thou understand that, Changeling, dangling thy Hands like Bobbins before thee? Why dost thou not stir, Puppet? thou wooden Thing upon Wires" (III, i). She uses hyperbole in the manner of Belinda, but without her charm: "Let me see the Glass—Cracks, say'st thou? Why I am arrantly flea'd—I look like an old peel'd Wall. Thou must repair me, *Foible,* before Sir *Rowland* comes" (III, v). This violence of language springs from the intemperance of her nature, and the result is a sort of bastard wit compounded of striking figures and absurd ideas. To this she adds a novel malapropism, as in her remarks to Sir Rowland, whom she wishes to marry: "But as I am a Person, Sir *Rowland,* you must not attribute my yielding to any sinister Appetite, or Indigestion of Widowhood; nor impute my Complacency to any Lethargy of Continence—I hope you do not think me prone to any Iteration of Nuptials" (IV, xii). In this character, she is better and wittier than Mrs. Malaprop, because her mistakes are not nonsensical but have an ingredient of sense in them.

One important fact about this comedy which we must note especially is that Congreve returns to the moralistic temper of *The Double-Dealer,* though not in so extreme a manner. Those who censure this play as an example of cynicism and moral indifference, as Palmer does when he speaks of the "dead level of conscience,"[4] misunderstand the play completely. It is generally assumed that the title of the play indicates a cynical acceptance by Congreve of the treachery, marital infidelity, and moral indifference that are "the way of the world." Actually, Congreve repudiates the way of the world, for he censures Fainall, Marwood, Petulant, and Witwoud, who conform to the world as it is. On the other hand, the two Truewits in the play, Mirabell and Mrs. Millamant, refuse to conform to the pattern of a world which is conventional and cynical in its human relations, which places fortune before love in matrimony, regards adultery as an accepted fact, substitutes a public display of affection for real love, and acclaims Witwoud as much as the Truewit. Fainall, both an adulterous husband and a cynical wit, is outwitted and defeated by Truewits who are not only more clever than he but more honest. In this last play, Congreve is obviously turning away from the naturalistic philosophy of wit comedy, and is making concessions to morality, good sense, and sensibility. Mrs. Millamant is the perfect female Truewit, but she has developed a heart; and Mirabell is still a striking and elegant Wit, but he begins to grow sententious and sober.

Congreve comes a generation after Etherege and Wycherley, and it would indeed be surprising if he continued to write the same type of play as they, with the same philosophical assumptions. *The Old Batchelor* and *Love for Love* still have the playful and libertine temper of true wit comedies; but in *The Double-Dealer* morality begins to rear its head, and in *The Way of the World* there is a shade too much of sense and sensibility. The increasing subordination of philosophical naturalism reflects the changing intellectual climate, as does the new stress on judgment and good nature over fancy and malice in wit.

It is not a far step from Congreve to Addison. But Congreve remained essentially a child of the seventeenth century, and was always a Truewit.

[4] Palmer, *Comedy of Manners,* p. 192.

as man and artist, though he moved among the Wits of the age of reason rather than among the rakes of Charles' court. He was, as Pope observed to Tonson, *"ultimus Romanorum."* [5] It is clear, from an examination of Congreve's life and work, that he was an intelligent, cultivated, and sensible Truewit, far different from the "manners" conception of him as a cynical stylist and "a professional funny man." The most fitting tribute to him are the words inscribed on a tablet by his dear friend Sir Richard Temple:

INGENIO,
ACRI, FACETO, EXPOLITO,
MORIBUSQUE
URBANIS, CANDIDIS, FACILLIMIS,
GULIELMI CONGREVE.[6]

[5] Joseph Spence, *Anecdotes, Observations, Characters of Books and Men* (London, 1858), p. 35.

[6] *Memoirs of the Celebrated Persons Composing the Kit-Cat Club* (London, 1821), p. 219.

Chronology of Plays

(The dates give the year of first performance.)

John Dryden (1631-1700)

1663 *The Wild Gallant* (comedy)
1664 *The Rival Ladies* (tragicomedy)
With Sir Robert Howard, *The Indian Queen* (heroic tragedy)
1665 *The Indian Emperour* (heroic tragedy)
1667 *Secret-Love* (tragicomedy)
With the Duke of Newcastle, *Sir Martin Mar-all* (comedy)
Adaptation with Sir William Davenant, *The Tempest* (comedy)
1668 *An Evening's Love* (comedy)
1669 *Tyrannick Love* (heroic tragedy)
1670 Part One, *The Conquest of Granada* (heroic play)
1671 Part Two, *The Conquest of Granada* (heroic play)
1672 *Marriage A-la-Mode* (comedy and heroic play)
The Assignation (comedy)
1673 *Amboyna* (tragedy)
1675 *Aureng-Zebe* (heroic tragedy)
1677 *The State of Innocence* (unacted dramatic version of *Paradise Lost*)
All for Love (tragedy)
1678 *The Kind Keeper* (comedy)
1679 With Nathaniel Lee, *Oedipus* (tragedy)
Troilus and Cressida (tragedy)
1680 *The Spanish Friar* (comedy)
1682 *The Duke of Guise* (tragedy)
1685 *Albion and Albanius* (opera)
1689 *Don Sebastian* (tragedy)
1690 *Amphitryon* (comedy)
1691 *King Arthur* ("Dramatick Opera")
1692 *Cleomenes* (tragedy)
1694 *Love Triumphant* (comedy)
1700 *The Secular Masque* (performed with Fletcher's play, *The Pilgrim*)

Also three odes for cantatas: *A Song for St. Cecilia's Day* (1687),
An Ode on the Death of Mr. Purcell (1696), and
Alexander's Feast (1697)

Sir George Etherege (c. 1635-1691)

1664 *The Comical Revenge; or, Love in a Tub* (comedy)
1668 *She Wou'd if She Cou'd* (comedy)
1676 *The Man of Mode; or, Sir Fopling Flutter* (comedy)

William Wycherley (c. 1640-1716)

1671 *Love in a Wood* (comedy)
1672 *The Gentleman-Dancing Master* (comedy)
1675 *The Country Wife* (comedy)
1676 *The Plain-Dealer* (comedy)

Thomas Otway (1652-1685)

1675 *Alcibiades* (tragedy)
1676 *Don Carlos* (tragedy)
Titus and Berenice (tragedy)
The Cheats of Scapin (farce)
1678 *Friendship in Fashion* (comedy)
1679 *The History and Fall of Caius Marius* (tragedy)
1680 *The Orphan* (tragedy)
The Souldiers Fortune (comedy)
1682 *Venice Preserv'd* (tragedy)
1683 *The Atheist* (comedy)

William Congreve (1670-1729)

1693 *The Old Batchelour* (comedy)
The Double-Dealer (comedy)
1695 *Love for Love* (comedy)
1697 *The Mourning Bride* (tragedy)
1700 *The Way of the World* (comedy)

Notes on the Editor and Authors

EARL MINER, the editor of this volume, is Professor of English at the University of California, Los Angeles, and associate general editor of the California edition of *The Works of John Dryden.* He is author of *Nihon o Utsusu Chiisana Kagami,* of *The Japanese Tradition in British and American Literature,* and of the forthcoming *Dryden's Poetry;* co-author of *Japanese Court Poetry;* and editor of John Ogilby, *The Fables of Aesop Paraphras'd in Verse.*

D. W. JEFFERSON, Reader in English Literature in the University of Leeds, is the author of *Henry James* (in the Writers and Critics series), of *Henry James and the Modern Reader,* and of articles on Dryden, Swift, Goldsmith, Sterne, and Ivy Compton-Burnett.

ARTHUR C. KIRSCH is Associate Professor of English at the University of Virginia and author of *Dryden's Heroic Drama.*

EUGENE M. WAITH is Professor of English at Yale University. He has edited *Macbeth* and *Bartholomew Fair;* he is author of *The Pattern of Tragicomedy in Beaumont and Fletcher* and *The Herculean Hero;* he has compiled the volume on Shakespeare's history plays for this series; and he has done an introduction to drama, *The Dramatic Moment.*

JOCELYN POWELL is Lecturer in the Department of Drama and Theatre Arts at the University of Birmingham. He has directed *Hamlet,* Marston's *The Malcontent,* and other plays for the Nuffield Theatre in Southampton and has written essays on such writers as Marlowe and John Lyly.

DALE UNDERWOOD is Professor of English at the University of New Hampshire and is author of *Etherege and the Seventeenth-Century Comedy of Manners.*

ANNE RIGHTER is University Lecturer in English at Cambridge University and Fellow of Girton College. She has written *Shakespeare and the Idea of a Play* and an essay on Francis Bacon published in *The English Mind: Studies in the English Moralists Presented to Basil Willey.*

ROSE A. ZIMBARDO is Assistant Professor of English at The City College of New York. She is author of *Wycherley's Drama: A Link in the Development of English Satire* and of articles on Shakespeare and on modern drama.

DAVID R. HAUSER is Executive Director of the Society for Religion in Higher Education. He is the author of articles on Pope, Blake, and Coleridge as well as on Otway.

NORMAN N. HOLLAND is Professor of English and chairman of the Department at the State University of New York at Buffalo. In addition to *The First Modern Comedies,* he has written *The Shakespearean Imagination, Psychoanalysis and Shakespeare,* and numerous articles.

THOMAS H. FUJIMURA is Professor of English at the University of Hawaii. He has edited Wycherley's *The Country Wife* and is author of *The Restoration Comedy of Wit* as well as of articles on Dryden, Etherege, and the Earl of Rochester.

Selected Bibliography

In addition to the works from which some of the selections in this book have been taken, the following books should be mentioned. Only a few works have been given that are not primarily critical and the copious literature of essays and articles is not included. There are numerous editions of the principal plays by all four writers.

Bonamy Dobrée. *Restoration Comedy* (Oxford, 1924, 1958); *Restoration Tragedy* (Oxford, 1929).

Arthur C. Kirsch. *Dryden's Heroic Drama* (Princeton, 1965).

Joseph Wood Krutch. *Comedy and Conscience after the Restoration* (New York, 1924).

John Loftis. *Comedy and Society from Congreve to Fielding* (Stanford, 1959).

Kathleen M. Lynch. *The Social Mode of Restoration Comedy* (New York, 1926).

Elizabeth L. Mignon. *Crabbed Age and Youth: The Old Men and Women in the Restoration Comedy of Manners* (Durham, North Carolina, 1947).

Frank Harper Moore. *The Nobler Pleasure: Dryden's Comedy in Theory and Practice* (Chapel Hill, 1963).

Paul and Miriam Mueschke. *A New View of Congreve's* Way of the World (Ann Arbor, 1958).

John Palmer. *The Comedy of Manners* (London, 1913).

Moody A. Prior. *The Language of Tragedy* (chapter on Restoration tragedy; New York, 1947).

John Harrington Smith. *The Gay Couple in Restoration Comedy* (Cambridge, Mass., 1948).

British Authors in the Twentieth Century Views Series

JANE AUSTEN, edited by Ian Watt—S-TC-26
SAMUEL BECKETT, edited by Martin Esslin—S-TC-51
BLAKE, edited by Northrop Frye—S-TC-58
BYRON, edited by Paul West—S-TC-31
CONRAD, edited by Marvin Mudrick—S-TC-53
JOHN DONNE, edited by Helen Gardner—S-TC-19
DRYDEN, edited by Bernard N. Schilling—S-TC-32
FIELDING, edited by Ronald Paulson—S-TC-9
E. M. FORSTER, edited by Malcolm Bradbury—S-TC-59
HARDY, edited by Albert Guerard—S-TC-25
HOPKINS, edited by Geoffrey H. Hartman—S-TC-57
SAMUEL JOHNSON, edited by Donald J. Greene—S-TC-48
BEN JONSON, edited by Jonas A. Barish—S-TC-22
KEATS, edited by Walter Jackson Bate—S-TC-43
D. H. LAWRENCE, edited by Mark Spilka—S-TC-24
MARLOWE, edited by Clifford Leech—S-TC-44
MILTON, edited by Louis L. Martz—S-TC-60
SHAKESPEARE: THE COMEDIES, edited by Kenneth Muir—S-TC-47
SHAKESPEARE: THE HISTORIES, edited by Eugene M. Waith—S-TC-45
SHAKESPEARE: THE TRAGEDIES, edited by Alfred Harbage—S-TC-40
G. B. SHAW, edited by R. J. Kaufmann—S-TC-50
SHELLEY, edited by George M. Ridenour—S-TC-49
SWIFT, edited by Ernest Tuveson—S-TC-35
DYLAN THOMAS, edited by C. B. Cox—S-TC-56
YEATS, edited by John Unterecker—S-TC-23

American Authors in the Twentieth Century Views Series

AUDEN, edited by Monroe K. Spears—S-TC-38
EMILY DICKINSON, edited by Richard B. Sewall—S-TC-28
T. S. ELIOT, edited by Hugh Kenner—S-TC-2
EMERSON, edited by Milton R. Konvitz
and Stephen E. Whicher—S-TC-12
F. SCOTT FITZGERALD, edited by Arthur Mizener—S-TC-27
ROBERT FROST, edited by James M. Cox—S-TC-3
HAWTHORNE, edited by A. N. Kaul—S-TC-55
HEMINGWAY, edited by Robert P. Weeks—S-TC-8
HENRY JAMES, edited by Leon Edel—S-TC-34
SINCLAIR LEWIS, edited by Mark Schorer—S-TC-6
MELVILLE, edited by Richard Chase—S-TC-13
O'NEILL, edited by John Gassner—S-TC-39
EZRA POUND, edited by Walter Sutton—S-TC-29
WALLACE STEVENS, edited by Marie Borroff—S-TC-33
THOREAU, edited by Sherman Paul—S-TC-10
MARK TWAIN, edited by Henry Nash Smith—S-TC-30
EDITH WHARTON, edited by Irving Howe—S-TC-20
WHITMAN, edited by Roy Harvey Pearce—S-TC-5